THE THIRTY-FIRST
OF MARCH

BRIDWELL TEXAS HISTORY SERIES

THE THIRTY-FIRST OF MARCH

AN INTIMATE PORTRAIT OF *Lyndon Johnson*

HORACE BUSBY

With a preface by Scott Busby
and an introduction by Hugh Sidey

University of Texas Press, Austin

Dolph Briscoe Center for American History

Requests for permission to reproduce material from this work should be
sent to:
   Permissions
   University of Texas Press
   P.O. Box 7819
   Austin, TX 78713-7819
   utpress.utexas.edu/rp-form

♾ The paper used in this book meets the minimum requirements of ANSI/
NISO Z39.48-1992 (R1997) (Permanence of Paper).

Library of Congress Control Number: 2004116942

   ISBN 978-1-4773-2747-0 (paperback)
   ISBN 978-1-4773-2748-7 (PDF e-book)
   ISBN 978-1-4773-2749-4 (ePub e-book)

doi:10.7560/327470

For Ellie
May she come to know and live her grandfather's
gift for making people happy about themselves.

PREFACE

On an overcast weekend in June 2003, I drove to my sister Betsy's house in Encinitas, California, to do something I had long resisted—sort through my father Horace Busby's papers and memorabilia. My sisters and I had moved him from Washington, D.C., to Los Angeles in 1997 because of his failing health. It had not been an easy transition for a man who had been a close associate and aide to Lyndon B. Johnson and who, after LBJ left the White House, remained for nearly three decades in the nation's capital, where he built a considerable reputation as a political consultant, publisher, and pundit. He died in May 2000 in Santa Monica. Betsy's garage became the repository for what was left of his possessions.

I had avoided making the journey for many reasons. The thought of spending countless hours in a hot, dusty garage digging through thirty-odd boxes of old papers wasn't exactly a drawing card. I knew Betsy, the most organized and meticulous member of our family, would want to look at—and discuss—every piece of paper and photo. Things might, God forbid, get emotional. But deep down I guess what I dreaded most was what the process would mean—bidding a final farewell to my father.

My procrastinations ended when Betsy called to say that LBJ biographer Robert Caro had contacted her, asking to see my father's papers. We agreed that the time had come to organize his writings and documents so we could donate them to the Lyndon Baines Johnson Library and Museum in Austin for the use of Caro and other historians.

We foraged through two long file boxes that first morning, sipping coffee, reminiscing. Then, at the bottom of a storage container, I found an unmarked blue stationery box. Betsy looked up as I opened it and saw my expression. "You found it," she said, smiling.

It was a manuscript my father had worked on for more than a decade about his long and extraordinary relationship with LBJ. For reasons his family and friends have never understood, he didn't publish it. My youngest sister, Leslie, who visited and helped our ailing father frequently during the 1990s, reported seeing an early draft of parts of the manuscript in black-ringed binders in his office. But when we all assembled in my father's place at the St. George near Georgetown to move him to California in 1997, we couldn't find a complete manuscript anywhere.

When we asked our father about the manuscript, he told us he had never finished it, didn't really like it, and had thrown away its various drafts. This shocked and saddened me, because no one in Washington or Texas had known Lyndon Johnson, the man and the politician, in quite the same way as my father had.

Horace Busby went to work for Congressman Johnson in 1948 at the age of twenty-four. He served on LBJ's staff in the House and Senate, during the vice presidency, and at the White House, where he was secretary of the cabinet from 1963 to 1965. He wrote many of the president's important speeches, including his civil rights orations, his announcement of the end of U.S. bombing of Vietnam, and—the heart of this book—his decision not to run for reelection in 1968. He also had a hand in drafting much of Johnson's Great Society legislation.

My father's relationship with Lyndon Johnson was often tumultuous. Tempers would flare, and he would abruptly leave Johnson's service—only to be asked to return. But a powerful bond existed between the two men. "More than any other member of his staff, Lyndon Johnson believed, Horace Busby thought and felt like him," wrote Eric F. Goldman in *The Tragedy of Lyndon Johnson.* "This did not leave Busby entirely comfortable, but at least with respect to a number of hour-by-hour situations, it was accurate and Busby was most often the man who served as LBJ's other self."

As I read these pages, I was flooded with memories and struck again by the closeness, the intimacy, of my father's relationship with LBJ. One section of the book especially affected me. The defining moment in Lyndon Johnson's life was the assassination of President

Kennedy in Dallas on November 22, 1963. It is an event seared into the consciousness of every American who lived through it, but it had a very particular effect on my family. I was twelve years old, a seventh grader at a public school in suburban Maryland. I remember the confusion and fear on the faces of my classmates when we were called back to our homeroom that afternoon. I remember many of the girls bursting into tears when the principal told us that Kennedy had been shot. And I remember the stares of hatred and words of anger that were directed at me because I was from Texas.

Betsy and Leslie were called into an emergency assembly at the National Cathedral School for Girls, in Washington, where many government officials and diplomats sent their daughters. They watched a phalanx of Secret Service agents enter the auditorium and quickly remove one of their fellow students—Luci Johnson, the vice president's younger daughter.

My mother, Mary V. Busby, was at The Elms, the vice president's residence in northwest Washington, doing research for Lady Bird Johnson, when news of the assassination broke. She spent several desperate hours on the phone with my father, who was at his office in downtown D.C. monitoring the news from Dallas on a wire service Teletype machine, and with telephone company operators in Austin, trying to locate the Johnsons' elder daughter, Lynda, who was a freshman at the University of Texas. Later that afternoon, my father joined my mother at The Elms. They stayed late into the night, awaiting the arrival of the newly sworn-in president, knowing their lives—and the lives of their children—would never be the same.

My sisters and I were watched over that night by our neighbors—Congressman Joe Kilgore of Texas and his wife, Jane. It was a night when a twelve-year-old boy and his younger sisters would have liked to be with their parents. There was so much we didn't understand. But for the next several weeks we hardly saw our father. Looking back now, I realize that I grew up resenting my father's absence during those traumatic days—and on many other occasions during my childhood and teenage years.

The discovery of his manuscript, and his firsthand account of events surrounding the tragedy in Dallas and its aftermath, stirred up all those old emotions again—then laid them to rest. Reading his story, I learned many things I hadn't known, but two stand out: during those dreadful nights and days in November 1963, his wife and children were constantly on his mind; and his hands were very full, counseling the new, troubled President of the United States.

The manuscript as we found it is incomplete. The missing period covers Johnson's race for the United States Senate in 1948, his controversial victory, and his rise to Majority Leader during the 1950s. There is some evidence from my father's correspondence, and from conversations he had with family friends, that he felt he had given his best recollections of that era to Robert Caro for use in his Pulitzer Prize–winning biography of Johnson. Perhaps my father skipped over those years in his writings because he disliked the idea of being redundant, or he thought he'd come back and fill in the gap later. Unfortunately, we will never know. A stroke and macular degeneration eliminated that possibility.

Still, the hundreds of neatly typed manuscript pages he left behind were clearly of historical value. In time, I've come to see the work as a gift to his family, one that allowed us to rediscover him. Far from saying good-bye to my father on that trip to Encinitas, I was given a remarkable second chance to know him better.

This book could not have been published without the encouragement and support of many friends and family members. Special thanks go to my sisters, Betsy Busby and Leslie Busby; my wife, Johanna Woollcott Busby; and my mother, Mary V. Busby. I am particularly grateful for the generosity and wisdom of Bess and Tyler Abell, Barbara Baldwin, Dr. Peter Birnstein, David Broder, Steve Fisher, Jonathan Gage, Wayne and Beth Gibbens, John Glusman and his staff, Drex Heikes, Robert Jesuele, Nick Kotz, Jack Limpert, Alex Linklater, Margaret Mayer, John McClung, Gary McDonald, Harry Middleton, Tim Richardson, Ric Robertson, Hugh Sidey, Michael Sheehy, Robert and Anna Sneed, Kenji Thielstrom, Donley Watt, and J. J. Yore.

Finally, I'd like to give a belated thanks to the unlikeliest Texan of them all, who, night after night, year after year, filled his smoke-wreathed den with fine words, clear thoughts, and prodigious stories for his inquisitive children, whom he loved from afar.

Scott Busby
Los Angeles
July 2004

INTRODUCTION

When I read through the copies of those manuscript pages rescued from a blue cardboard box in California, "old" Buzz, my friend of so long ago, rose up, and as if he were standing beside me, I could hear his soft chuckle again and see the intelligence in his eyes and his modest body padding quietly through the shadows in those majestic corridors of the United States Capitol.

Horace Busby, thirty-three then, wasn't "old" and he was never really "Horace." He was Buzz, a term of deep affection and respect. He knew a lot about the volcano in our midst named Lyndon Baines Johnson. He could dispense his insight with candor and humor better than anyone around the Senate in those wonderful days when the United States stood astride the world with wealth and power.

When I was a young reporter assigned to make political sense out of Congress, I needed guidance and had no idea where to go, until some of the old hands, like Connecticut's Prescott Bush and Georgia's Richard Russell, told me to get ahold of Busby for the true understanding of Johnson.

There were a dozen years in my life when understanding and writing about LBJ was near the center of my universe at *Time* magazine. And Buzz had written his speeches and talked out his issues and run his errands and sometimes for hours just sat in silence with the brooding LBJ. "You feel each other," I once said to Buzz, who smiled and replied, "Yes, especially in the silences." In these pages he writes, "It was this solitary Lyndon Johnson that I came to know best." A rare privilege granted; a trust carried out to the end of the lives of both men.

It was a wild and often crazy journey from Johnson the Majority Leader of the United States Senate, when on some days he seemed to have more influence in the world than President Dwight Eisenhower, through the sterile land of his vice presidency, and then to the heights of the White House, and finally—the focus of this fascinating and singular memoir—the night of March 31, 1968, when on national television he gave up the presidency. "I can't get peace in Vietnam and be president too," Johnson told Buzz.

In fact, the president had floated the idea to several people around him that he might not run for a second term. I rejected the notion as another effort by this power-nurtured egomaniac to win sympathy for the burden he carried, as did others.

Buzz knew better. There was something building inside Johnson, and sooner or later it would emerge. At Johnson's behest, Buzz had written some exit lines three months earlier and had held on to the secret. On March 31, 1968, he was ready for the real drama, and he crafted some of the most famous political lines in history.

Buzz spent all of that day in the White House. He felt the deep stirrings of the pivotal time, never certain until that evening that Johnson would actually step offstage and in so many ways give up life itself. Buzz was with him every inch of the way, knowing the internal torment of the man and understanding that a second elected term would be politically devastating for LBJ. This is the book's intimate and powerful story.

As I read through those manuscript pages, I was again in the grip of Buzz's mind. His sentences were gentle and revealing, easy to follow, and always with the special feel of a soul mate. Too often historians try to resurrect the past from memos and box scores, and they fail to grasp the inner struggles of the people they write about, which more times than not are the most important things in any story—especially in and around the presidency. Buzz's account of many epic moments in Johnson's life—joining John Kennedy's ticket, the assassination of Kennedy, Johnson's political abdication—are the best writings yet done about LBJ. Buzz had a touch of the Texas High Plains poet in him, casting his subject in the long ranks of history.

From his days as a reporter and then from the years of residing near Johnson with a view of some of the world's great power dramas, Buzz developed an engaging wariness about many of the cataclysmic predictions made by statesmen and scholars. For a while he kept a list of the world calamities confidently enumerated by the seers—such things as the collapse of the international banking system, the inexorable spread of communism. Almost none of them occurred, either within the time or in the form predicted, much to Buzz's delight. "You guys," he once told me with his usual good nature, "just don't know as much as you think you do, and most of the people don't listen anyway." Buzz always walked on the ground despite so many temptations to stand above it.

To Buzz's evangelical parents the newspaper business was the land of the devil, but to Buzz it was a marvelous boot camp for the real world.

Before he began working for LBJ, Buzz knew about the rambunctious congressman from Texas's Tenth District. At first he eschewed Johnson's overtures to him to come to Washington as a congressional aide. He'd never met the man. But Johnson wanted him, sight unseen, and Buzz was beginning to sense the excitement in the country that lay beyond Austin. After several months of thought and many talks with friends and colleagues, Buzz succumbed to the entreaties, and in 1948 he headed east in a shiny new car, crossing the South and the Eastern Seaboard through land and history he'd never seen before, and on a fateful March day was ushered before the legendary Lyndon Johnson.

Whether it was then or later that Johnson explained himself is a little vague. But as Buzz related it to me, Johnson told him that as he'd gotten to know the people in Congress, in both House and Senate, he'd found that the important and powerful members seemed to have at least one thing in common in their offices. "There was always a little guy over in the corner," explained Buzz, quoting Johnson, "who was tucked away with his books and with cigarette ashes on his tie, and it turned out he was the one who came up with the great ideas for his boss. I want you to be that man in this office."

Buzz did smoke a lot, and he did read a lot, and he did have a surplus of ideas for a better society ("One a day," ordered LBJ), but I am not sure I ever detected cigarette ashes on Buzz's tie. He was not a disheveled man. He sometimes held his cigarette in his lips so high he burned his eyeglasses, and often I thought he was infected with the same adoration of Franklin Roosevelt that possessed Lyndon Johnson, to the point that LBJ sometimes played Roosevelt with a pince-nez over his long nose and a rakish cigarette holder clamped between his teeth.

When I arrived to get the traditional newsman's full-Johnson introduction—nose thrust into my face, arm squeezing, shouts of patriotism—I was forewarned, because the story of the meeting of Johnson and Buzz ten years earlier had already reached mythical proportions around the Congress. The most delightful part of it was that Buzz found thirty-seven books on Winston Churchill piled on and around his desk, and the orders from Johnson were to read them "and be my Churchill."

Did he read them, I wanted to know. "Of course not," he told me. "But I had a better idea of what he wanted. Johnson did think in the grand terms of Winston Churchill." Johnson's Great Society was as sweeping as any Churchillian vision. His understanding of segregation became as profound as that of any public figure.

The March 31 speech not only ended Lyndon Johnson's pursuit of power but it also ended Buzz's days of counseling at the presidential level. He walked off into the private sector as a consultant and an editor of a newsletter, rich with the lessons he had learned, full of humor from his days beside Johnson, wise in his view of the future. Buzz foresaw the Republican Party's rise in the Old South and the powerful partnership being forged by the media, Hollywood, and academia. He viewed it all as another act in the great and wonderful political drama in which he had taken part. Before his health failed and he went to California to be with his children, we would still lunch, talking and laughing about the absurdities and the beauties of our political system and its people. This book is a colorful journey down many of the byways of those eventful years.

Hugh Sidey

THE THIRTY-FIRST
OF MARCH

— 1 —

PROLOGUE
The Sunday Shift

Shortly after midnight, on Sunday, the thirty-first of March, in 1968, the telephone rang at my home in rural Maryland, twenty miles north of Washington, D.C. An operator at the White House was calling. Her message was brief.

"The president," she said, "would like for you to be here this morning at nine."

Did she have any idea why? "Not a clue," she confided, her voice cheery and conspiratorial, "not a clue." Were others also being summoned? Was there, perhaps, to be a group meeting for some purpose? "Nope, no evidence of it, not from the calls through the switchboard tonight." The operator had no other information: Before retiring for the night, the president had asked her to relay the message about time and place; that was all she knew. I was prying, of course, as one learns to do, and the operator laughed understandingly.

"It's like old times, Mr. Busby," she said. "You've drawn the Sunday shift again."

In other years, while still serving as one of the president's special assistants, I frequently drew what the staff referred to as "the Sunday shift." That meant being called in by the president to share with him the loneliest hours of his week. Sometimes the summons came from Camp David, the secluded retreat of presidents in the cool mountains of Maryland, not far from Washington. A Sunday there meant long walks through the deep forests; a few games of bowling, at which the president competed intensely, determined to win; and at twilight, a quiet time before the log fire, listening as he reflected on the problems the week ahead would bring. At other times, during vacations, the calls came from his ranch home, and one knew to expect a day of casual driving over the dry southwestern hills, admiring his cattle, as westerners expect guests to do; counting the young deer when they broke from the underbrush and went leaping across the open pastures; and occasionally, when he yearned to leave the ranch, the president would ask you to take the wheel and drive past the reporters watching at every gate while he ducked from sight, hoping to escape to freedom beyond the fence. But when he was alone at the White House, the patterns of such Sundays with the president seldom varied.

At the start of the morning, one expected a quiet hour in the refuge of the small, square bedroom on the second floor of the Executive Mansion. Lying beneath the covers of the high canopy bed, out of sight of the constant eye of security, servants, and staff, the president invariably began his day turning through the thick Sunday newspapers. He glanced over the pages, reading aloud columns and editorials which caught his eye, chuckling at some, fuming at others.

Several times each morning he was likely to pause, coming alive with some fresh idea the news suggested. "Why can't we do this?" he would ask, laying the papers aside. Then he would excitedly sketch out his thoughts for a new government program to meet some need identified from the morning reading. While the exuberance still ran strong, he would reach eagerly for the telephone and rouse a surprised cabinet officer. "It has been suggested," he usually began, carefully avoiding—as presidents must—what might be construed as a direct command. However, after he had outlined the idea and begun to listen, his face would gradually show deepening dejection: he was hearing that, for one reason or another, the idea could not be implemented. The president might try another line of argument or start calling around in search of a more amenable official, but the answers would continue to be discouraging. At last he would put the telephone down, grumbling, "Who in the hell is supposed to run this government, anyway?" With a shrug, he would usually pour another cup of Sanka from the silver pot on his breakfast tray, take a warm sip, and return to his reading.

After a while, he would glance at the clock and come bounding out of bed. "We're going to be late for church." With the practiced timing presidents acquire from their many public appearances, he would race through the morning rituals: shaving, showering, and dressing. All the while he could be confident that a limousine awaited at the entrance, engine running, right rear door open, the temperature inside adjusted to the exact degree of his preference. The route through the downtown streets—cautiously different each Sunday—was planned and rehearsed to the minute, so that he arrived just as the church doors were closing for the morning services to start. Whoever drew the Sunday shift could expect to hear the president whisper, as you hurried down the aisle beside him, "Be sure to put some folding money in the plate; everybody'll be watching." And later, when the collection plate began passing along the seat rows, he would whisper again, "Slip a bill to him," nodding toward the Secret Service agent seated at the end of the pew, "so he'll have something to put in, too."

If his mood was buoyant and the weather favoring, he would delay the return to the White House as long as he could. The weekend automobile, smaller and less conspicuous than the regular limousine, would turn down through Washington's Rock Creek Park and follow the Sunday traffic out toward the residential neighborhoods. He would press a button at his side, raising a glass between the rear seat and the front seat, where the two Secret Service agents sat, and in privacy, he would talk of many things. But his eyes were always on the people outside, going freely and unrestrainedly about their Sunday lives.

On his own orders, the president's automobile observed all traffic lights. "You only lose votes," he liked to joke, "when you turn on sirens and red lights and make people get out of the way." Frequently, while the driver waited for a signal to change, children in a car alongside would recognize the tall man in the rear seat of the shining black Lincoln. He readily returned their waves and smiles, and the children would shout, "It's the president!" But their harassed mothers would neither believe the children's cries nor dignify the foolishness by turning to look for themselves. "Watch this," the president would say playfully, lowering his window, and as the limousine pulled away when the traffic light changed, he would lean out to make a gallant bow toward the unbelieving mother so that the kids would be proved right.

The Sunday drive might go everywhere or nowhere. Wherever the black car went, however, Halfback, the unmarked Secret Service chase car, followed one length to the rear, carrying six alert young men over the quiet Sunday streets, their hands resting lightly on the out-of-sight firepower of a Marine platoon. The office was never far away. One of the agents in the front seat would signal for the president to answer the telephone concealed in the armrest at his side. He usually answered tersely and listened intently. Most of the time only a few words were sufficient in reply. Sometimes, though, as he returned the telephone to its cradle, the president rapped on the glass, pointed with his finger, and the driver turned back toward 1600 Pennsylvania Avenue. The duties of the presidency do not observe Sunday as a day of rest.

Back at the White House, if there was no crisis to attend to, you joined the president for lunch in the second-floor dining room: soup, a meat course, and salad, served always on the fine china identified by the names of the presidents whose First Ladies had brought it to the mansion. The afternoon usually brought a long walk, around and around the great circular South Drive, and the president's mood would become ebullient in the open air. Sometimes he would decide to lead a boyish expedition through the silent White House, exploring the historic rooms, discovering concealed doors and hidden stairwells, lifting up chairs and tables to search for the makers' marks; and at the end, the two of you would stand for a long while in the hush of the Lincoln Bedroom. Or there might be a mischievous tour of the empty staff offices in the West Wing with the president reading through his assistants' unanswered memoranda or searching around the secretaries' desks for boxes of candy, from which a forbidden sweet could be taken without the First Lady present to frown sternly about the calories.

But still the duties of the office were never far away. Wherever the president might go on his Sunday afternoons, messengers found him, silently handing him brown envelopes from the Situation Room. He would stop to read the contents, sometimes handing the message to you to share with him, other times somberly folding it into his coat pocket and striding rapidly to his Oval Office to begin telephoning the officials who could tell him more of the developments involved.

At nightfall, if the world had not intruded on the presidential day, invited friends—a cabinet officer and his wife, an old friend from the newspaper world, someone from his home state, perhaps a prominent person in town for the weekend, people with whom the president could be at ease—usually gathered on the family floor. Everyone came determined to be relaxed and informal, to keep talk away from serious concerns. But amid the laughter and trivial talk, you could watch his face and see that the duties of the office were beginning to call again. At the theater downstairs, after dinner with the guests, he might try to be interested in the movie, and occasionally he would be. Twice he sat through *Seven Days in May*, the story of a president fighting to prevent a military takeover of the United States; and when a guest asked his reaction, the president said, without smiling, "It scares me." But on most occasions, the unreality would be too much. In the darkness, the man with the burdens would slip away, back to the bedroom, and you would go with him. There, in silence again, you would stay for two hours—or maybe for much longer—reading, as he handed them over, each of the day's accumulated memoranda and reports.

The items in "Night Reading"—some secretaries called it the "Pillow Pouch"—came from throughout the executive branch. Heads of departments and agencies knew they could always reach the president—and obtain his decision—through these communications placed beside his bed. Many nights the items numbered into the hundreds, and each required a penciled answer before the chief executive slept.

At midnight, or at one o'clock—or sometimes after two—the light would go out. He would thank you for coming, say good night, and you would call the White House garage for a car to drive you home.

Since morning, you would have been at the side of the most powerful man in the world, listening as he talked of prime ministers and kings, of senators and congressmen, of preachers and charlatans; of war and peace, of live dreams and dead hopes; of happy times past and other times ahead; and of the proper size for cuff links, of the respective merits of various hair tonics, of the price of sirloin as opposed to club steak.

But when you reached your own house and your wife awakened to ask what you and the president had been doing all day, you could answer only "Nothing" and fall off to sleep. The Sunday shift was over.

On this last day of March, however, I knew that the Sunday shift at the White House would mean a very different kind of day.

At the White House, history would be made before midnight came again.

Thirty seconds past the hour of nine tonight, the President of the United States would be going before the television cameras to address the nation. His purpose, as announced to the press on the previous day, was to review American policy in Southeast Asia, where the combat forces under his command were engaged in the nation's longest and most divisive war. His actual purpose, however, was far more specific. The president intended not only to review American policy but to reverse it. Seated at his large desk in the Oval Office of the West Wing, the president—speaking as commander in chief—would stun the nation and surprise the world by announcing that, after three controversial years, American bombing of the Democratic Republic of Vietnam was being halted north of the twentieth parallel.

It was a high-stakes gamble. Thus far, since the start of American intervention, the government of North Vietnam had consistently rejected overtures leading to the conference table. Officials at Hanoi made it clear that there would be no negotiations until the bombing ended, unconditionally. Now, hoping to open the way for the start of peace talks, the president was largely meeting those terms. If the move succeeded, it could mean, in time, the return of American troops from the burned and bloody jungles half a world away.

On Saturday, when the president himself telephoned unexpectedly, I had learned for the first time of what was to be announced. For a moment, I was jubilant. Such a startling reversal of American policy must mean Hanoi already had sent assurances that the proposal would be accepted.

"No," the president replied, when I asked the obvious question, "we have heard nothing from Hanoi, not a whisper, not a wink." I was taken aback. If there were no assurances, how did the president rate the chances for success? "I don't know, I don't know," he said, his words coming slowly and heavily. "It's only a roll of the dice." After a moment he added, with a sudden tiredness, "I'm shoving in all my stack on this one."

The world of power is an emotionless world. Whether at the center or on the periphery, one never registers shock or surprise. I was thoroughly stunned by what I had just learned, and by the words and tone I had just heard, but I said nothing.

The decision was final. All the president's advisers and associates close to the heart of national policy were undoubtedly in concurrence. It would be no help to the man in the White House for anyone so far from the center to badger him with questions. When he asked if I would take time on a Saturday afternoon to read the draft proposed for his television address, I readily agreed—and began to wonder, as one does, whether that was the only reason for the president's call.

The start of the last March weekend was bright and warm; spring had arrived just in time for the beginning of Washington's annual cherry blossom week on Sunday. When the president spoke on the call from his desk, he dwelled on the sunshine, the blossoming of the trees, and the coming of the new flowers, which he could see in the garden outside his Oval Office. He would have been more acutely aware than anyone else that the speech on Sunday night might be the most important of his presidency. His countrymen could accept the decision and applaud it, or just as easily, the decision could be construed a thousand ways that were not intended. A president can never know the consequences of his words at home or in the world. Yet listening to him speak, I sensed that other thoughts must be stirring in his mind.

A long silence came into our conversation. I made no move to interrupt it. When he spoke again, the softness was gone from his voice. Very firmly, he asked, "What is your judgment on how we are doing?"

Over many years, at many stations in his career, I had heard that question often. This was not the President of the United States asking for opinions about war or peace or high national policies; this was the man in the presidency asking for—and expecting to receive—the candid answer of a friend about the state of his national leadership. It was not easy to give.

The office of the presidency does not encourage directness in addressing its occupant. However long and durable the friendship with the man, one is careful in addressing the president—careful about being presumptuous, careful about being too authoritative, careful about saying, "You should do this" or "You should do that." But in this instance, I thought I knew what must be stirring in the mind of the president. For him, 1968 was a year of crucial decision. Already he had occupied the office for four years: his achievements were many, and his pride in those achievements was very great. But as it does on all presidents, the office had turned on the man. America's agonies abroad and torments at home were centering squarely on him. He stood at the eye of a strange and swirling storm of unrest and division, and with him stood the future of the office he held, the nation he led, and the causes he had chosen to champion in the world. The year of 1968 was pressing him to decide how he could most faithfully keep the trust that was his.

Two courses were open to him. In this year of national elections, he could go to the people seeking a renewal of their mandate for another term in the presidency. No one realistic in his appraisal of the powers of the office could doubt that such an effort by the president would succeed. If success served him, though, would it also serve his trust? Would his victory be the nation's victory? Or would it only set the storm to swirling more angrily through a society already anxious and tense? Only the president himself could answer questions such as these. Only the president himself could raise for consideration the other course open to him—the course of laying down his political life.

Once, in a time that now seemed long ago, the president had been considering that course, and I had been privileged to sit with him, listening as he debated away an afternoon, trying to decide if he should relinquish the powers he held. But from that day, two and a half months earlier, until now not another word had been spoken of the matter. Now time had almost run out. Because of the inexorable schedule of American politics, if he was to make this decision—and take this step—he must do so soon, before the month of March ended.

Very tentatively, uncertain whether I was overstepping that thin line of presumption which surrounds the awesome office, I recalled the course the president had been considering as the year began. Abruptly, it was a new conversation. This thought was his thought—the thought foremost in his mind on this springtime Saturday. I had not transgressed; on the contrary, this was the unrevealed purpose of his call.

Questions came rapidly, and the conversation moved swiftly. It was by no means certain that, with the most important decision of his presidency already to be announced on Sunday night, he should or could consider a further announcement of even greater consequence. But he concluded that Saturday morning call with words we both fully understood:

"I am going to send a driver out to your house with a copy of the speech for Sunday night. It'll take him at least an hour to get there. While he's on the way, I wish you would sit down and write out for me what you and I were talking about in January. Have the driver bring it back in here to me. I want to look it over, and I may consider using it."

I thought that he had forgotten, but I would never forget what we were "talking about in January."

— 2 —

THE BEGINNING OF THE DAY

An early Sunday stillness rested over the Maryland meadows as I started on the drive that would take me to the White House for the appointment at nine with the President of the United States. I could not know what lay ahead, there on the family floor of the Executive Mansion, or how the day might end. It was entirely possible, I knew, that before midnight came again, I might be witness to—and, in the most peripheral way, participant in—a historic decision. One hopes for such experiences, but one does not really expect them. When you are awaiting it, and watching for it, history almost never comes.

This day belonged to another decision, the decision to halt the bombing in North Vietnam. The men who had participated in its making would be possessive and protective, impatient at the intrusion of still another decision, unconcerned for any talk of how the announcement might be received by the people. When the president sought their counsel on his own decision, as I was sure he must, their answers would be curt. "Not today, Mr. President." "Let's wait awhile, Mr. President." "The concerns are exaggerated, Mr. President." When I drove this way again, returning home after the Sunday shift was done, it was most likely that I would be greeted with my wife's usual question—"What did you and the president do all day?"—and I would be able to offer the usual reply, "Nothing."

Whatever the end might be, on the thirty-first of March, twenty years were coming down to a single day for me.

In another March, back in 1948, I had driven into Washington from Texas to join the staff of a young congressman whom I did not know—Lyndon B. Johnson of the Tenth District of Texas. The first hours remained as vivid and memorable as the last hours were soon to be. Congressman Johnson, Senator Johnson, Majority Leader Johnson, Vice President Johnson, and President Johnson were all vivid, completely different, and memorable men; I had known all of them and, in varying degrees, understood each of them. But mine was not the usual story of closeness, constancy, and worshipful devotion that associates of public men have to tell.

It was a far more real story: of trusting intimacy and sulking estrangement, of laughing good times together and name-calling quarrels, of moments frivolous and trivial, and of awesome hours that made the heart pound. I thought, in the living of it, that I was only sharing the story of another man, an extraordinary man of extraordinary capacities, towering one moment, slouching abjectly the next; a man bedeviled by grand and innocent visions almost beyond mortal reach, and a man beset by petty doubts and cynical suspicions of himself; yet a man who, for all of this, wrought very large works upon his times. I laughed with him when life was sweet, sorrowed for him when life went sour; I worked with him, argued with him, felt for him both pride and pity; and when the power was his, I chose to turn and walk away. I did not know, through most of this, that in sharing his story, I was sharing history. Thus, in the telling of it, as in the living of it, the story cannot be changed; it must be told as it was lived.

Along the way of my association with Lyndon Baines Johnson—perhaps because I came and went as I did—the experiences often seemed to be distinct parts of a single day. The day had a beginning, a morning, a midday, and a time of darkness at noon; then there was an afternoon, and a coming of dusk. On the morning of the thirty-first of March, 1968, knowing the purpose for which I was being called to the White House, I thought that I might be going to share the long day's last hours. And I was.

Why I had been called for that purpose I could not know—and will never know. But I did recognize that, in some way, I brought with me something of what had gone before, and that was not unimportant. Of the thirty-sixth President of the United States,

more than of any other man I have known, it was always true that
without a knowledge of what had gone before, the present was
beyond understanding.

This story of the thirty-first of March at the White House
begins, then, where it must begin—at the start of the day which
was to last for twenty years.

On March 10, 1948—my twenty-fourth birthday—I cleared out
my room at the old, white frame Austin apartment house where I
had lived since my senior year at the University of Texas. The elderly
landlady, prim and powdered for the occasion, sat in the swing on
her shaded porch, smiling her approval as I went back and forth,
carrying the accumulated belongings of college life out to my new
car; she was very proud that one of her boys was going off "to help
run the country." When it came time for me to leave, she walked
with me to the curb, admonishing me about the perils, spiritual and
physical, lurking in the Godless East. "Now do everything you can,"
she said firmly, as her unexpected but long-remembered parting
words, "to make sure we don't have another old war." I promised
that I would and drove away.

A few blocks from the house, I took time for a last nostalgic
drive around the campus while the chimes in the Tower played
the noontime concert; then I proceeded on to the State Capitol,
where my pressroom colleagues of the past year were generously
treating me to a farewell cheeseburger at the nearby short-order
cafe. Our conversations were lively and reminiscences long; and
when friends among the state officials stopped by the table, they
made me promise that someday I would return to Texas. "It is
my observation," the old chief justice of the state supreme court
admonished, in all seriousness, "that the Texas in a man begins to
wear thin after two years away from God's country."

Late in the afternoon, when the talking was done and the friends
were gone, I said a private farewell to the good years and headed
out the highway toward Washington, D.C.

Six days later I arrived in the nation's capital. It was to matter
considerably, before that first day in Washington came to an end,
that through the years, other young men making the same journey
from Austin, for the same purpose, usually managed to travel the

distance in less than three days. But that lesson did not come until after my insights into Congressman Johnson were already beginning.

It was noon on Tuesday, March 16, when I finally reached my destination—504 Old House Office Building—on Capitol Hill. I timed the arrival at that hour purposely. If Lyndon Johnson was at all like other Texas politicians, I knew he would welcome the chance to begin our association over a long, leisurely lunch. I could tell him about election year politics back home, and of course, he could tell me about the duties of my new position on his staff, duties which remained only vaguely defined. Then I could sightsee around the Capitol awhile, get settled wherever I was to live, and be ready to start to work the following morning. As I soon learned, however, my new employer was not like other politicians, in Texas or anywhere else.

Thirty minutes after I opened the door into Congressman Johnson's spacious three-room suite of offices, I was pointed toward a desk and told to begin immediately on my first assignment.

The congressman was not on hand to greet me. An important debate in the House of Representatives, on extending wartime rent controls, would keep him occupied at the Capitol during the afternoon. However, Walter Jenkins, his young assistant, welcomed me, introduced my new associates on the staff, and invited me to his own heavily burdened desk, hidden behind a makeshift partition in the "workroom" of the suite.

Almost immediately, the telephone began to interrupt our efforts at conversation. A buzzer would sound, and Jenkins, stopping in midsentence, would instantly grab for the receiver, answering very crisply, "Yessir." On each call, he listened intently, snapping out frequent "Yessir"s but saying little else as he rapidly filled the pages of a notebook with shorthand; then, as abruptly as he began, Jenkins clipped off a final "Yessir" and, to my amazement, resumed our conversation almost precisely at midsentence. It was an awesome, electric, and formidable new world, entirely foreign to my Texas experience; and I was too impressed, at the moment, to realize either that the calls were from Congressman Johnson or that they concerned me. While Jenkins could not have been more casual or more cordial between calls, I grew edgy waiting for the buzzer to intrude again. After the third or fourth such call, I stood up from my chair, suggesting that it might be best if I waited in the reception room, which seemed much more serene. But Jenkins stopped me.

"Over there," he said, pointing across the room, "is a desk we have been saving for you. You will find some books on it. Mr. Johnson wants you to begin reading them immediately."

At the end of six days of highway driving, I hardly expected to plunge so precipitately into the affairs of the nation. However, I had been told all along that my principal duties in Washington would be "to read, think, and come up with new ideas." The reading, at least, was about to begin, and I welcomed the opportunity to learn what sorts of books young congressional assistants were expected to peruse. More important, the subject matter would tell me much of Congressman Johnson's priorities among the major issues of the times. But the sight that awaited around the desk by the windows was overwhelming.

On top of the small typewriter desk there were four books, neatly tied together with cord—a reasonable quantity for the start of a research project. But behind the desk, on a small table, there were more books; still other volumes were piled high on a filing cabinet, and on the floor, stack after stack rested along the wall. I looked back to Walter Jenkins for some sort of guidance, but the telephone had his concentrated attention again. Thoroughly taken aback by the wholly unexpected magnitude of this first task, I pulled out the desk chair, intending to sit down and begin examining this array. When I did so, still more books tumbled from the chair seat onto the carpet. There were books everywhere, all shapes and sizes, all lying in wait for me.

I knelt beside the desk to retrieve the fallen volumes and glanced, for the first time, at the titles in my hand. My face must have reflected my utter bafflement as I began slowly looking over the other volumes, confirming my worst suspicions. All the volumes—I quit counting at thirty-seven—were related to a single subject. Incredibly, my first assignment from the congressman of the Tenth District of Texas was to begin reading what had to be every speech of, as well as every book written by or about, Sir Winston Churchill.

Still kneeling, I heard a stern voice from the doorway connecting into the reception room.

"All right, Busby," the voice barked as I jumped. "Let's quit daw-dling and get busy." At that point, nothing would have surprised me, but I turned to see, with some relief, my only contemporary in the office, Warren Woodward. A classmate at the University of Texas who had himself joined Congressman Johnson's staff only the previous week, Woody had earned in college a justly deserved reputation as a heartless and tireless practical joker. His broad grin reassured me that this had to be, could only be, some sort of first-day joke. But when I demanded to know the point of the prank, Woodward's grin waned. Motioning for me to follow him into the corridor outside, he whispered, "Hold on to your hat, it's not a joke."

Around the corner, out of earshot of the office, he broke into unrestrained laughter. "Buzz," he said, barely able to speak, "you aren't going to believe this man Johnson. He's not real, I tell you, absolutely not real."

Then he told this story of the books:

On his first morning in the office, Woodward answered his initial summons into Congressman Johnson's presence. Call the Library of Congress, the congressman directed. Tell them to send over all their books by, or about, Winston Churchill, and copies of all his speeches, too. Woody did as he was told. In a short while, the first of a daylong procession of messengers arrived with a pushcart of selected volumes; by evening Woodward could no longer see over the books stacked on his desk in the reception room, so he sought further instructions. "Sir, what do I do with them now?" he asked. "Read 'em," the congressman replied sternly. "Your job in this office, son, is to learn to write like Winston Churchill speaks." Near panic—"I could see my whole life passing before my eyes," Woody exaggerated as he retold the experience—Woodward hastily and desperately pled mistaken identity. "I can't write anything but my name," he told the new boss. "Were you possibly thinking of Busby?" The congressman readily agreed; he had indeed intended the assignment for "that other boy, whatever his name is." "If he ever gets here," Congressman Johnson ordered, "you tell him that his job is to be my Churchill."

Still laughing at the preposterousness of the episode—a laugh-ter in which I was not ready to join—Woodward wiped his eyes and extended his hand. "Congratulations," he said with mock seriousness. "You are, from now on, our Blood, Sweat, Tears, and Toil Department."

I wondered then how it all would someday end.

Surprising as the events of my first hour in Congressman Lyndon B. Johnson's offices were, any more conventional and prosaic introduction into his world would have been a bit disappointing. After all that I had heard about him during my few years in Austin, I never doubted that my new employer would prove to be an improbable man.

Universally among his constituents the young congressman was accepted as a "miracle worker" in Washington. He could, by popular legend, accomplish anything: command the reopening of an Air Force base after the Pentagon had ordered its closing, speed the discharge of a son awaiting release from wartime military duty, or have an apologetic state official knocking at the door to hand-deliver an overdue old-age pension check. Much to the annoyance of his colleagues in the Texas congressional delegation, residents of other districts thought nothing of asking "Lyndon" to do what their own congressmen had not been able to accomplish, and most often, he succeeded. Furthermore, the image one formed of him as a power in national affairs was formidable.

While his importance in Texas could be disputed—and was, after the death of his patron Franklin D. Roosevelt—no one questioned Congressman Johnson's influence and impact in Washington. His name appeared regularly—and favorably—in national magazines and syndicated columns; visiting lecturers, knowledgeable about affairs on the Potomac, invariably told Austin audiences that their congressman was "one of the ten best in the House of Representatives," a young man "who is going far"; presidents—not only FDR but now Harry S. Truman—took him into their counsel; and on occasion one read, at least in the newspapers of his district, that he was under consideration for the cabinet. But when his constituents talked of "Lyndon," they invariably talked not of the man's attainments but of his personality.

This was not inconsequential. The Johnson personality, and the many tales in circulation about its more volatile manifestations, overshadowed all else about him—his politics, his performance, his genuinely remarkable public record. His friends and campaign workers freely acknowledged that it limited his future, or at least made the going harder. "No telling where Lyndon could go," I once heard a friendly lawyer say, "if he could just control that personality of his."

It was difficult, without having been exposed to the man or to the personality, to be fair in assessing this factor. In later years, after I had come to know him well, it would still be difficult to be fair: one seemed always to be somewhere between laughter and tears, or occasionally rage, over this personality which—try as its owner might—would never accept the bridle and bit of conformity. Fair or not, the talk I had heard, the images I had formed, of Lyndon Johnson's personality caused me to approach my association with him in a state of considerable wariness.

Around Austin, one grew accustomed to hearing what were referred to as "Lyndon stories." At backyard social gatherings on summer nights, when conversation slacked, someone would raise his voice and ask, "Have you heard the latest thing Lyndon did?" Everyone, men and women, would draw chairs closer and add enjoyment to the evening's watermelon by listening to the newest, and retelling the oldest, of the "Lyndon stories."

Most commonplace, of course, were accounts of his explosiveness in dealings with important community figures. All manner of conferences among Austin's staid, parochial old-family bankers and businessmen crashed to an end when, after an hour of desultory conversation brought no progress toward agreement, Congressman Johnson told the assembled symbols of wealth and prominence, "Gentlemen, you can go to hell!" Quite often, he was more explicit. One patriarch, never known to be bullish on the twentieth century, heard out the latest of the congressman's new schemes for fostering Austin's postwar growth and development; then, condescendingly, he avowed that he and his friends, and his family, liked Austin just the size it was. A long nose came leaning in, almost touching the patrician face. "Your brain has been clogged up for thirty years," the congressman shouted, "and it would be a service to the city if you poured in a can of Drāno to open it up."

Barons of banking and business were not the only targets. On one occasion, a leader of the local Daughters of the American

Revolution undertook her annual April pilgrimage to the DAR's national meeting in Washington. Walking through the Capitol with a contingent of friends from other states, she spotted her congressman approaching along the corridor. Buxom and bristling with the regalia of her office, she stepped into his path. "I'll just bet," she said coyly, "you don't remember my name." Without breaking stride, so the story went, Congressman Johnson shot back: "Lady, you are absolutely right. I don't have the least idea who you are."

Another "Lyndon story," especially popular after World War II, concerned a young entrepreneur, eager to climb to the top rungs of Austin life, and especially ambitious, as nearly everyone knew, to crash the inner circle around Congressman Johnson. When his first child was born, the man had the happy inspiration to share the tidings with the man whose favor he so coveted; at two o'clock in the morning, from the hospital, he telephoned the congressman's residence, cheerily reporting the new arrival. A cold steely voice interrupted. "What did you name it?" Brightly, the new father advised that the boy would be named "Junior." Forthwith, the congressman promulgated what came to be known irreverently as the Johnson rule on new babies: "In the future, on new babies," he decreed, before slamming down the telephone, "make it a practice not to call me before ten in the morning, unless you are naming them after me."

Other communities might have reacted differently to the image these "Lyndon stories" projected, taking them as evidence of simple boorishness, arrogance, ill temper, or poor manners. Many old-family Austinites did, in fact, savor and repeat the stories—along with some they invented—as confirmation of their oldest bias: that Lyndon Johnson was a man of no breeding, one of the "riffraff" visited upon the "better people" by the pestilence of the New Deal's class revolution. But that was part of another story, which I was to learn somewhat later.

Overall, Austin bore little resemblance to other communities: a small and beautiful capital city, populated with state employees, lawyers, university professors, and students, it was uncommonly liberal and tolerant, wise in ancient ways about public men. Whatever other feelings he riled up, Lyndon Johnson and his personality evoked in the community a consuming fascination. Politicians—Austin knew them all—did not and could not behave this way. Amateurs and professionals alike kept wondering: how long could he last, how far could he go, rebelling against the protocols of his cautious and guarded profession? Unless the laws of political physics were repealed, the consensus seemed to be that someday Lyndon Johnson's personality would bring him down.

My own view was, for the most part, the view of the congressman's political peers. Since coming to Austin as a student, I had gotten to know most of the principal political figures in state affairs: governors, lieutenant governors, attorneys general, legislators, and lesser officeholders. A summer devoted to the virtuous but not victorious gubernatorial campaign of Dr. Homer Price Rainey, dismissed as president of the University of Texas because of his defense of academic freedom against a reactionary board of regents, introduced me to the smoke-filled rooms of Texas liberalism. A year as a political reporter around the Statehouse brought me into daily contact with the talk, big and small, of the practicing politicians. In this world I knew best, Lyndon Johnson was a constantly recurring topic of conversation.

His fellow politicians retold the "Lyndon stories" with high and appreciative glee. However abrupt his outbursts, the congressman's determination to say what he thought when he thought it, to suffer fools poorly and to repulse presumption bluntly, and to refuse deference to the patriarchs who demand deference from even the highest-ranking public officials—all these traits evoked a sort of secret envy among men who, faced so often with similar situations, wished for the courage to emulate his responses. But the matching of his personality's unreality with political realities baffled everyone.

Lyndon Johnson would do almost nothing a Texas politician— liberal or conservative—was supposed to do. He seldom invoked the glories of the Alamo, ignored the conventions of the Sons of the Republic of Texas and the Daughters of the Confederacy, and was not the kind of man to be asked to deliver a states' rights address on San Jacinto Day, commemorating the Texas victory over Mexico on April 21, 1836. Grave suspicions lurked around the Statehouse that he was apostate on many teachings of the true Texas dogma: he spoke well of federal aid to education; he lacked fervor in defending Texas tidelands; he was deemed soft, by some, on issues such as civil rights and socialized medicine; and on one or two occasions, he had stirred a home district tempest by implying that the United States should try more cooperation with the Soviet Union.

The Johnson apostasy that most confounded other politicians related to his attitudes toward the state's sacred cows: the oil industry, private utilities, and the conservative employers' associations. No officeholder, it was believed, could defy these powers. Young Congressman Johnson defied all three and survived.

In his first year in Congress, he was one of only three Texans to vote for the first minimum wage legislation. After the next election, he was the only one of the three remaining in Congress. By his second term in Congress, he had succeeded in driving the private power utilities out of Austin and out of his district. During World War II, a test came on oil. Producers sponsored legislation raising the Office of Petroleum Allocation price ceiling on crude petroleum. Out of all the oil-producing states, only Lyndon Johnson's vote was recorded against it.

Such politics made no political sense: he gained no votes, he incurred unrelenting enemies. Before the oil vote, one friendly Democratic oilman—until the 1950s Texas millionaires were the bankroll of liberal Democrats—journeyed to Washington to dissuade his friend "Lyndon" from "political suicide." "Be absent, play sick, leave town," he pleaded. "Your vote won't affect the outcome, but it will destroy your future." Predictably, the congressman replied to the important contributor, "Screw you."

Governor James V. Allred, the spirited and combative bantam who gave Texas a New Deal of its own, regarded himself as the congressman's mentor. But he shook his head sadly over his protégé's fatal flaw: an unwillingness to compromise. "If Lyndon would only learn that politics is the art of compromise," Governor Allred told me in 1946, "he would make life so much easier for himself—and for all his friends." He illustrated with an episode which, to the governor, still seemed beyond belief.

In 1936, a year before he sought election to Congress, Lyndon Johnson presided as administrator over the National Youth Administration program in Texas. Word reached Allred, then in his first term as governor, that Administrator Johnson was about to make a grant to Prairie View State Normal College, the only state-supported senior college for blacks. Texas New Dealism, like FDR's Washington New Dealism, gave a very wide berth to racial issues. Allred, more appalled for Johnson than by his action, summoned the twenty-seven-year-old to the Statehouse.

"I know that out at Johnson City, where you come from, there aren't any coloreds," the governor began, carefully and correctly avoiding the inflammatory, and in those days insulting, terms "Negroes" and "blacks." "But you've got to understand, son, you're playing with something that would tear Texas apart; the people just aren't ready for federal money to start helping colored children through school." Allred went on at length—"at my persuasive best," he would say, laughing in recounting the experience—and concluded with an appeal to self-interest. "If you make the grant, you have no political future in Texas from then on—you'll be run out of the state."

"Know what that rascal did?" Allred liked to ask, affection mingling with exasperation. "He stood up and said, 'If that's all, Governor, I must go. You are so wise, so judicious, so fair-minded, so progressive, so Christian, that you have persuaded me. I must hurry back to the office before the money goes out to Prairie View—and double it.'"

If Lyndon Johnson was brash, reckless, even foolish in the eyes of his political peers, something about the man caused the power brokers to keep their hands on their political wallets. He might have voted wrong, behaved wrong, said what were considered the wrong things to the wrong people, but he had a personality—another and distinct public personality—which, it was just possible, might take over the state.

Congressman Johnson, as countless stories testified, was at his worst before small audiences, the individual encounters which are so much a part of a politician's success and survival. But, in vivid contrast, he was at his best before large audiences.

On the stump, before a campaign gathering, few men in Texas—before or after World War II—were his equal at moving and motivating an audience: orchestrating their applause to the rhythm of his words, cuing up their emotions to shake their fists or hiss at the mention of the people's enemies, and mobilizing them to march on the polls and smite down their foes—and his. Several times, long before I knew him personally, I stood on the edge of the downtown Austin park to hear him, and to watch him in action. Shouting, pounding, now whispering, now thundering around the stage, disdaining microphones and loudspeakers, he transformed sedate summer-night audiences into perspiring, foot-stomping, emotional mobs. Never careful with his voice, as politicians must be, he let his words come out raw and grating, but this only added a guttural and convincing meanness when he took after "PUP," a term he fashioned for the forces of evil: Petroleum, Utilities, and Privilege.

When he concluded, audiences never wanted to depart. They crowded toward the platform, and he came lunging out among them, coatless, drenched with perspiration, touching and being touched. Sometimes, as I once witnessed, he fell out of sight, beneath the crush of the young and the old struggling to be near him. If the "Lyndon stories" were true, Congressman Johnson might not be able to reach the well-born and well-placed and well-fixed across the width of a conference room; but in the public arena, where he could live by and be measured by his own codes, he reached the people. He was theirs and they were his, and with them he could overcome.

In 1946 his greatest test came. For the first time in his elective life, Lyndon Johnson faced an election contest without FDR in the White House to support him, or to save him. All the past closed in upon him: the defiance of the rules of Texas politics, the rebellion against the protocols of political behavior. Oil, the power trust, the conservative business lobbies, brought up their forces; so did the well-born, well-placed, and well-fixed of Austin. For a year or longer in advance of the battle, the consensus prevailed in Austin that Congressman Johnson could not survive the first postwar elections.

He bet everything on his ability to reach the people. Once campaigning began, he absented himself from the Tenth District, remaining in Washington, above the battle. It was necessary, he announced aloofly, that he be about the nation's business, supporting the program of the president; he had no time for politics. Two months, one month, before the voting, nothing could lure him into the contest; even two weeks before election day, he still had not been seen. Then came the electrifying announcement: fortuitously, the agenda of the nation would permit him to come home for the ten final days of the campaign, so that he could "visit" with his friends in each county seat. Neither the district nor the state ever saw quite such a virtuoso performance.

The incredible spectacle of "Lyndon" silently waiting out his doom fifteen hundred miles away had brought his constituents to the edges of their seats; word of his sudden coming brought them to their feet. Wherever he went, the little people were out in greater numbers than ever before, and he gave them what they had come to hear. "PUP" had his opponent—petroleum, utilities, and privilege had their candidate—but the people had him, the faithful public servant who had toiled at their labors without thinking of himself. The little people shook their fists, stomped their feet, and let tears run down their cheeks, while the opposition—which had been so close to victory—gnashed their teeth.

On the closing night of the campaign, the opponent spoke to an empty park with, it was said, the array of old-family guests on the platform outnumbering the listeners in the audience. Of course, the small attendance might be attributable, some cynics thought, to the fact that, at precisely the same hour, free watermelon parties were being staged on virtually every city block, and Lyndon Johnson stopped by each one, accompanied by the reigning cowboy movie star, Gene Autry.

When the votes were counted the following day, Congressman Johnson had won the hardest race of his career with 73 percent of the vote. It was a detail of that victory that, after a raging argument in full public view, he did not again speak to his young campaign manager for six months because the count was not 75 percent.

It was a time and a place soon to be remote but never irrelevant. In that time, at that place, the nature of the man was being forged. For Lyndon Johnson, life was a battle, and he fought it daily, hourly. His enemies were those who already had theirs, born to it or come to it by other means. They patronized him, mocked him, despised him, and tried always to bring him down. And wherever he met them—across a conference table, in a corridor, over a telephone, or in the chambers of Congress answering a roll call—he warred with them, confident that he could reach the people, and together, they and he would overcome.

While I could not know it before I knew the congressman himself, the "Lyndon stories" told much of the man who had been, and of the man who was to be.

Another, entirely different category of "Lyndon stories" was most on my mind as I prepared to meet him for the first time. These were the stories told by my recent colleagues in the pressroom at the State Capitol, and they were in a class apart.

The capitol pressroom at Austin, with bureaus of three national wire services and more than ten metropolitan dailies, was the summit of political coverage in Texas. To work there was to be smothered in constant solicitude—much of it liquid and hundred-proof—from all officeholders and office seekers. One became accustomed to great deference and accepted it as a just due. But one Texas political figure regularly gave capitol newsmen not tokens of esteem but the back of his hand: that, of course, was the Tenth District congressman.

A senior bureau chief who regarded himself as one of the real powers of Texas accosted Congressman Johnson at a political convention and asked a long, characteristically obtuse question. The Johnson lips, witnesses reported, set in a thin, tight smile, and the teeth clinched. "You know what you need?" the congressman asked, with cloying sweetness. "You need a nice, tall dose of warm salt water to flush out that constipated mind of yours." On another occasion, a reporter followed the congressman to his hotel room; at the door, turning the key, Congressman Johnson chose simply to ignore the reporter's presence and questions. An angry battle of nerves began: the reporter, hopping mad, pounded against the door, but no acknowledgment came from inside. After a long interval— which had grown, in the retelling, to one hour—the door abruptly jerked open and the congressman leaped out. "I'm not in here," he shouted to the stunned reporter, "and if you say I am, I'll say you are lying."

Lyndon Johnson was notorious for guarding his privacy, and that led to everyone's favorite pressroom story. A young reporter telephoned the Johnson office routinely, merely to confirm that the congressman would speak, as announced, at some political meeting the following day. A yes or no would have sufficed; instead, the congressman, through a secretary, communicated that it was "none of the press's business what he ever was going to do the next day." By late afternoon, a heated argument had developed, over virtually nothing. The reporter staked out the Johnson residence. When at last he saw the congressman emerge onto his back patio, the newsman came boldly across the lawn to confront him. What ensued was a mad Marx Brothers chase, through shrubbery, over furniture, and around the house—the reporter in full flight as the Tenth District congressman came running at him, waving his arms and shouting in the manner of a chicken farmer, "Shoo, shoo! Git, git!"

Congressman Johnson certainly did not invariably erupt at the first sight of a newspaperman, but even when he granted an interview, reporters were nervously aware that they raced a short and burning fuse. Understandably, one became conditioned by the "Lyndon stories" to meeting the congressman with some trepidation. I had been spared such a meeting during my own brief journalistic career and had still to see this storied personality for myself. Against this background, however, I could not profess to be surprised by the improbability of my arrival in the office of this improbable man.

— 3 —

THE BOMB THROWER

It would never have occurred to me to seek employment with Congressman Lyndon B. Johnson—and, in fact, I did not seek it. The job just came walking in one afternoon.

On a day shortly after the start of 1948 an Austin man, prominent as a writer and commentator on Texas affairs, stopped at my desk in the capitol pressroom. "Could I see you for just a minute?" he asked.

When I offered him a chair, he waved it aside and motioned for me to come with him. "This is private," he explained.

Notepad and pencil in hand, expecting to be given a tip on some news development, I followed him into the broad hallway and down two flights of stairs to the Capitol's marble rotunda. There my visitor leaned against an ornate column and, with a certain sorrowfulness, looked me over for a long moment before he broke his silence.

"You wouldn't be interested in going to Washington to work for Lyndon, would you?"

There was no introduction, no forewarning: only the stark and surprising question. I did not know what to say. Thoughts of a new job were far from my mind; I had no personal acquaintance with the congressman, or any of his political associates; my general impression of him evoked no enthusiasm, and I had not the vaguest idea what working in Washington for a congressman might entail. But the visitor gave me no chance to speak.

Quickly, he began reciting the essential details of the job offer he had come to present. The duties were curious: "You will be expected to read, think, and come up with new ideas." The salary was low: "Three hundred dollars a month, and that comes out of the congressman's own pocket." The one fringe benefit struck me as appalling: "Since the pay is less than you are getting now, the congressman will let you live rent-free at his house—you can have your own bedroom on the third floor." And, apparently, a yes-or-no answer was expected on the spot. "If you will fly, you can be in Washington tomorrow night."

I knew this must be entirely serious. My visitor was Paul Bolton, one of Congressman Johnson's closest advisers at the time and a man not given to idle humor. Before Bolton completed his recital, however, I was shaking my head negatively. But he held up his hand and still did not allow me to speak. "I know, I know," he said, cutting me off. "You are going to say you don't think you like Lyndon. Everybody says that. I'm not saying you will or you won't, but I wouldn't be here if I didn't think this was a good opportunity for you." Bolton leveled his eyes at me from behind his owlish glasses. "Let me tell you the whole story," he said, "and don't you say no until I'm through."

Over the next two hours, the two of us moved around the big granite State Capitol—from the rotunda down to a secluded corner by the post office, then to a hard seat on an unused back stairway, and eventually to the coffee counter at a drugstore across the street—while Bolton talked about Lyndon Johnson. It was the first time I had heard an objective discussion of the man, and I listened with increasing interest.

The starting point was the congressman's age. "Lyndon will be forty this year," Bolton explained, "and you know how men are when they reach that age—they begin to think life has passed them by." Such thoughts had been dominating Congressman Johnson since he had passed his thirty-ninth birthday in 1947: maybe he had chosen the wrong career; he might not be cut out for political life; and in any event, on his present course, he could see no future for himself in Texas or Washington affairs. Shortly before Christmas, he had called his close associates together and announced his decision: on January 1, 1948, he planned to announce his retirement, and he would return to Austin to manage the family radio station.

As Congressman Johnson analyzed the future of his political

career, he had come to a dead end. He had no prospect of reaching any position of leadership and influence in the national capital, at least not before the 1960s; and he would be an old man then, almost sixty. On the House Armed Services Committee, he could not expect under the seniority system to advance to the chairmanship for twenty years. Any significant role in the leadership of the Democrats in the House was blocked by the presence of the former Speaker Sam Rayburn in the reigning hierarchy. Mr. Rayburn, Bolton explained, was Congressman Johnson's friend, but he went on, "Lyndon says one Texan is enough Texans for the Democrats, and they won't take another one."

Furthermore, in the Johnson view, the country was entering a "long Republican era." For the first time in sixteen years, Republicans held control of both House and Senate, and now were preparing to take the White House in the elections of 1948. "Lyndon thinks the stand-patters are taking over," Bolton reported, "and he believes it will be fifteen years or so before anything progressive is done again, if then." The young man from the Texas Hill Country had moved at the center of Washington in its most exciting years—a companion and confidant of FDR, a friend of the famous and glittering personalities of New Deal life, a participant in the great events of the century. Now he could not accept serving out his days concerned only with strikes, investigations, Communist hunting, and budget cutting. "Lyndon," Bolton added with an indulgent smile, "is basically a big spender."

Congressman Johnson's friends argued against the decision or, at least, against announcing it on January 1, 1948, as he wanted to do. He should not abandon public life, they contended, for many reasons. Despite the state's conservative drift, his Central Texas seat in Congress remained secure, and he probably would have no opposition for reelection in 1948. If he dropped out of office now, he likely could never reenter politics successfully; Texas tradition ran strong against political comebacks. Thus, his retirement would default the future of Texas politics to what his people called "the Roosevelt haters"—Lyndon Johnson was the state's last surviving New Dealer under the age of sixty, and a number of his counselors and patrons hoped, in the postwar era, to build a strong liberal force in Texas, with him as the base. But the congressman was not moved.

National affairs, not state affairs, he insisted, were what he knew and all he cared about. He did not want to be the center of a party-building effort and had no desire to become—as some of his supporters wanted—governor of Texas, "messing around with ticky little issues." Lyndon Johnson wanted, he made emphatically clear, to be free of politics, to be his own man again, and to do "whatever I damn please."

In a final attempt to dissuade him, the council of friends hit him, as Bolton put it, "in his weak spot." They appealed to his sense of duty—not to politics or to Texas but to the country. From the beginning of his service, eleven years earlier, the thrust of his career had been devoted to the battles against American isolationism. In 1937, at President Roosevelt's personal request, he had accepted assignment on the House Naval Affairs Committee; in that role, he became FDR's acknowledged lieutenant on Capitol Hill during the long struggles to win appropriations for a two-ocean Navy over the growing isolationist opposition. In 1941, on the eve of Pearl Harbor, the congressman again responded to FDR's personal request by challenging—and almost defeating—an isolationist Texas governor in a race for the United States Senate. Out of that campaign, Lyndon Johnson won his statewide identity in Texas. When few political voices were being raised on behalf of military preparedness, he toured the state in April 1941, saying, "It is later than you think." For many of the young men who went off to fight the war, Congressman Johnson was a symbol of the kind of modern, internationalist, forward-looking leadership they wanted Texas to have.

Congressman Johnson's friends would not let him forget 1941—or what he stood for as a result of his public position against isolation. "We told him," Bolton recalled, "that the real showdown over America's course in the postwar world is still to come, and he can't quit now." One participant in the discussions also "stung him," Bolton said, by saying that if he retired Lyndon Johnson would be "running out on Roosevelt." The arguments were telling. Congressman Johnson agreed not to announce his withdrawal on January 1, although he reserved the right to do so later.

Anyone who knows Lyndon Johnson, his friend Paul Bolton told me, comes to understand that one must go behind his words to find the real motivations and purposes of the man. No one among those hearing the news of his imminent retirement fully accepted that only a lack of opportunity for personal advancement in Washington accounted for the congressman's depression. The causes must be deeper and more complex. Each associate had a theory; even at the closest range, it seemed, every man came to his own conception, and his own understanding, of Congressman Johnson.

Bolton, a sensitive and perceptive person always more interested in his friend's philosophy than in his politics, had this personal explanation. Basically, Congressman Johnson was simply not satisfied with the nature of his work in the House. "What Lyndon knows best, what he feels most strongly about, is the kind of work the New Deal did in the thirties," Bolton said. "He wants to be involved putting people to work, keeping kids in school, clearing out the slums, opening parks—that sort of thing." As a twenty-seven-year-old youngster, Lyndon Johnson had wangled appointment as administrator of the New Deal's National Youth Administration program in Texas. In that capacity, he had his first taste of this kind of activity, and in Bolton's judgment, "that's all Lyndon has ever wanted to do since."

However, in peacetime America, the congressman stood well away from the mainstream of domestic policies. At root, the committee assignment FDR chose for him was responsible for this impasse: on the Armed Services Committee, Congressman Johnson had little opportunity to participate in major domestic legislation or to pursue his own "natural interests." These, Bolton told me, were programs and policies directed to the nation's postwar needs in education, health, housing, conservation, rural electrification, and other such domestic sectors. "These are the fields where Lyndon would like to leave his mark." But it rankled the congressman that, thus far, he had left no mark at all on America's domestic policies. No major domestic legislation bore his name or imprint; he had no platform from which to speak about such concerns.

"Lyndon told us," Bolton recalled with a chuckle, "that he didn't want to spend the rest of his life 'sitting on my tailbone, listening to those sonofabitching admirals and generals and chicken colonels testify about bombers and carriers and air bases.'"

The analysis offered by Bolton came, in time, to be accepted by other participants in those Christmastime conferences. After more than a decade involved with war, preparedness, and defense issues, Congressman Johnson wanted new and broader horizons—activities which would permit him, in his own favorite phrase, "to do something for the folks." The congressman himself readily agreed. If he thought he could participate effectively and constructively over a broader range of national issues, that would be incentive to reconsider his retirement decision.

At this point, the question came down to one matter: How? How could Congressman Johnson best be started on what would be, in effect, a fresh career? For other public men, the answer might have been different. For Lyndon Johnson, however, those who knew him best believed that the first step had to come with his staff.

"Lyndon is not a creature of his staff, as some politicians are," Bolton told me, "but more than other men I have known in public life, he relies on his staff to help him go wherever he is going."

In the late 1930s, at a time when the staff role in political offices was still small and concerned with routine, Congressman Johnson became the talk of Capitol Hill with his office full of bright young men, mostly recruited from among the student leaders at the University of Texas. He adopted for himself the concepts and patterns of staffing which FDR had introduced into the White House; and at one time the congressman, characteristically, was thought to have more assistants than the president. But World War II dispersed the original staff, and since V-J Day, of the pre-war assistants, only Walter Jenkins had returned to the office. If the congressman was going anywhere, into new fields, new interests, new pursuits, it was in the nature of the man that he must have new—and additional— staff "to help him go wherever he is going."

Expansion of the Johnson staff was controlled by the Johnson pocketbook. His stenographic force alone—double the size of the typical congressman's office—drew most of the salary appropriation for the Tenth District. Thus, Congressman Johnson would have to pay himself for whatever staff was added. He scaled his goal down to a frugal two new positions. The job descriptions he prescribed told much about the man.

Congressman Johnson wanted one assistant "who is presentable and has a good personality." He would have a desk in the reception room, welcome visitors, deal with the departments, travel with the congressman, and in the main "leave a good impression." Unspoken in this description, however, was a familiar need of Lyndon Johnson's. Sensitively aware of the impressions he made himself, he wanted someone on his staff who could be for him what he felt he could not be for himself: poised, polished, gracious, easy and effective in light social conversations with others, preferably a bit debonair and sophisticated, and able to handle not only substantive matters but also the social situations that the congressman himself found so confounding. For this position, my friend Warren Woodward was being recruited.

The congressman, however, saw another need—for a staff assistant unlike any he had employed in previous years. In words I would long remember, Bolton quoted Congressman Johnson's description of the person he sought: "This fellow doesn't have to have any personality or looks. I don't care if his socks droop, or his shirt's open, or his tie's crooked. Fingernails ought to be clean, of course. But it's not his job to meet people or put up a good front. I'm going to keep him back in a corner, out of sight. I want him to read, think, and come up with a good new idea every day. I'd like for him to have enough heart to be able to cry a little, and I wouldn't mind if he had a mean streak—not too much, but enough. If I'm going to take on all those smart sonsabitches in Washington on this domestic business, what I've got to have is a bomb thrower."

Bolton looked at me and laughed.

"You," he announced, "are the bomb thrower."

The conversation had run late into the afternoon. Bolton and I were by now strolling around the grounds of the Texas Statehouse, pausing to kick aimlessly at the sidewalk or to watch the birds coming into the trees at twilight. A job with Congressman Johnson ran against all my instincts, all my ambitions, but Bolton's long discourse had intrigued me immensely. The congressman's "natural interests" were, very largely, also my own; the unexpected insight into the man's career dilemma stirred some sort of empathy; and, for the moment, the impressions created by the "Lyndon stories" seemed less important. Washington, I knew, was in my blood; for as long as I could remember, back to the day in March 1933 when I listened on coast-to-coast radio to Franklin D. Roosevelt's first inaugural address, I had wanted to be there in the national capital, to see the great men, to witness the great events, and perhaps to be close when great decisions were being taken. A job with a Texas congressman, of course, offered little promise of fulfilling those ambitions, but at least it would take me to the East for the first time. I found myself more interested than I meant to be.

"Paul," I asked, "does Lyndon know you are talking to me?"

"He told me to come. The offer is firm."

"But," I protested, "the man doesn't know me."

"No, he doesn't," Bolton agreed, "but that doesn't matter. Lyndon remembers your editorials in *The Daily Texan*."

Two years earlier, during my senior days at the University of Texas, I had served as editor of the student newspaper, *The Daily Texan*. The times on campus were tempestuous. A wartime confrontation between liberal faculty and reactionary regents—a confrontation which had precipitated a historic march on the State Capitol by the student body—had left the university divided, seething, and the center of all political eyes in Texas. Academic freedom had emerged as the foremost issue of state affairs. In the long tradition of editors preceding me, my uncompromisingly liberal editorials in *The Daily Texan* became a part of the controversy. I knew Congressman Johnson was a reader; once, during a period when the paper was under fire, he wrote a warm and encouraging letter from Washington highly complimentary to the editorial policy. From that perspective, I could understand why he might, without knowing me, think I would be a "bomb thrower." However, I found it far more difficult to comprehend what manner of man would offer me a job in his office and a room in his home sight unseen.

"No, I'm not kidding," Bolton said. "He doesn't know anything else about you, he hasn't made any inquiries about you—he's just going on your editorials."

While my first impulse had been negative, this clearly was not an offer to reject on the spot, not without thorough consideration.

"How much time do I have?" I asked.

"Lyndon wants everything yesterday," Bolton answered. "But if there is a chance you might accept, I think he'll wait for a little while."

I asked permission to discuss this with my friends, former professors, and the various statehouse acquaintances who knew much more about Congressman Johnson. Bolton agreed, on the condition that I not mention the fact that the congressman still had not decided whether to seek election to another term. I promised to give my answer in a few days.

Deciding whether I wanted to go to Washington presented no problems at all: of course I did. Among my generation of young Texans, the eastering urge ran strong. Except for one who departed for California, most of my closest friends from student days at the University of Texas were already in the East or on the way, setting out—as Texans have a long history of doing—to become arbiters of taste for New Yorkers as editors, critics, and authors. It was becoming embarrassing, in fact, to encounter old classmates and have them ask, in surprise, "Are you still in Texas?" But the primary drawback to the job in Washington was Congressman Lyndon B. Johnson.

Politically, the views of the Tenth District's young New Dealer were much nearer my own than those of any other public figure in the state. While I thought his actions strangely reckless, the congressman's provocative votes against the Texas sacred cows—oil, utilities, conservative employers—were intriguing and thoroughly appealing. Like the statehouse politicians, I found the behavior portrayed in the "Lyndon stories" unbelievable and unexplainable but, nonetheless, refreshingly honest. Obliging, conforming politicians, of whom I knew many, are bland, unexciting men, often very boring in private; whatever else, Congressman Johnson, as an employer, would not be flat and dull. But there was no doubt, from my knowledge of community opinion, that Lyndon Johnson was regarded as—in the favorite term of that day—"a character."

When I began my rounds, soliciting counsel from former professors, townspeople, political figures, and pressroom friends, I encountered considerable caution on just this point. His politics and performance were one thing, but Congressman Johnson's personality was quite another—and it influenced what people thought of his associates. "I'd go slow," a *Dallas Morning News* correspondent counseled. "Lyndon can be such a damn ass, and he makes so many people mad, that it might hurt you down the road to have his name on your record."

Out at the university, I encountered this reserve very pointedly among my former professors. "You can do better than that," a favorite journalism prof said, adding, "He only wants a press agent, and you aren't the type." When I defensively presented the imposing job description—arguing that I would be expected "to read, think, and come up with new ideas" rather than be a press agent—the professor responded with an incredulous snort. "Think? In Lyndon Johnson's office? Don't fall for that."

The chairman of the journalism department, Paul J. Thompson, was even more sobering. A dour Missourian, affectionately called "Spike" because of his temperance lectures to errant male undergraduates, Mr. Thompson faced a courtly gentleman's dilemma. Lyndon Johnson could not be all bad, because he had married a graduate of his department, Miss Claudia Taylor. Claudia, in Mr. Thompson's opinion, was one of journalism's finest products. "A girl of strong character," he used to tell his classes, "with a good head on her." Her choice of a mate, however, did not please Miss Taylor's former professor. After much evasiveness, Mr. Thompson came bluntly to the point. "If you leave the profession to work for a man of Mr. Johnson's reputation," he declared, "I am very much afraid you will never be able to get a job on any of the major newspapers in Texas."

The negative reactions in these early conversations were discouraging. I wanted to accept the job, solely as a vehicle for going east and beginning a career in Washington, but I did not want to be foolish. The mixture of forlorn head shaking and loud guffaws which greeted the idea clearly suggested, though, that for an association with Congressman Johnson, there might be an unexpected—and unnecessary—price. But these reactions, I realized, were coming primarily from persons who knew Lyndon Johnson barely, if at all. So I turned to his political peers, men who did actually know the congressman.

Politicians might laugh about Congressman Johnson, repeat their own versions of "Lyndon stories," and on occasion, denounce him for his heretical liberalism, but when I told my story, they were quick to recommend that I accept. Lieutenant Governor Allan Shivers, the state figure whom I knew best and longest, strongly urged me to take the job. "He'll work your tail off"—Shivers laughed—"but you'll learn more from him in thirty minutes than you will around here in ten years." Governor Beauford Jester worried that I might not return to Texas. "Our heaviest burden in the South is the loss of our young minds who desert their homeland for the North," he said. But if he were my age, the governor went on, he would catch the next train. "You'll hear all sorts of stories about him," he conceded, "but remember, Lyndon is one of a kind." Then he added with a wink, "Who knows? Lyndon just might end up as president of these United States someday."

Austin's most Olympian state official was Colonel Ernest O. Thompson, the stiff and starchy chairman of the powerful Texas Railroad Commission, which regulated the oil industry. In the colonel's eyes, few men in public life measured up to—or approached— the standards he set himself for courage, fortitude, and bravery under fire; the congressman was no exception. "All gall and no guts," he pronounced. "Got a good head, but it's not connected to any backbone." My face fell, but the colonel sheathed his knife. Few politicians had spine, he explained, so I should not be bothered. "Lyndon needs boys around who'll stand up to him," he concluded. "I recommend you accept, and when you see him tell him Ernest Thompson sends his highest regards."

One source of counsel I did not seek out was old Tom Martin, a wily Hill Country legislator who regularly enlivened sessions of the House of Representatives at Austin with stormy personal privilege speeches attacking Lyndon Johnson. Martin's particular complaint was that the congressman should not be regarded as a true Texan, and I had laughed through many of his dead serious tirades. Word spread around the Capitol that I was considering the job with the congressman, and in due time, the pressroom was shaken by Tom Martin's mule-skinning voice bellowing my name. As my colleagues silenced their typewriters to listen, Tom stood at my desk, orating loudly.

"Son," he stormed, "Lyndon Johnson is an easterner, not a Texan.

He went off up there to Washington and started running with the fast set—and now he dresses like 'em, acts like 'em, thinks like 'em, votes like 'em, and is one of 'em. Lyndon's no 'count, and never has been, but don't let that stand in your way." Tom Martin leaned closer. "You'd be a fool, boy, not to fall in with 'em yourself—after all, it's the easterners who run this country."

The attitudes I encountered in Austin were not greatly different from those I was to hear from Lyndon Johnson's political peers through the years ahead. He was baffling, broke all the rules, trampled on conventions and customs of his profession, and evoked a sort of wonder rather than awe in his colleagues; some of them disliked his company and disapproved of his politics, but as a rule, fellow politicians were far more tolerant and respectful of him than those removed from the public arena. But what I learned from my conversations did little to bring into clear focus any portrait of Congressman Johnson.

The few days in which I had promised a decision became a few weeks and a few months. Whenever Paul Bolton called or came by to check on my progress, I told him—mostly as a term of convenience—that I could not decide what the job offered as a "future." His reports finally touched off the short fuse in Washington. At the capitol post office one morning in late February, I found waiting my first and only communication about the job from Congressman Johnson.

In a "Dear Horace" letter, the congressman wrote:

> There is a wealth of material here and with your imagination and initiative I think we could make an excellent team. I know you could expand your contacts, widen your influence and render a service to Texas if you were here.
>
> ... We could start you at $300—that comes out of my own pocket—and if you choose you can stay at our home without charge until you find just what you want. I will do what I can to see that you know all the people that are worthwhile, and I think in a very few weeks you would be very happy that you made the decision to come.
>
> If you plan to do this let me know, because I am putting off doing a lot of work until you get here.

Under the provocation of my long-extended delay in saying yes or no, the congressman exhibited commendable restraint—up to that point. But a P.S. had been added to the letter, and I sensed that its waspish tone was nearer to pure Johnson:

> I don't know what the future holds for any of us—who does? I do know that if you fit in as Paul thinks you will, there will always be plenty of work to do in the public interest and I think we will always have enough for bacon and beans. Frankly, Horace, I think it is a great opportunity and you can make it as permanent as you like.

I read the letter several times, absorbed. Obviously, my stall about the future had gotten through, and he made short shrift of it. But I was most taken by the phrases he sprinkled through the letter—"imagination and initiative," "render a service," "plenty of work to do in the public interest." Until then, I had thought of the job not in terms of the public interest but only in terms of Lyndon Johnson. I liked the new thought.

When I reached my desk in the International News Service bureau, I handed the letter, without comment, to my bureau chief, Bill Carter. A native of New York, Carter was still emerging from culture shock over his transfer the previous year from Manhattan to Texas; however, until now he had carefully avoided offering any opinion, or even any comment, on my decision. He read the letter carefully and handed it back.

"Go," he said. "Johnson is big-time. He's going somewhere. You don't want to waste your life around the clowns and baboons down here."

I picked up the telephone and called Paul Bolton.

"I guess I'll try your job."

— 4 —

SNOWSTORM IN MISSISSIPPI

One evening early in 1960, at the start of the national election year, I met Senator Lyndon B. Johnson at the majority leader's office in the Capitol. When his work was completed, we rode together in the long black limousine to his home in Northwest Washington, and as I had hoped, there was an opportunity to discuss with him a matter of some importance.

A national magazine had requested an article, to be published under his byline, giving his views on the presidency—his conception of the office, how it could and should be used to meet the challenges of the 1960s, what he would do if he were to be elected the thirty-fifth President of the United States. Senator Johnson already had declined the publication's invitation. However, those of us who were interested in persuading him to become an active candidate for the Democratic nomination regarded the opportunity as too valuable to be rejected. My purpose was to change his mind.

As we rode through the Washington streets after the evening rush hour, I raised the matter with him. "I don't like it," he replied. "No man ever ought to say what he would do if he were president." I knew, of course, that "if" always irritated him, and I had a suggestion ready. The article could be written to express only his conception of the office of the presidency. I grew a little expansive, outlining my own thoughts. Many such articles were being written by or for other prospective candidates, and the literature of the scholarly journals offered much on this theme. The presidency, I was saying, repeating the popular views, is a "bully pulpit," as Theodore Roosevelt called it; it is an office for educating the nation and elevating the people's goals and aspirations; and on and on. I was, of course, speaking to a man who had been close to the presidency and its occupants through all his Washington life. After a few moments he cut me off in midsentence, unimpressed with the lofty theorizing.

"The presidency," he said very firmly, "is a man."

Of course he was right, and no presidency was to confirm that view more convincingly than his own. On the thirty-first of March 1968, when he came down to the hours of choice about his continued occupancy of the office, it was relevant to remember the man as I had first met him in another March, twenty years before.

On the afternoon of March 16, 1948, surrounded by the collected works of the Right Honorable Winston S. Churchill, I settled down at my newly assigned desk in 504 Old House Office Building to await the first face-to-face meeting with my new employer, Congressman Lyndon B. Johnson. I recognized, of course, that the story of my initial, incredible assignment would, when I recounted it someday to the friends I had left behind in Texas, add another and very lively episode to the repertoire of "Lyndon stories" so popular around Austin. I did not immediately suspect, however, that more was still to come. Or that before the end of this unforgettable first day in Washington, I was to become a central figure in the "Lyndon story" that would live on, as a sort of summarizing legend, long after other tales of this improbable man were forgotten.

Although I remained unaware of any of this, the singular reception Congressman Johnson was planning for me had been set in motion back in January. "Lyndon wants everything yesterday," Paul Bolton had told me then, asking, in effect, for an on-the-spot answer to the Washington job offer. But this hardly seemed consequential when Bolton patiently accepted my request for a few days to think it over. When my indecision ran on and on, through the weeks of January and February, Bolton, the kindliest of men, gave no deadlines, made no attempts to force the issue; neither did he hint of the increasingly agitated telephone calls from Washington, demanding to know "when is that boy from the university going to make up his damn mind."

Bolton, alone in the Johnson world, knew both parties to the agreement he was trying to consummate. A quiet, reflective, deeply intelligent University of Missouri alumnus, Paul Bolton was philosophical, not political; he served, it was said, as "Lyndon's owl," trying—with great effect—to broaden the young congressman's range of intellectual interests and to channel more purposefully his phenomenal energies and abilities. Ten years older and far more secure than the congressman, Paul Bolton treated his friend Lyndon's tempestuousness with amused and detached indulgence. As for myself, Bolton had become a friend and senior counselor during my editorship of *The Daily Texan* at the University of Texas. He applauded my rather militant editorial prose during the campus controversy and described me to his large radio audience as "an outwardly placid and pleasant little fellow, who runs his newspaper with more prickly independence than any other editor in Texas." He also formed an interesting personal assessment.

At one point during the weeks of my indecision, I raised with Bolton the possibility that I might not get along with the volatile congressman. Bolton conceded that could be the case. "Lyndon is a prima donna," he admitted, "but I wouldn't worry about that. After all, you are a little bit of a prima donna yourself." Then he laughed, savoring a thought which intrigued him very much. "I would like to be in a corner of the room the first time you two tangle."

The prolonged procrastination was highly provocative to the congressman. When he wrote in late February, his letter was, as I sensed and confirmed later, the end of his patience. However, my prompt affirmative reaction—together with Bolton's assurance that I intended to depart in one week—soothed things, briefly. Then I told Bolton that I must postpone departure for another week. An incredulous Lyndon Johnson learned that, instead of heading for Washington, I was heading west to the McDonald Observatory to cover an unexpected national assignment on what astronomers would learn when the earth made its closest pass of the century to the planet Mars.

On Wednesday, March 10, assured that I was finally on the road, a relieved Paul Bolton reported the news to Washington and promised that I should be arriving on Saturday or Sunday, within the customary three days required for the long drive. Saturday, a Johnson office workday, passed with no sign of the new assistant.

On Sunday afternoon, Congressman Johnson himself opened the office and began awaiting my arrival. After several hours a messenger came bearing a telegram dispatched at noon from Meridian, Mississippi, less than one full day's journey from Austin. It read: DELAYED BY SNOW AND ICE. ARRIVING MIDWEEK. ALL IS WELL. BUSBY. The congressman's thoughts were not recorded in their fullness, but his words registered indelibly upon those who heard them, and they were to enrich the comic-opera afternoon of my eventual arrival at his office.

Other priorities had intervened along the way to occasion the message from Mississippi. For one thing, I had developed a very specific dread of being quartered at the Johnson residence, in "my own bedroom on the third floor." The rent-free offer was generous, and in housing-scarce Washington it might be inescapable, but at the age of twenty-four, I placed considerable value upon living my own life. Driving away from Austin after the long afternoon with my pressroom friends, I realized it would never do to motor up to the Johnson home—to my Texas mind, the unheard-of third floor suggested a mansion—with trunk and both seats of my automobile overflowing with the artifacts of four college years. I made what I considered a happy and rare decision: I would detour 180 miles north to my hometown of Fort Worth, and leave with my parents some of the cartons of books, record albums, newspapers and magazines, photographs, letters, plaques, study lamps, and such.

The detour also served another important purpose. Both my parents were near collapse over the news that I had decided to enter the employ of Congressman Johnson. My father, an old-school Church of Christ evangelist, had accepted admirably my first career decision, to enter newspapering: "It's the shortest road to hell." But the second career was confirming his fears. From his own church friends in Central Texas, my father knew that Congressman Johnson drank whiskey, danced, played forty-two, and "whooped it up at parties sometimes." Furthermore, as Dad set out in a plaintive eight-page letter, "Lyndon, you know, is a Digressive." This mattered most of all.

"Digressives" was the term applied by members of the Church of Christ to members of the Disciples of Christ, or Christian, Church. It was not a term used in any spirit of brotherly love. At the turn of the century, a bitter schism had rent the congregations of the Church of Christ across the nation: modernists, who were to form the Disciples of Christ, began moving pianos into the Lord's houses, and fundamentalists, unable to find biblical authorization for instrumental music, began moving out, retaining the Church of Christ name. In Texas, as in most of the Bible Belt, church and state were never far separated, and this old schism still simmered in politics. Church of Christ members could advance no higher in public life than to the position of school superintendent, but "Digressives" faced no such ceiling; in fact, one had reached the governorship during the 1930s, and it was especially galling that he had switched from the Church of Christ to the Disciples of Christ before entering politics. My association with a Digressive congressman would, I knew, be a burden on my father wherever he went in the brotherhood, and I thought the overnight detour to Fort Worth not only would be compassionate but might also spare me a steady flow of eight-page letters.

The evening with my parents went as expected. They were reassured that I showed no outward evidence of a dissolute life. Dad found some comfort from the fact that "Frank Roosevelt"—whose church affiliation he had forgiven because "Episcopalianism is religion in its lightest form"—had seen some good in Congressman Johnson. At their bedtime Bible reading and prayers, I joined my parents for the last time, and my father prayed, "Guide and protect Horace Jr. in the strange city, and set Mr. Johnson on the path of right." I knew my strategy had succeeded.

When morning came, however, an unseasonable Texas blizzard had glazed the highways with ice. Since Mother intimated that the Lord might be trying to tell me something, I took no chances and went back to bed. On Saturday, at last, the journey resumed. Born and raised in Fort Worth—"The City Where the West Begins"—I was taught by parents, and even public school teachers, to disapprove of our neighbor city of Dallas, twenty-five miles away: it was not western, not even truly Texas; it was eastern, effete, and unfriendly, and we lived for the day when its arrogance would be humbled by virtuous Fort Worth's greater growth. But on the morning of my departure, I felt differently about Dallas: when I passed under the landmark triple underpass, one of the proudest showpieces of North

Texas since the 1930s, and saw the tall buildings of downtown rising above me, I sensed for the first time that I might be on the way to a far larger experience than I had anticipated.

That feeling grew stronger throughout the first day. From Dallas eastward, each mile of the way was new. I had never seen East Texas, or Louisiana, or the Mississippi River—and I approached the Deep South with both excitement and a very real trepidation.

A Texas boyhood could be very different from those in the states of the Old Confederacy. My father's father wore the gray; my mother's mother saw Sherman's troops burn the family home in Alabama. But these people moved west as war refugees, and many of those who found their way to Texas remembered the South as a dark and bloody place, and despised it. "Mr. Lincoln was our greatest president," my Confederate grandmother taught me, "because he stopped the killing." In this spirit, they taught their children Texas history, not southern history. At Fort Worth's Lorenzo de Zavala Eighth Ward Elementary School—named, of course, for a signer of the Texas Declaration of Independence—I spent the 1930s learning the songs of the Texas Revolution, participating in annual reenactments of the Mexican surrender at the Battle of San Jacinto, and in two successive years reciting before a rapt gathering of the PTA the full text of Colonel William Barret Travis's last letter from the Alamo. But it was only after I had been in Washington almost one year that I learned by asking an Alabaman—who was outraged at my ignorance—the meaning of the term "Lost Cause."

Conditioned by years of reading liberal journals, I half expected to find, when I crossed the Mississippi at Vicksburg, a Ku Klux Klan lynching party waiting. Instead, I found history, American history, not Texas history, at the Vicksburg Battleground and National Cemetery. The journey came to a standstill. Through a long afternoon there, and through other hours on the days to follow, I left the highway to feast on the past: Jackson, Montgomery, Atlanta, Kings Mountain, Thomas Jefferson's home, Monticello. The congressman, I was confident, would understand. But to keep him from worries about the possibility of an accident I dispatched—thoughtfully, in my own view—the brief telegram from Meridian, Mississippi, explaining about the snow and ice which had delayed the start of my travel back in Texas.

In Congressman Johnson's office early in my first afternoon, I began sensing that something must be awry. My new colleagues smiled at me when they saw me looking out from around the Churchill books, and occasionally they asked trivial questions about the weather in Texas. Only my old friend Warren Woodward, however, engaged in conversation. Walter Jenkins in particular seemed unusually reserved, almost aloof, and I thought it unusual that neither he nor anyone else had me take advantage of the congressman's absence to complete the usual forms required of new employees. But then the congressman's own continued absence became puzzling. The telephone calls, which continued to occupy Jenkins, had to be from Congressman Johnson himself, but the House had completed its voting and adjourned for the day, and night had come over Washington. Then I heard the door open and close in the private office, and I thought my meeting was near.

Congressman Johnson's arrival at his desk, behind the closed door, sent his staff into spasms. Buzzers were sounding, telephones ringing, red and green signal lights—indicating when he was on a call—were flashing above his door; stenographers went racing to and from Jenkins's desk depositing stacks of freshly typed letters, and Jenkins, traveling at higher speeds than anyone else, raced to and from the congressman's inner office. It was apparently very grim business: no one—except Woodward—smiled or spoke. Shaking his head ruefully and laughing with reckless irreverence, he called in to me: "Now you see why they call him the Blanco Blitz."

The state of near frenzy went on for more than an hour. I might as well have been still on the highway, or out sightseeing in Washington: no one looked my way or spoke. Then Walter Jenkins returned from one of his sprints and, with a sudden formality in his voice, summoned me to his desk.

"Mr. Johnson will see you now," he said. He lit a cigarette nervously, blew smoke toward the ceiling, then looked at me very coldly. "I think I should tell you, before we go in, that I honestly do not know what he may say to you about the future of your arrangement with us."

It was a thunderclap. The import of the announcement could not have been more starkly clear. But why? What had so suddenly gone wrong? What had I done?

My confusion seemed to soften Jenkins slightly. He took another nervous draw on his cigarette and turned toward me again, showing a little pity. While he was sure there must be some explanation, Jenkins suggested, Mr. Johnson himself had driven from Austin to Washington many times—and it never required more than three days.

"But I sent you a telegram," I protested.

"Yes, Mr. Johnson received your telegram himself." Jenkins obviously did not want to say more, but he blew out another mouthful of smoke, and a sort of smile played around his lips. "When the message came, Mr. Johnson called the United States Weather Bureau himself, and asked them to check their records."

Jenkins seemed to expect me to understand something from this remark, but to me it was the most incomprehensible turn yet.

"The Weather Bureau," he announced, rising from his chair to deliver the coup de grâce, "told Mr. Johnson that the last time it snowed in Meridian, Mississippi, in March was before you were born."

I was stunned, outraged by the stabbing innuendo. I came to my feet trying to explain that the snow and ice had occurred in Texas, not in Mississippi, from where the telegram had been sent. But I was too upset to speak, and Jenkins, now motioning for me to follow him, delivered his final line. "Mr. Johnson said then, 'I don't think I am going to like this Busby boy.'"

With that, the two of us headed for the presence of the man who was to be either my new or my near employer. As we hurried, at Jenkins's gait, through the hushed center reception room, I caught a glimpse of the good Protestant Warren Woodward at his desk, solemnly crossing himself on my behalf.

presence of a mature, adult member of the Congress of the United States, a mover and shaker on the Washington scene, a friend and counselor of President Franklin D. Roosevelt. But I knew instinctively that the Honorable Lyndon B. Johnson did not, as a matter of everyday routine, sit so stiffly behind his desk, holding his head so awkwardly, just to balance precariously across his long nose the pair of pince-nez glasses he was wearing. Neither would any man, engaged in such a commonplace chore, be straining so visibly and uncomfortably to keep upright, at a perpendicular angle, out of the corner of his mouth, this six- or eight-inch cigarette holder now clenched between his teeth. Walter Jenkins's bursting laughter told me that for himself, as well as for me, this was a show, a marvelous show, complete with props.

The act went on with unwavering aplomb and finesse. At least twenty-five letters were awaiting signature, and the congressman made a production of each: the same elaborate concentration, the same sweeping reach across the desk toward where I stood, the same deliberate and calculated avoidance of any glance in my direction. Once he interrupted the ritual to extinguish a cigarette; without looking, he pointed the holder toward the ashtray, pressed a button, and the cigarette ejected with perfect aim. A few moments later, after he had inconspicuously touched the fingers of his right hand to the wrist of his left arm, a startling buzzing sound broke the silence and continued until he unhurriedly stopped the alarm on his wristwatch. He was demonstrating all his gadgets. I knew, by then, that I must be in for the full treatment, and I wanted to join Walter Jenkins in his laughter.

All the heat had gone from my emotions. The congressman had his own image of me: it was misleading, I thought, and based on misinterpretations, but given what he assumed I must be like, this was a singularly persuasive way to deliver the message: a man of such great importance was not to be taken so lightly.

Twenty-five minutes passed before the signing of the final letter. Jenkins and I remained standing where we had waited throughout the episode. The congressman leaned far back in his chair, this time looking directly at me—and through me—with a cold, impassive, and unseeing stare. He pressed a button for his secretary, Mary Rather. Pert and pretty, tiny Mary came bouncing through the entrance behind us and began collecting the trayful of signed letters. With her back turned toward Congressman Johnson, she quickly surveyed the scene, realizing what was transpiring; she hurried out—in fact she ran—but did not quite make it: before Mary Rather could open the heavy door, she burst into laughter.

The moment had come. Congressman Johnson could evade no longer the unpleasant business of dealing with me. He returned the pince-nez glasses to his coat pocket, rested the cigarette holder on the ashtray, and fastidiously went over the desktop, brushing and blowing away specks of dust. Then he bounded to his feet, reaching both hands across the desk to clasp mine, and with his broadest, warmest, most transparently insincere grin, he said: "Horace, how good it is to see you. Please"—he gestured toward the chair beside me—"don't stand. You've had a tiring trip."

The world had spun again.

I'd never met a congressman before and had no sure idea of the proper salutation. In haste, I fell back on the greeting which would have been normal in the pressroom at Austin: "Hello, Lyndon."

He continued pumping my one hand in both of his and drew me over the desk before he released the very firm grasp. "You must be very thirsty," he said, his voice registering elaborate concern. "Could I get you a drink of water?"

I did not want a drink, but before my "No, thank you" caught up with him, he charged around the desk, bound for a small lavatory fixture in the corner of the room. Then he was back, still smiling, and his six-foot-three-inch frame towered over my five feet seven inches as I gulped down the tumbler of tap water. He took the glass, gestured more insistently for me to be seated, and moved the chair closer to me. "Please, Horace. Don't stay on your feet."

I felt a little foolish, since Walter Jenkins remained standing, but I did as I was told. Congressman Johnson downed a glass of water himself and hurried back to his own chair.

"I am so anxious," he began, "to hear about how things are in Austin, and how they are with yourself. I know you have much to tell me."

The performance of the last half hour simply had not happened. A different man occupied the tall chair, a man animated, spirited, overflowing with apparent friendliness, and smiling all the while in what I learned his staff identified as the "Chessie Cat grin." He appeared to be waiting eagerly for my first words.

I began with some appropriately light remark, trying to demonstrate both my wit and my determination that two could play at this game. But I got no further. "Yes, yes." He nodded after my attempted humor. "That's very good." Then, once again, his demeanor changed.

The smile left his face. He fished out a smaller cigarette holder and lit up again. From another pocket, he removed a second pair of eyeglasses—conventional glasses with rims and earpieces—and began twirling them idly. He appeared thoroughly organized, at ease and reflective.

"There are several things I should tell you about your work here."

He held up one finger. "Point One," he said. "If you don't already think so, in a few weeks you will begin to think that you are smarter than I am. That's fine, that's the way I want it to be. Young men who work for me are of no value to me unless they are smarter than I am." The finger leveled in my direction, and he spoke emphatically. "But if you think you are smarter than I am, be sure you don't just think so—be damn sure you are."

Two fingers opened up on his large right hand.

"Point Two. At Austin you saw the Texas Legislature in operation, and that was valuable experience," he said, "but don't expect Congress to be the same. You'll find a different breed of men in any Congress than in state legislature—better quality, better informed, harder working, and on the whole, a hell of a lot smarter." An edge came into his voice. "Your professor friends at the university might not think so, but you always remember this: for a man who works at his job, four or five terms in the House or two terms in the Senate are equivalent to anybody's Ph.D."

The fingers continued to open, and he kept on counting off the points he wanted to make—"Point Three," "Point Four," "Point Five." In essence, I was on my own. He wouldn't tell me what to do; I was there to tell him what to do. Read all I wanted, tell him who I wanted to talk to and he would arrange it, give him my best judgment about what ought to be done for the country—and he would try to do it.

By now, I was taking a reporter's notes on this discourse. However, at my side in the next chair, Jenkins, relaxing for the first time since my arrival, occupied himself—to my gratitude in later days—by transcribing the words in shorthand as Congressman Johnson spoke.

"Point Six." The congressman gazed steadily across the desk. "From what I know of you, you are very independent. Don't lose that. It does me no good to have people who only agree with me, and I have never had that sort. If you think I'm wrong, say so; when you disagree, speak up. But when you have differences with me, don't go out and talk about it to every Tom, Dick, and Harry who happens along before you talk to me."

A genuinely warm smile lightened his face, a smile I was to see many times as a preface to his next words: "One thing Roosevelt always told me is very good advice." Utterly unconscious of what he was confirming about the performance a few moments before, he began demonstrating the Rooseveltian manner, and even the voice. "The president would stick that long cigarette holder straight up—you'd think it was going to set fire to his eyebrows—and he would cock that big head back, looking down through those pinch-nose glasses; then, he would say"—and now the words came in FDR's familiar cadence—" 'Lyndon, my boy, it is my observation that the men who serve me best, and the ones I respect the longest, are those who have a passion for anonymity.' "

Congressman Johnson liked that thought, or some memory it recalled, and he lingered over it in silence before resuming.

"Point Seven," he began, but abruptly withdrew it. "No, I guess that's enough points. I think it might be helpful if I gave you some idea of how I feel about the country's problems."

The chair behind the desk turned until Jenkins and I could see only the back. Congressman Johnson faced the dark windows, raised his long legs, and rested his feet on the table beneath the windows.

"Roosevelt is gone," he said. "We never finished what he started out to do, and I'm not sure, the way the country seems to be going, that we're going to do much about the things that most need doing. The economizers are in the saddle, and after November, they'll have the reins.

"We ought to be doing something for our schools, but we won't. We ought to be doing something for our old folks, but we won't." One by one, the sentence structure seldom varying, he worked through a long listing of the issues he regarded as most important—jobs, housing, hospitals, soil conservation, water, rural electrification, farmers, and more. His tone remained unchanging, and he spoke with resignation until the list ran out.

"I don't know what I can do, or anybody can do," he said. "We don't seem to have the ideas like we used to have, and if we had the ideas, I'm not sure we could get the votes."

Still facing the windows, his feet on the table, Congressman Johnson turned to another subject. "You probably are wondering if we are going to have another war," he said. "The thing in Czechoslovakia looks bad. Italy, France, Berlin—it all looks bad in Europe. World War III? I don't think so, but I don't know so.

"We aren't prepared. It's 1941 all over again. The atom bomb has given us a Maginot Line psychology. It's powerful, too powerful to use again, but that doesn't mean there won't be more wars. When an aggressor knows you're muscle-bound, he's going to come edging across the border, nibbling away—like Hitler did—taking it in little bites nobody wants to fight about, until he's chewed up all of it.

"Isolationism? Yes, I think that's a danger, the real danger. The people are tired of controls and taxes and government. They want to keep their money home. I think the Marshall Plan will pass, and we'll get some help for Europe—but we'll pay a price for it at home. The isolationists will start picking off the liberals who vote for aid, and we'll go back over the same old road."

Another silence began, and it continued long. I thought he might have concluded. But his chair turned suddenly, and he was leaning on the desk, his eyes showing a new liveliness. "Of course, you understand," he said, "we can't wait forever about the Negroes. They fought the war, they got better jobs, they proved themselves. They want for their children the same thing I want for mine. The haters are determined to keep them down, but they won't stay down forever."

In Texas I had never heard a man in public life say such things, whether before an audience or in private. I was surprised, fascinated, and at the moment, none too certain what it meant.

Other than the economy issue, he continued, the Negro issue was, and had been through all his years in Washington, the greatest single roadblock to domestic legislation. "It's messed up some way in every question that comes along," he said, "and you can't get a domestic bill through because somebody stands up and starts yelling, 'Nigger, nigger.'" Change, he insisted, must come in the South and also in the North. "Force won't change any of it," he added, "but it has to change—we've got to get it off our back."

Abruptly, he stopped and rose from his chair. Since I had entered the room, feeling so different than I felt now, I had met not one but two, and possibly even more, Lyndon Johnsons. I wondered how many others there might be within this improbable man. For the moment, though, it was clear from his manner that the introductions were over.

Once more the broad "Chessie Cat grin" fixed on his face. He shook hands again and told me that he was "very proud" to have me on his staff, and that he appreciated my coming. Nothing was said—either then or later—about my telegram from Mississippi, about my late arrival, or about the mountain of Churchill books waiting on my desk. Following Walter Jenkins, who seemed anxious for us to withdraw, I started for the doorway, but Congressman Johnson called to me.

"One more thing," he said. "In the past, it has been the practice of the young men in the office, at their own choice, of course, to call me 'Congressman.' None of those close to me call me 'Lyndon.'"

I took due note of the instruction and never again spoke of him—or thought of him—as "Lyndon."

Outside the inner office the reception room stood vacant, but Jenkins and I could hear laughter coming from a gathering of the staff in the adjacent workroom, where I had been assigned a desk. All the office force was gathered around, and Mary Rather stood in the center reenacting the scene she had witnessed on her quick visit to collect the mail. Jenkins burst in on the scene waving a fist in the air. "He made it," Walter shouted, "he made it."

Everyone crowded about me now, shaking hands, offering congratulations, and appearing relieved, as if some prolonged burden had been lifted from the office. Walter Jenkins, lively and spirited for a change, began recounting his version of the encounter, and after he had set the stage, he asked: "What did you think when you saw those glasses and that cigarette holder?"

I felt a little foolish answering with the truth, but I summoned up the courage to tell them, as they waited expectantly: "Well, I know it's silly, but I had the idea that he was trying to look like President Roosevelt."

My colleagues clapped their hands and laughed louder than ever. I knew that my answer must be correct. After a moment, Mary Rather spoke, her voice both disapproving and understanding. "You'll learn after you've been around for a while," she said, "that every so often, when the mood comes over him, Mr. Johnson just likes to play president."

My first day in Washington was not yet ended, nor were my insights into Congressman Lyndon B. Johnson.

Amid the general merriment and excitement following the unexpectedly successful conference with the congressman, members of the staff lowered their guard. No one was posted to watch the door from the congressman's office. The senior staff members became engaged retelling—for myself and Warren Woodward—their own brand of "Lyndon stories," affectionate but wholly irreverent accounts of episodes similar to my experience. At the big point of one such story all eyes turned to see, standing in the doorway, a very disapproving Lyndon B. Johnson.

No one knew how long he had been standing there or what he had heard. Understandably, there was some hard swallowing and nervous shifting from one foot to another. Adopting the air of a man deeply wronged but still tolerant, he looked over the group and said: "I don't hear any typewriters clicking."

It was, I noted, already seven-thirty at night. Typewriters, however, started clicking immediately at every desk. But he had come to see me.

"Horace," he began, but his nose turned up as though he had smelled a dead fish. "What do people call you?" he asked. "I'm sure they don't call you that."

Warren Woodward intervened. "On campus, everybody called him Buzz."

"That's better," he said. "Yes, I like that." Then he went on. "Buzz, as you know, I wrote you that you could stay at our residence. Mrs. Johnson and I would be pleased to have you come and make yourself at home." My hopes were sinking, but this was hardly the time to tell him that I did not want to live at his home. "However," he continued, "I had a chance to think it over during your long trip, and I decided you would prefer to have a place to yourself. So, you and Woodward are going to stay together where I lived when I first came to Washington—over in the basement of the Dodge Hotel."

It sounded like nothing at all, but this was wonderful, and I thanked him as he turned away. He left the office, without his coat or hat, and the typing stopped again. But this time the congressman returned by telephone: if Woodward and I had no other plans for the evening, why didn't we go on out to his house and visit with Mrs. Johnson until he arrived for dinner?

The Johnson residence in Northwest Washington proved not to be the mansion I had imagined. Hidden away on secluded Thirtieth Place, it was an unpretentious but very appealing red-brick structure which did, indeed, have three stories—like most single-family residences in Washington and none that I knew in Texas. At the door, I began searching in the dark for a doorbell, but Woodward told me the protocol.

"The Johnsons," he said, "never lock their door, and you are expected just to go on in."

We did, and a voice called from the living room. "Gentlemen, is that you?"

It was a splendidly warm voice, rich with the accents not of Texas but of some more southern origin. I followed Woody and came into the presence of Mrs. Johnson, the lady I had heard referred to only as "Claudia."

Mrs. Johnson was seated in a tall wing-back chair near the door, waiting for her husband. As she waited, she was reading a book. Her large, dark eyes were warm, like her voice, but unlike her speech, the eyes showed nothing of the South: they were capable of great intensity, as I became acutely, and awkwardly, aware during the next several minutes while they took my measure—against what background of husbandly comment I did not want to imagine.

In Texas state politics, one became accustomed to the demure, self-effacing helpmates who stood to the side, smiling, making frequent reference to "Daddy," and exchanging comments about the weather. This, I knew immediately, was not that sort of woman.

When I took my seat on the sofa, near Mrs. Johnson's chair, she laid aside the book and said, "I'm so glad we have a *Daily Texan* editor with us, and I want to hear all about the university."

Until now, my only knowledge of Mrs. Johnson and her interests came from an episode in 1944, during the controversy at the University of Texas. On the morning of Dr. Homer Rainey's dismissal as president by the board of regents, students had convened for a mass meeting to protest the action. This led to a strike, shutting down most of the civilian classes. Later, virtually the full student body began a funeral march on the State Capitol, bearing the coffin of "Academic Freedom" to the governor's office. It was a rare and moving sight: some five thousand students, each wearing a black armband, moving slowly, in eerie silence, through the streets in a miles-long procession. Austin's sympathies were such that police patrolling the line of march threatened to arrest local citizens who tried to break through to go about their business.

When the funeral march reached the downtown business district and turned toward the capitol grounds, thousands of local citizens stood along the curbs. One woman came off the sidewalk, however, and approached the student body president, who was leading the procession. She extended her hand, saying, "I'm Mrs. Lyndon Johnson, and I want you to know my husband and I are with you." When the student body president looked, he saw that she had left in his hand a twenty-dollar bill.

Mrs. Johnson's interest in the well-being of her alma mater had not waned. Her questions were acute, penetrating, and numerous. When her husband finally arrived, well past nine, she greeted him with an effusive, open-armed "Darling," asked very briefly about his day, then returned to the questions. "Darling" took his chair across the living room, listening in none too enthusiastic silence. I was about to meet another of the Lyndon Johnsons.

Student demonstrations at the University of Texas had, in the past, contributed significantly to the state's political history. During World War I, Texas was governed by an immensely popular banker turned populist, Governor James "Farmer Jim" Ferguson. In a fight with the board of regents, Ferguson vetoed the appropriations for the University of Texas. A student march on the Capitol set in motion events which led to the governor's impeachment and removal from office. Since "Farmer Jim" held his strength among the tenant farmers, laborers, and others in the lower economic levels, the University of Texas incurred their smoldering wrath. I had some inkling from the past that Congressman Johnson, graduate of the small state teachers' college in San Marcos, near Austin, harbored the expected small-school bias toward the university as a large, arrogant, overbearing "Texas Harvard," but I did not know that his boyhood political hero was Governor Farmer Jim Ferguson.

Mrs. Johnson led her questioning back to the events of the earlier student demonstrations, and I began recounting with considerable gusto and pride how students had brought down the most popular governor in the state's history. There was an ugly rumble from across the room.

"You goddam smart snobs at the university make me want to puke." The congressman was half out of his chair, glaring at me. "Your bunch out there destroyed the best friend the poor people of Texas ever had or ever will have. It's nothing to be so proud of—one of the sorriest moments in Texas history."

I thought that I had blown it for sure. The reaction itself was not unfamiliar; I had heard it with similar intensity from among "Ferguson men" who, after thirty years, still remained a factor in state affairs. But this was an intense, combative response, as though old "Farmer Jim" were still alive and active. Few things, I was to learn, so stirred Lyndon Johnson as others rejoicing over a public man being hounded out of public life.

Mrs. Johnson's eyes flashed as she quickly appraised the living room crisis, but her poise remained perfect. "All that is so very interesting," she said, and not missing a beat, she added, "and I am sure your trip to Washington was just as interesting. Tell me about it over dinner."

I knew that I had met a most remarkable woman.

6

THE KEEPER OF THE FLAME

The Washington to which I had come in the springtime of 1948 was not a happy place.

Since the end of World War II three years earlier, the course of national affairs had gone dismally: strikes, shortages, inflation, continuing controls, kept the country ill-tempered and contentious. In 1946 Republicans swept back into control of Congress on the simple slogan "Had Enough?" President Harry Truman struck no sparks: crude and banal to some, ineffectual in the eyes of many, he lacked the charisma and class of the man he succeeded, and old New Dealers, convinced time had ended when FDR died, stood over the grave waiting for a new messiah to arise and lead them back to the Remembered Land.

While locusts shut out the sun over the Potomac, the skies were also darkening ominously across the Atlantic. In the short span between January and March 1948, during the time of my debate about accepting the position on Congressman Lyndon B. Johnson's staff, the world situation surged to the fore. Wars raged from Malaya to the Middle East. American arms and advisers were turning the tide of the Communist guerrilla struggle in Greece, but in Indochina a Vietnamese movement had begun to harass the French. Dominating all other concerns, however, "the bear that walks like a man"—Washington's much-used euphemism for the Soviet Union—had begun foraging into Western Europe only three years after V-J Day.

In late February, Czechoslovakia fell to a Communist coup.

Italy appeared in genuine danger of being lost to the West after the national elections in April. France's future remained far from certain. Allies were feeling the tightening pressures of the Soviet vise around Berlin. On March 10, the day of my departure from Texas, the former Czech foreign minister Jan Masaryk, a particular favorite in Washington, died in a fall from his apartment window in Prague. While Communists announced the death as a suicide, American interpretations insisted that Masaryk had been murdered, and a new gravity infused the tragic event. When I reached Washington, a resigned air of reluctant crisis pervaded the nation's capital.

The tense world situation had changed Congressman Johnson's course. His intentions to pursue his "natural interests"—the activities in domestic social legislation which had been outlined to me in January—were overridden by the threat of war abroad. This was clear within twenty-four hours of my arrival.

On March 17, my first full day in his office, Congressman Johnson—the events of the previous day all apparently forgotten—devoted his entire morning to trying to secure a scarce gallery seat so that, at noon, I could hear President Truman's emergency address to a joint session of Congress on the world crisis. His efforts succeeded, of course, and after the speech we hurried back through the connecting tunnel to the Old House Office Building to discuss the president's message.

The Truman address had bristled with unusual militancy. Some Republicans complained, publicly, that it was an election year oration and, privately, that it was calculated to arrest erosion of the Democrats' Catholic support in the northeastern states. FDR's former vice president Henry A. Wallace, rallying the Democratic Party's peace blocs against the man in the White House, dismissed it as showing the influence of Wall Street and the militarists. But for my new employer the fire bell was ringing again.

All of Lyndon Johnson's Washington life, until the brief postwar years, had been devoted to supporting presidents against their adversaries in just such situations and on this issue of confronting aggression. Passing years and changing generations were, of course, to erase the national memory of the late 1930s and of the inexorable march toward war as the Rhineland, Sudetenland, Austria, and

Czechoslovakia fell before the Nazis and the democracies did not respond. But the memory of those years still burned within men such as Congressman Johnson. As FDR's lieutenants, they had fought and would never forget the struggles in Congress and in the public arena to "quarantine the aggressors," to make America "the arsenal of democracy," to fortify the islands of Wake and Guam, to arm the "broomstick army," and to save the military draft by one vote in the House only three months before Pearl Harbor. The shadow now falling across Europe was, to Congressman Johnson's eyes, the same shadow of aggression under which he had lived his legislative life. His first action when he returned to his desk was to dictate a letter to the White House, pledging President Truman full support and cooperation.

"It looks like Hitler all over again," he said, with visibly deep feeling, "chapter and verse." He foresaw what the situation meant to domestic reform. "Congress never wants to spend anyway," he told me, "but give 'em the excuse of war talk, and you can't milk a drop out of the tit for anything to help the people." Until much later, neither the congressman nor his new assistant was to have much time for education, housing, health, conservation, or "coming up with new ideas."

That was my introduction to Congressman Johnson's working world. As a pattern it would reappear again and again, weaving through his public career to the end: at times when he was preparing to "leave his mark," as Paul Bolton had put it, by "doing something for the folks," wars and rumors of war invariably intervened to delay the dream.

Crisis is a stimulant, some would say an intoxicant, for centers of power. Unhappy as were the events of springtime in 1948, and uncertain as was the outcome, Washington came alive, pulsing and throbbing with a grim but curiously welcome sense of hovering cataclysm. "It's like old times," one heard at social functions, and a newcomer on the scene had the feeling that many of the men who once held power had not been so much at home in Washington for the past three years.

This was not Congressman Johnson's response. He met the world crisis by lengthening his already long working day, devoting himself to enactment of the Marshall Plan, development of a larger

Air Force, and reinstatement of the wartime draft, which President Truman had urgently requested.

Work was Congressman Johnson's compulsion, dominating his life and his relations with others. Somewhere along the way in life, someone or some circumstance had filled Lyndon Johnson to brimming with specific and merciless doubts of himself. Associates knew this and debated endlessly over the source; outsiders very often sensed it. The drive of the man, which could be such a fearsomely powerful force, was less a drive to succeed than a drive not to fail. Towering over all other doubts, however, was his fear that he might have inherited a tendency to be "lazy." He was determined never to be found out.

At the office his pace was obsessive. Every letter received from Texas by noon must have an answer in the mail before the office closed. Every telegram, whatever the hour of arrival, must have a telegram in reply the same day. Typewriters and telephones were never to stop. He entered the workroom and typewriters slowed; he snapped his fingers and whispered tersely, as if the world were outside listening, "Let's function! Let's function!" Coffee breaks might be entrenched in 434 other congressional offices, but he guarded his doors—and his secretaries' desks—against the iniquity, concerned more for appearance than for productivity. What would visitors think if they saw members of his staff away from their desks, drinking coffee and engaged in conversations? "I can't afford to have my office look like one of the departments," he said.

Congressman Johnson meant to make a good impression by working so relentlessly; instead, in all his offices, the impression he left was consistently bad. On Capitol Hill, where his reputation as a driving taskmaster overshadowed his role as a considerable achiever, introduction as a new member of Lyndon Johnson's staff evoked, invariably, spontaneous and embarrassing expressions of genuine sympathy from outsiders.

I did not approve his working style and did not adapt to it, but— for what reasons I never knew—Congressman Johnson directed none of his explosiveness at me. From the first month to the last year of our association, my colleagues were to complain that I led a privileged life in his employ: setting my own pace, keeping my own schedule, sharing the best times, spared the worst times. Certainly that was true, and while the future was not to be without its flaring moments, a measure of independence helped our relationship to endure.

Among his employees, Congressman Johnson never appeared the ogre outsiders imagined. Unfettered in his responses, innocent and uninhibited in his schoolboyish impulses, yet brilliant and untiring in pursuit of his ideals, he made other employers seem pale and deadly dull. Whenever his office door opened, one expected the unexpected.

Shortly after I arrived, he bounded out of his office one morning, his arms loaded with dozens of tie boxes. "All the men, come into the workroom," he barked. Jenkins, Woodward, myself, and Glynn Stegall—the congressman's senior employee—dutifully reported. "I've been noticing," he said bluntly, "that none of you know how to tie your ties." To correct the condition, he had gone out and purchased a selection of fashionable Countess Mara ties; for the next hour, he conducted a solemn class in the art and science of tying Windsor knots. I was exempted from his demand for absolute perfection at this skill. "Newspapermen," he explained, expressing a lifelong belief, "were born to look a little seedy."

Other impulses would strike. Stenographers were ordered away from their desks and dispatched on ten minutes' notice to a stylish hairdresser's. The congressman had made the appointment himself after looking over the stenographic room and concluding: "I can't work well when every time I look up I see an Aunt Minnie." A Hollywood makeup artist whom he chanced to meet somewhere advised the congressman that his left profile would photograph more favorably than the right: destroy all right-profile photographs, he directed with some urgency when he returned to the office.

A chauffeur, he decided, might befit his status, so he recruited Walter Bayer, a young part-time employee. Shaken by this unexpected new role, Bayer went at the task with all the caution and conservatism of his Texas German ancestry. The congressman at his side engaged, as was his custom, in "talking" to each car ahead: "Move over, black car." "Slow down, blue car." "Dammit, red car, get out of the way." The new driver's anxieties mounted, and his caution became too much. In Rock Creek Park, at forty miles an hour, Congressman Johnson gave the signal silently, and without

a word, the two of them somehow managed to trade seats so that
the congressman took over the wheel.

The flavor of the man was both rich and singular. Since I was not
involved in the stream of constituent affairs—answering calls and
letters, or pursuing problems with the executive agencies—he found
me to be an available companion for long hours of conversation.
His foremost interest lay in the study of successful men. Over the
hours in his office, he would analyze why one Washington figure
succeeded or another failed. His approach was that of a novelist.
Out of the whole of a man's life—his origins, parentage, marriage,
career, successes, failures, and frustrations—he constructed a character, delineating both strengths and flaws; the ends to which men
came were the workings and interworkings of all these elements.
"If you are going to understand a man," he explained, "you have
to know all of him—not just the part he lets you see." No subject
still occupied him more than Franklin D. Roosevelt.

Congressman Johnson managed to be worshipful without being
reverential toward his old chief. FDR had succeeded greatly, in
his view, yet he had also failed greatly. While war had brought
the New Deal to a halt, FDR himself—after his landslide victory
in 1936—had contributed to the loss of momentum for needed
reforms. Roosevelt, in the Johnson view, had communicated too
much arrogance, grown careless of the sensibilities of Congress, and
had not kept his house in order. The prominence of the big-city
bosses in Democratic Party affairs cost votes in Congress; so did
the frequent personality conflicts and quarrels among New Deal
cabinet officers and others; also, Mrs. Eleanor Roosevelt's interests
and associations were often more hindrance than help. "A president,"
Lyndon Johnson would say often, "who doesn't keep the reins tight
on those around him can't get a damn thing done."

A source of relaxation for the congressman was his store of often-
told Roosevelt stories, experiences he remembered with relish from
his hours in the company of the late president. High on the list of
favorites was the story of FDR and Ambassador Joseph Kennedy.

Joe Kennedy, among New Dealers of Congressman Johnson's
vintage, evoked a knee-jerk response: disloyal to the chief, ruthless,
personally ambitious, not a man to be trusted. On the eve of World
War II, Kennedy became highly controversial; as ambassador to

England, he sided with American isolationists, and it became known that he was approving of Hitler's policies toward the Jews in Germany. At the peak of the controversy, Kennedy returned home to vacation with his family at Hyannis Port. Congressman Johnson, as he recalled it, was sitting at FDR's side when a call came from the ambassador reporting his arrival in New York. Roosevelt asked Kennedy to come to Washington; the ambassador demurred, but the president insisted—and Congressman Johnson liked to repeat the dialogue, imitating the cloying consideration of the Rooseveltian voice. Finally, Joe Kennedy acceded, and FDR put down the telephone, saying to the young man at his side: "When he gets here, I'm going to fire the sonofabitch."

Such stories of Roosevelt the actor enthralled Lyndon Johnson. His favorite he repeated to me—in complete innocence—only two weeks after my own memorable first evening in his office:

William Bullitt, ambassador to France, was, like Kennedy, a perpetual problem to FDR. On some occasion Bullitt returned to Washington and tried to persuade Cissy Patterson, publisher of Washington's anti-Roosevelt *Times-Herald*, to expose certain secrets in the private life of Undersecretary of State Sumner Welles. "Say what you will about Cissy," Congressman Johnson said, "she may have been a reactionary, but she was a patriot." Miss Patterson went to FDR and exposed Bullitt's duplicity. Again, Congressman Johnson happened to be with Roosevelt as the president prepared for a face-to-face confrontation with the ambassador. "I will have them usher Bill in to my desk," FDR said, with great glee, "and I will leave him standing there while I sign letters. I won't invite him to sit down or even acknowledge his presence for twenty minutes. Then I'll give him a big smile and pretend I hadn't noticed—but that bastard is going to understand by then who is President of the United States."

Other men, many other influences, molded and shaped Congressman Johnson, but the Roosevelt legacy was the flame burning within. A fine distinction had to be drawn, however; while he venerated the man, the program of the New Deal was the legacy he kept with more fervor.

The intensity of this commitment was not commonplace. Washington at this time still sheltered the famous figures of the New Deal.

Wherever one went in the company of the congressman—and it was his practice that young assistants accompanied him everywhere—the gatherings were resurrections of the 1930s. Names which had already found their way into the history books of my college courses filled the rooms: Tommy Corcoran, Ben Cohen, William O. Douglas, Thurman Arnold, Milo Perkins, Sam Rosenman, Stephen Early, Abe Fortas. FDR had drawn them to Washington as young men; they were still active and vigorous, only three years out of power. But Lyndon Johnson, the youngest of all in what *Life* magazine once pictured as "The Roosevelt Party," conceived the legacy and trust in a way different from that of many of the old New Dealers. They dwelled on the power and when it would return; he dwelled on the program and when it would succeed.

On Sunday afternoons during the springtime of 1948, the Johnson residence was filled with the old New Dealers. Congressman Johnson seemed to be virtually the salon keeper, maintaining the ties. Others at these gatherings talked of old struggles against business and new clients from business; Congressman Johnson circled the living room, arms pumping, nose bobbing in the faces of his guests, asking, "Why can't we do this?" "What's wrong with this idea?" His idea of the moment might be a nationwide Rural Electrification Administration telephone system to serve every farm home, or a new National Youth Administration to ensure jobs for returned war veterans, or something else. The New Dealers, most of them, would shake their heads negatively, and he always appeared saddened that the fight had gone from his friends.

"Lyndon," one of the most prominent of the Sunday afternoon assemblage told him in my hearing, "you've got to come down out of the clouds. The country doesn't want more of the New Deal now." "You're just out getting rich," he shot back. "You aren't thinking of the people anymore." And he turned away sulking.

The world of the congressman from the Tenth District of Texas was unlike any other I had ever known: exciting, significant; sober and grim at times, uproarious at others; but always dominated by the unexpected. In May 1948, only two months after my coming, the world ended as improbably as it had begun. I was on my way back to Texas to turn the pages of a new chapter in his career.

Congressman Johnson was returning home to tend the flame.

7

MAN ALONE

L yndon B. Johnson opened his campaign for the Democratic nomination to the United States Senate late in the afternoon on May 22, 1948, at Austin. It was twilight in Washington when he telephoned with the news.

"I've hit the cold water," he told Walter Jenkins, "just like I had good sense."

The self-deprecation was characteristic, of course, but in this instance, it seemed justified. Odds against Congressman Johnson's success were almost impossibly high. Opinion polls showed that only 27 percent of the state's eligible voters could correctly identify the name of Lyndon Johnson. An even smaller percentage of Democrats favored his nomination over that of the former governor Coke Stevenson. The survey by the state's most respected opinion analysts, Joe Belden and Alex Louis, presented still more sobering details.

Congressman Johnson could count on majorities in eight of the ten counties of his own Tenth District, since the predominantly German counties were unreliable even when he ran unopposed; otherwise, the balance of the state's 254 counties and twenty-one congressional districts were pro-Stevenson territory. Belden and Louis advised that no Texas candidate had ever overcome such a formidable lead by an opponent during the brief sixty days of primary campaigning. It appeared all but inevitable that when Lyndon Johnson reached his fortieth birthday, on August 27, 1948, he would be making preparations to start on a new career as manager of the family's radio station at Austin.

Adversity had a singular effect upon Lyndon Johnson. He became resigned and relaxed, almost lighthearted, treating the situation with detachment. On his telephone call from Austin, this mood prevailed: he laughed at himself, reminisced about campaigns of other politicians, and spoke of the Senate race decision as one which others had made, not himself. His only direction was for Washington staff members to proceed at once to Texas. When he talked with me, however, the events of my arrival in March were very much on his mind.

"It's May now," he said. "When can I expect you? In July? Or in August?"

I departed the following morning, retracing the route of my leisurely March journey in only two and a half days. The early return to Texas was far from welcome. Sixty days in Washington were not nearly enough. I was still pressing my own vintage from the arbors of the old New Dealers, and the taste was too sweet to relinquish so soon. Furthermore, there were weekend trips to be made, exploring the East: New York still had not been visited, and, unknown to the congressman, I had been carefully contriving to attend the Democratic National Convention at Philadelphia in July. As staff members often are, I was annoyed at my employer for disrupting my own plans, but I thought the unscheduled experience might bring one compensation.

Congressman Johnson was acknowledged to be a master campaigner. In his only previous statewide race, he had overshadowed four formidable performers and established himself as one of the state's best vote-getters. No clown or comedian, and certainly no stereotype of the old-school courthouse politician, Lyndon Johnson was regarded as tough, wily, and skillful, a potent campaigner who hit hard and drove remorselessly toward victory. Hard-nosed politics, as it came to be called, has an indefinable appeal to the young, and while this was not the way I had expected to spend my summer, I considered myself fortunate to have an inside view of the most professional campaign organization in my home state.

At Austin, when I reached the end of my full-throttle journey from Washington, I found the electric, do-it-yesterday urgency I expected. On the edge of the downtown district, one of the capital city's turn-of-the-century mansions was being outfitted as state headquarters for the Johnson campaign. Telephone installers, office supply salesmen, printing firm representatives, and others hurried in and out of the executive offices; managers and volunteers alike ran more often than they walked from place to place; a movie-set tempo prevailed, with much shouting, tension, and excitement. Only the congressman's irrepressibly mischievous brother, Sam Houston Johnson, remained an island of calm.

Sign painters were busily lettering a red, white, and blue banner proclaiming, "Elect Lyndon B. Johnson, He Gets Things Done." Sam, however, was solemnly trying to persuade the artists to paint in the 1941 campaign slogan: "Franklin D. and Lyndon B." Straight-faced, Sam told me, "It may be a little out of date, but it has more sex appeal."

Apart from Sam, this was not the typical slow-paced Texas politics—it was politics as it should be practiced, and I was thoroughly captivated. If he could spare a moment from his own hard-driving schedule, I hoped to see Congressman Johnson himself and draw my own first assignment for the campaign. But Congressman Johnson was not on the premises.

On the executive floor of the headquarters, I made the rounds, renewing acquaintances with the high command: Claude Wild Sr., a highly regarded professional campaign manager, who had directed the first Johnson campaign for Congress in the 1930s; John B. Connally, the handsome, intelligent, and tough-minded former assistant who functioned as the congressman's political alter ego; and three close Connally associates, J. J. "Jake" Pickle, Charles Herring, and Dub Singleton. When I inquired about the congressman's whereabouts, Connally only shrugged. "Hell, I don't know," he said. "I haven't seen the bastard in three days."

Connally's attitude was reflected by his associates, none of whom seemed perturbed by the candidate's absence. But before I could learn more about their apparent nonchalance, Mrs. Sarah Wade, the switchboard operator, summoned me to her desk in the lobby. "Congressman Johnson," she announced, "wants to see you at his apartment immediately."

Directions in hand, I departed promptly for the Johnson residence. At that time, the congressman owned no ranch home; it was almost a decade later, in fact, before I first saw what became his much-publicized homestead on the Pedernales River at Johnson City. My destination was Congressman and Mrs. Johnson's gracious cut-stone and clapboard residence in the northwest section of the city, near the crescent of lakes and hills which caused William Sydney Porter to identify Austin in the O. Henry stories as "The City of the Violet Crown." Two apartments in the long, rambling structure were rented to friends, including John Connally and his young family; a third apartment on the upper level was occupied by the congressman's former college roommate, Willard Deason, and his wife, Jean. Bill and Jean kept one bedroom available for the landlord's use and obligingly made themselves scarce while he was in residence. When I reached the house on Dillman Street, I found Congressman Johnson there, waiting upstairs in the living room.

It was a puzzling contrast to the campaign center downtown. No assistants scurried up the stairs. No secretaries transcribed correspondence. No telephones rang. Blinds were drawn against the Texas heat, and except for the hum of a window fan, the apartment was still and hushed. Congressman Johnson was alone.

Subdued and calm, he lay motionless on a long sofa beneath the broad picture window, drawing on an ever-present cigarette as he gazed reflectively out at the nearby hills. He made no move to rise when I entered. In a gesture typical of political campaigners, he extended his left hand, saving the right hand for hand shaking which lay ahead. As we shook, he grinned sheepishly.

"Well," he said, "I guess we ripped our britches on this one."

The fires which I expected to find burning were banked. Around the room there was no evidence of campaign activity: no wall maps, no voter registration lists, no telegrams and letters, not even the usual neatly bound reports from the opinion polling firms. Neither was there any assignment waiting for me. Congressman Johnson only wanted someone to talk with in the solitude of his retreat.

After my experiences in Washington, the role of being a good listener came easily and naturally. He poured me a cup of coffee from the silver pot which he kept beside the sofa, and I took up a chair across the room. No inquiries were made about my journey, or my brief visit to the headquarters. His voice barely audible, he began surveying the odds against him in the Senate race: no organization, no managers, no workers, no issues, no money.

In 1941, when he made his first race for the United States Senate at President Franklin D. Roosevelt's request, Congressman Johnson risked nothing in terms of his public career and political power. He ran in an off-year special election, which did not require him to relinquish his position in the House of Representatives. If he lost, he still held his seat and his seniority. In 1948, however, he was gambling everything.

At the end of the year, he would surrender his House seat and his committee assignments. If the Republicans regained the White House in November, as he expected, there would be no prospect of appointment to a position in the executive branch. He foresaw no place for a Texan in the affairs of the Democratic Party's national structure. Any future for him in public life rested on the outcome of a Texas primary in which he was a virtually hopeless underdog. As he reviewed his situation, he seemed intent on making certain I understood that he had realized the odds against him before he took the step which appeared to have ended his political life. When the black recital was done after an hour, he looked directly at me for the first time since I'd entered the room.

"You're a realist," he said. "Do you think I have a chance?"

I did not think he did, but I began a prudently equivocal and evasive answer. He was on his feet immediately. Towering over me in district attorney fashion, he shook a finger toward my face. "The truth now," he barked. "The whole truth and nothing but the truth."

My reply came weakly. "No, sir. Not much chance."

"That's right," he said, nodding vigorously in agreement. "Little Lyndon"—a favorite reference to himself during this period—"doesn't have the chance of a snowball in hell."

His spirits brightened perceptibly. He smiled broadly, stretched his arms over his head, and yawned. After a moment, the irony of his predicament brought on laughter, and he hurried out to refill the coffeepot so we could continue the conversation. From the kitchen, still laughing at himself, he called out to me. "It's like my daddy always told me: 'If a fella starts trying to climb a pole, he usually ends up showing his ass.'"

A new Lyndon Johnson strode back into the living room. Some burden had lifted, and all solemnity was gone. In an incongruously gleeful mood, he vanquished further thoughts and talk of the campaign; his ebullient spirits went soaring off into the uproarious retelling of the stories of a political lifetime. The congressman rarely told outright jokes; he drew his humor from life. For another hour, he entertained me—and himself even more—satirizing the gestures and voices of Washington's more celebrated figures, not sparing even his hero, FDR. After he had resigned himself to the likelihood that his career was ended, a sense of release stirred through him: nothing could be more amusing than the posturing and pomposity of politicians, and he marched around the room skillfully playing out all the parts in dramas he had witnessed in Congress and at the White House.

The afternoon was marvelous fun, but I had come to start on the campaign, and I grew eager to see this most professional of professionals begin to concoct his political magic. Only when the telephone intruded upon our conversation for the first time did I realize that this performance was itself some essential part of Congressman Johnson's singular act.

Telephone apparatus around a Johnson household was never simple. At the Austin apartment, the living room instrument had a thirty-foot extension cord, equipped to plug into connecting outlets which were spaced throughout the apartment, on the patio outside, and even in the flower beds. Wherever Congressman Johnson went around the premises, he wagged telephone and cord at his side; if he became engaged in an extended conversation—one-hour and even two-hour calls were not uncommon—the extra-length cord permitted him freedom to prowl around a wide perimeter as he talked. On this afternoon, the cord was plugged into an outlet behind the sofa where the congressman reclined; however, the instrument itself rested on a table beside my chair. When it rang, I reached automatically to answer it, but Congressman Johnson began gesturing excitedly for me to leave it untouched.

The congressman's eyes fixed on the receiver from across the room, and a wicked sort of smile moved over his face. Touching a finger to his lips to signal silence, he whispered to me, "One of them down there is having an attack of the smarts." I took this to mean that one of the managers at the downtown headquarters must be telephoning with some suggestion about the campaign. The congressman allowed ten rings, then his eyes narrowed combatively and he shook a reproving finger at the offending instrument. "Telephone," he said, addressing it sternly and personally. "I'm gonna fix you."

With that, he reached behind the sofa and triumphantly jerked the cord from its connection. A smugly satisfied smile suggested that he had scored a small but gratifying victory.

Two months in the employ of the Tenth District congressman had instilled caution in me. I sat very still, trying to show no sign of surprise or interest. The congressman, however, hardly acknowledged the matter; while the smile continued to flicker over his face, he volunteered no explanation, and our conversation went along without pause. It was not until sometime later that I learned the significance of what I had witnessed.

On the previous day, it developed, Congressman Johnson had appeared at his headquarters. The seasoned veterans of Texas politics were busily occupied with campaign fundamentals: recruiting workers, arranging appearances, scheduling itineraries, procuring automobiles and sound trucks, ordering pamphlets and placards, buying radio time, soliciting contributions. While the candidate acknowledged the necessity for such activity, it nonetheless bore down upon him that the managers were managing him: deciding where he should go, when he should be there, whom he should see, what he should say. Other politicians might welcome such industriousness on their behalf, but Lyndon Johnson had a different chemistry; he could not abide being managed, and as happened sooner or later in all his campaigns, he went to war against his own managers.

At first, he was content with sabotage. When schedule makers proudly presented a tentative itinerary for his first week of travel, he discarded it with a roar. "You're trying to murder me," he shouted. "A Hereford bull couldn't live through that schedule." All other plans submitted to him met similarly anguished wails, until John Connally intervened; he had been through this before, and he wisely instructed the staff to disclose no plans to the candidate. Sensing conspiracy, the congressman went on the offensive. At noon he sulked in his private office, declining to lunch with Connally and his associates; when they returned he toured the offices, announcing,

"I must be an idiot, because only an idiot could attract so many idiots as I do." But he saved his cavalry charge for the afternoon staff meeting.

When the managers, emboldened by Connally's example, began to counterattack, demonstrating where the congressman's criticisms were wrong, the candidate listened only briefly. In the accepted manner of the "Lyndon stories," he rose from his chair and moved toward the door. "You smart sonsabitches think you know everything," he snarled through clenched teeth. "Well, all right, let's just see how smart you look without a candidate."

Angrily he stormed from the room, and the managers waited until they heard his Chrysler drive away before they began to laugh. If this was predictable conduct, it was also predictable that he would not answer his telephone, or speak directly with anyone at headquarters, for at least three days. Yet the candidate's seclusion was neither so petulant nor so purposeless as it appeared.

On the eves of his campaigns, Lyndon Johnson was much like a concert hall artist in the last hours before a performance. He had a compulsive need to withdraw, be alone and apart while he established some private communion with the people whom he would soon be facing. It was this process that I witnessed for the first time during my stay at his Austin apartment.

Isolated from his own campaign, Congressman Johnson brushed aside reality: it was too bothersome. Gradually, as he began to talk with increasing animation, it became evident that he had considerably more hope about the outcome of his race than he had initially admitted. "The people," he said, "are going to decide this election, and by God, I am for the people—p–double e–p-u-l."

On his scale of values, very little mattered except being "for the people." He scoffed at the electioneering techniques popular among campaign professionals. "This goddam public relations business is a pile of manure," he argued. "A little pimply squirt at a typewriter can't win any votes. You have to go out with the people, let them press the flesh, look you over, size you up. You can't fool 'em—when they look you in the eye, they can tell whether you are for the folks or for the interests."

Once, I interrupted his reverie with a question about which issues he thought would be effective in his campaign. He dismissed the prevailing Texas concerns: economy in government, centralized government, and states' rights. "The people aren't interested in those old bones," he declared. Then, pacing the floor, he began calling out a list which I would hear many times over the next twenty years.

"People are good," he said. "What the average folks want is very simple: peace, a roof over their heads, food on their tables, milk for their babies, a good job at good wages, a doctor when they need him, an education for their kids, a little something to live on when they're old, and a nice funeral when they die."

I commented that this would be difficult to write in a campaign speech, and he shook his head in amusement. "You're thinking like a public relations man," he explained. "No good political speech comes out of a typewriter. It has to come from the heart."

Any mention of speeches brought one memory to Congressman Johnson's mind: the golden voice of his hero, Franklin D. Roosevelt. On his feet now, the congressman paced the floor, smiling, thinking back over the past. Then the words began to come.

"For twelve years," he repeated, pitching his voice out to an unseen audience, "this nation was afflicted with hear-nothing, see-nothing, do-nothing government." I recognized the line: it was from FDR's memorable Madison Square Garden speech, closing the 1936 presidential campaign. Confident of victory over Governor Alf Landon of Kansas, the Old Campaigner spoke boldly that night, savoring the rout of the wealthy Liberty League industrialists who were denouncing him as "a traitor to his class." Congressman Johnson relived the moment: holding his head high, smiling jauntily, intoning the words from memory.

"The nation looked to government but"—and now his voice repeated FDR's tone of scorn—"the government looked away. Nine mocking years with the golden calf and three long years of the scourge. Nine crazy years at the ticker and three long years in the breadlines. Nine mad years of mirage and three long years of despair."

It was evident that he relished the rhythm of FDR's carefully crafted cadence. Now his voice grew stronger and the Hyde Park accent more pronounced. "Powerful influences strive today to restore that kind of government with its doctrine that that government is best which is most indifferent. Never before in all our history have these forces been so united against one candidate as they stand today. They are unanimous in their hate for me—and I welcome their hatred."

He delivered the last clause powerfully. Then he whispered an aside to me: "Get this now—the greatest lines in any political speech." The Rooseveltian pose resumed; he waited, it seemed, for the cheering to end, and then he continued.

"I should like to have it said of my first administration that in it the forces of selfishness and lust for power met their match, and"—his face began to beam—"I should like to have it said of my second administration that in it these forces met their master."

It was a moving performance. When he concluded, Congressman Johnson stepped to the window, lighted a cigarette, and stood silently, looking out at the bright blue Texas sky. I did not intrude upon his solitude.

Over the days ahead, I came to understand that my new employer paid a price for these private moments. His closest associates had no patience with these withdrawals; as they saw it, he was only escaping reality, and they disparaged his moodiness to his face. Before the summer ended, several of his senior advisers heatedly told him—sometimes in the presence of others—that he was being "childish," behaving "like a woman," not conducting himself "as a grown man should." He rarely replied directly to such thrusts; deeply hurt and dispirited, he only retreated further and built his walls higher. The times apart and alone meant more to him than he could make others understand.

8

"THE CANDIDATE HAS DISAPPEARED"

It was this solitary Lyndon Johnson that I came to know best. Extroverted, gregarious, and roughshod as he could appear at times, the Tenth District congressman sheltered a sensitive, introspective, and unaccountably fragile self inside. This self required an audience of its own, one that would be neither approving nor disapproving; for reasons I never understood, I was drawn into that role, and it was the one role which survived to the end of our relationship. However, on the second night of my stay at the Johnson apartment, I abruptly fell from grace.

On my return from Washington, I had no apartment awaiting in Austin. When Congressman Johnson invited me to share his bedroom, I readily accepted. It was a narrow room, converted from a sunporch, with two bunk beds built head-to-head along the interior wall. On the first night, this arrangement went well, as far as I knew. I thought nothing of it when, the following morning, the maid told me she had been instructed to remake my bunk so that my head would be away from the congressman's. On the second night, the congressman and I retired late after fourteen hours of arduous communion with the people, and I slept soundly. At two o'clock in the morning, however, I awakened to find the congressman standing over me, shaking my shoulder.

"Get up," he said softly. "I've made you a nice pallet in the other room."

This information was less than pleasing. Grumpily, I demanded to know why it was necessary for me to move.

"You can't sleep here anymore," he announced, smiling very solicitously. "You breathe too much."

That was the end of my stay. After an early and wordless breakfast with the congressman, I reported to campaign headquarters for my first assignment. To my surprise, I learned that I was "to handle the press." In most statewide campaigns, press relations were regarded as a critical responsibility, requiring a staff of seasoned professionals. It was characteristic of Johnson campaigns, however, to accord no special significance to this sector. Wholly inexperienced and untested as I was, and with a considerable distaste for the duties of a publicist, I was nonetheless handed the responsibility of serving as a one-man press office for the statewide effort. Almost immediately, my recent colleagues in the State Capitol pressroom began heckling me with a noisy clamor for advance copies of Congressman Johnson's speech opening his campaign for the Democratic nomination to the United States Senate.

In the traditions of Texas politics, opening speeches were uniquely important. By the textbooks, Texas was a one-party state; since the years of Reconstruction after the Civil War, Republicans had been elected to no public office outside the German bloc counties, and victors in Democratic primaries went uncontested in the general elections. Actually, however, politics functioned somewhat differently: each major statewide candidate became the center of his own party, with his own set of managers, volunteers, financial supporters, and partisan newspapers, and with his own personal platform, calculated to attract a groundswell of statewide support. Opening speeches, broadcast over statewide radio networks, served as showcases for presenting the platform of each candidate, and capitol correspondents expected to receive copies several days in advance for line-by-line scrutiny.

Congressman Johnson's opening speech was set for Saturday, May 22. He would return to Austin's Wooldridge Park, scene of his many past triumphs, and launch his campaign before a cheering crowd of hometown partisans. On Tuesday, when I asked for a copy of the text, my friend Paul Bolton, who was responsible for writing the speech, buried his head in his arms. "Tell the press," he said, after a long silence, "that there may not be any speech."

Unwittingly, I had touched a raw nerve at campaign headquarters.

Since my departure from his apartment, Congressman Johnson had continued his isolation, admitting none of his senior advisers other than Paul Bolton, but as the opening of the campaign drew near, a nasty, no-holds-barred Donnybrook raged between candidate and counselors over the opening speech. Bolton explained the conflict succinctly: "Lyndon wants to make an old-time, fire-eating New Deal speech," he said, "but John Connally, Claude Wild, and everybody else won't let him."

It was a fight over fundamentals. Congressman Johnson had outlined his own platform: federal aid to education, higher old-age pensions, expansion of public power through rural electric cooperatives, establishment of consumer cooperatives to combat high prices, "a blacktop road in sight of every farmhouse," plus many other proposals. His managers objected: the program contained "too many promises," ran against the mounting public resistance to more spending, gave too much emphasis to federal activities, and most seriously, from a political viewpoint, expressed no opposition to any of the national programs so unpopular in Texas. It was obligatory, the managers contended, for candidates to denounce the Truman civil rights program, especially the Fair Employment Practices Commission, and to come out against the Wagner-Murray-Dingell Bill providing for a system of national health care, which the powerful Texas Medical Association labeled "socialized medicine." Congressman Johnson, however, would not yield.

"I didn't come down here to run for governor," he shouted at Bolton, when he heard the views from downtown. "Tell those smart-asses I'm not going to start sucking up to the oilmen and all the other conservative bastards. I am for the people."

The standoff continued. Two days before the speech, Connally and Wild began maneuvering adroitly. They summoned two men of impeccable liberal credentials: the former governor James V. Allred, architect of the state's own "little New Deal" during the 1930s, and the onetime state senator Alvin Wirtz, who had been Harold Ickes' undersecretary of the interior and was a personal friend to both FDR and President Truman. Congressman Johnson could not refuse to see these two advisers, it was assumed, and both men were of the pragmatic school that believed "you have to be elected first."

Governor Allred met the wrath first. Chuckling over the problem, and discounting it, he telephoned Congressman Johnson from my desk to arrange an appointment. When he heard Allred's voice, however, the congressman immediately recognized the plot against him. "I knew you were in town," he told the astonished former governor. "I opened the window and smelled you." Allred pleaded. "Lyndon, you've got to come down out of the trees," he said. "This is serious business, and time is running out." "If you are so damn smart about politics," the congressman fired back, "why aren't you in the Senate?" Allred, who had run for the Senate six years earlier and lost narrowly, had no answer.

The exchange was duly reported to the campaign strategists. Alvin Wirtz grew livid. One of the few men around who could outmatch the Tenth District congressman in face-to-face invective, Wirtz departed for the apartment announcing, "I'm going to tell that sonofabitch how the cow ate the cabbage." Several hours later, he returned with a surrender: "Lyndon says go ahead and write what we think he ought to say, and he'll read it."

On Saturday night, at Wooldridge Park, a dispirited Lyndon Johnson took the platform to begin the most important campaign of his career. He delivered the lines hoarsely and ineffectively; neither the words nor the cadence was his, and several times he lost his place as he turned the pages. It was the poorest Johnson performance I had witnessed, and immediately after the speech he hurried back to his seclusion.

A meeting of district managers was scheduled for Sunday morning. Most of the men were young, rising lawyers, contemporaries of John Connally at the University of Texas. Supporting the liberal Tenth District congressman carried a high risk for most of their careers, but as veterans of World War II, they shared a determination to overcome the isolationist views which W. Lee O'Daniel and Coke Stevenson epitomized. When their candidate addressed the eager volunteers, however, he made only a half-hearted attempt to motivate them; it was evident that he had no faith in the campaign he had begun the previous night, or in himself. Shortly after the meeting, however, he took Warren Woodward and departed for Amarillo, in the Texas Panhandle, to begin his on-the-road campaigning.

A pall lay over headquarters the following morning. The doors to the executive offices remained closed; telephones were silent; the anticipated deluge of letters and telegrams from supporters did not materialize; and not even Sam Houston Johnson could manage a smile. The career of Lyndon Johnson had apparently come to an end on Saturday night.

I sat in the empty pressroom at the front of the old house, idly clipping newspapers. The report from Amarillo came in thoroughly discouraging: the congressman had seemed distracted and preoccupied when he spoke, received little applause, and had departed early with Woodward on the overnight train to Dallas. Mercifully, none of my newspaper friends called to needle me about the congressman's poor showing, and I had nothing of consequence to do.

Early in the afternoon, automobiles began arriving in the parking lot outside, driving in at high speeds, slamming to a halt, and disgorging passengers who hurried inside, taking the steps two at a time. I recognized several of the visitors as key political figures in Austin, but I had no word of what might be under discussion upstairs. At four o'clock, however, I received a summons from Claude Wild, the campaign manager. "Could you come up?" he asked. "We have a matter of some importance."

Wild's face was grave. He motioned me to a chair at his desk and carefully closed the doors to his office.

I waited with my pencil ready, prepared to take notes for a possible press release, but Wild gestured negatively. "What I am going to tell you doesn't go out of this room," he said. "In fact, I want you to get lost so the press can't locate you to ask questions."

I folded the paper and put it into my pocket.

"Busby," he said finally, "we have a problem on our hands. It seems the candidate has disappeared."

In later years, I learned to accept announcements such as this routinely, even to expect them. A Johnson campaign was not a Johnson campaign without such trademarks. But the news now came as a thunderclap.

The story offered no clues. Congressman Johnson and Woodward were last seen boarding the Pullman at Amarillo. At Dallas, a group assembled at noon to hear the candidate, but he did not materialize. His manager, Bob Clark—brother of the then United States attorney general, Tom Clark—checked hotels, motels, and residences of Johnson friends to no avail. There was some evidence, however, that he must have reached Dallas. Mrs. Johnson had arrived there earlier to be with him, but now she, too, had disappeared.

At five o'clock, the newsmen began to call. While I declined to talk with them, I insisted to my colleagues that I must have some statement by six o'clock. John Connally put on his hat and left. "If the sonofabitch doesn't call by six," he instructed, "go up to the pressroom and tell them he has withdrawn from the race."

I returned the press calls and promised some announcement by seven. A few minutes before the hour, a collect call came from Warren Woodward. At least half the staff listened on extension lines as he made his report. "You fellas are never going to believe this," he began. "I'm in Rochester, Minnesota, and I just put Golden Boy to bed at Mayo Clinic."

On the long train ride across the Texas plains, Congressman Johnson had concluded that he must have a kidney stone. He had learned from a morning newspaper that a famous woman pilot, Jacqueline Cochran, was in Dallas. When the train arrived, the congressman had his plans formulated. He dispatched Woody to find Mrs. Johnson and take her to Love Field. The congressman himself set out to locate Miss Cochran, confident he could persuade her to undertake a "mercy flight" to Mayo. It was a current Johnson fetish that most pilots were "a little crazy," and he would fly only with the best. The scheme succeeded, but when Woody suggested a call to headquarters before the departure, the congressman laid down the law. "If you touch a telephone the next ten days, you're fired," he declared. "I don't want any of those people in Austin to know where I am."

Over the following week and a half, the congressman received the medical attention he required. But mainly he found what he had flown more than one thousand miles to seek: solitude which permitted him to develop a concept of the campaign he would make.

9

TIME OF TRIUMPH

Austin to Boston, 1960

While the welcoming crowd of his Texas neighbors cheered and applauded the new vice presidential nominee on his return from Los Angeles in July 1960, telephones inside the LBJ ranch home began ringing angrily. A few loyal friends called to offer congratulations, and to wish him well. But these were the exceptions. The senator who had departed for the Democratic convention as his home state's favorite son returned now as its prodigal, and many past associates and supporters were anxious to disown him, in hasty, bitter terms.

Over the last few months before the convention, Lyndon Johnson had become what he had never been in Texas: a popular figure. State pride, the prospect of having a Texan as president, and a genuine respect for his attainments as majority leader overcame the state's traditional suspicion of his nonconforming national liberalism. For the first time in their association with him, his managers, contributors, and well-wishers basked in their loyalty to the senator. Defeat only enhanced the man; it was, after all, a clash between regions, and the Texas psyche could accept the outcome as foreordained. But then he had done the one thing his supporters were certain he would never do: subjugated himself and his powerful position to assure—as Texas saw it—national victory for the man, the family, and the amorphous eastern group which had inflicted defeat on him and his region. It was the ultimate betrayal.

Along with others on the staff, I sat in the office of the ranch house, screening the incoming calls and trying to shield him from the virulence of the outbursts. Catholicism, liberalism, civil rights, were never mentioned. This was a family falling-out, and the old acquaintances dwelled on "Lyndon's" own "lack of character," "disloyalty to those who stayed with him," and weakness for "the glamour of the Kennedys." The senator knew, without being told, what was being said, but he could not resist lifting the receiver on an extension telephone to eavesdrop. He did so just in time to hear a prominent Houston lawyer thundering, "Tell him for me, that Texas is through with him, the country is through with him, and I am through with him." It was not Saturday night whiskey talk: to the best of my knowledge, the two men never spoke again.

The next few days brought no calming of the storm. Quietly, Senator Johnson slipped away, leaving Texas behind; with Mrs. Johnson and a few close friends, he departed for the cloudless skies of Acapulco. There, far away from politics, he played out the familiar role of a man alone, contemplating what he had done and what the future might hold. A week later, I was watching the proceedings at the Republican convention when he telephoned immediately after returning to the ranch. "Who," he wanted to know, "do they say Nixon is going to pick to run against us?"

I took that to mean he regarded Richard Nixon's selection of vice presidential running mate to be his own direct opponent. At that stage of the convention, commentators were still discussing three possible selections: Secretary of the Treasury Robert B. Anderson of Texas, once a liberal law professor in Austin and brain truster of the Texas New Deal, who despite his latter-day Republicanism remained one of Lyndon Johnson's best friends; United States Senator Thruston Morton of Kentucky, an articulate and intelligent border state leader, greatly underrated outside the Senate; and United Nations Ambassador Henry Cabot Lodge of Massachusetts, a man of presidential timbre, attractive, popular, patrician, yet often diffident and condescending to the rough-and-tumble of politics. The majority leader summed up his feelings in a quick sentence.

"I hope it's not Anderson, I'm afraid it's Morton. I wish, oh, how I wish, it would be Lodge," the congressman said, adding with a laugh, "he's just my meat." Interpreted, the remark meant that, in the Johnson view, Anderson would make Texas and other southwestern states difficult for Democrats to hold; Morton would penetrate the South and add strength for the Republican ticket everywhere; Lodge alone among the three would win no votes for Richard Nixon and, quite possibly, become a liability. Senator Johnson was to get his wish.

The days of solitude under the tropical sun stirred Lyndon Johnson's campaign fever. Whatever else, he determined to carry Texas for his friend John F. Kennedy, and he returned from Acapulco with an idea to start toward that goal.

If Catholicism was to be a telling issue anywhere in Texas, he reasoned, it would cut most deeply in the traditionally Democratic rural areas of the state's Protestant "Bible Belt." Such areas feared Catholics, the senator observed, because "they've never met one." So he conceived the idea of chartering a commercial airliner, "filling it to the gills with editors of small-town weeklies," and flying off to Hyannis Port, Massachusetts, to meet Kennedy. "If they feel him, smell him, and look him in the eye," he explained, "they'll damn sure come home knowing the Pope's not going to be running the White House."

The trip would also serve another purpose. A national campaign was developing. The role of the vice presidential candidate was, thus far, not discussed. A meeting with the new Democratic Party leader seemed urgent to establish the basis of a working relationship.

When the expedition was announced at Austin, statehouse sages had a field day predicting disaster. The most prominent local lobbyist, noted for his irreverent wit about political figures, reflected the new Texas attitude toward the state's senior senator. "When Lyndon lands up there on Cape Cod," he said, "Ol' Joe Kennedy's going to have the battleship *Missouri* anchored in the bay for the signing of the surrender."

Forty editors and reporters in tow, Senator Johnson departed Austin aboard a chartered Viscount, bound for a meeting with the man who had defeated him for the Democratic presidential nomination less than a month earlier. Characteristically, however, he altered the flight plans at the last minute to include a stop at Kansas City for lunch with the former president Harry Truman. On the eve of the Democratic convention, Truman had bitterly denounced the Kennedys, charged that the Los Angeles proceedings were rigged, and publicly canceled his plans to attend. The majority leader thought it would be a welcome gesture if he could arrive at Hyannis Port with a cordial message from the old Missourian promising full support to the ticket. It was a sound idea, even if hastily improvised, but going against it was the tradition that such undertakings by Lyndon Johnson usually became adventures in misadventure.

The familiar pattern first appeared at the Kansas City airport. Unknown to any of us, local employees of Continental Airlines, which was flying the charter, were on strike, and before he realized it, the vice presidential nominee of the Democratic Party had committed the cardinal sin of crossing a picket line. "Oh, God," he sighed when informed of what had occurred, "what will Kennedy say about that?" Downtown, at the Hotel Muehlebach, matters were not much better.

President Truman was in no mood to kiss and make up with the Kennedys. Barely civil in his audible statements during a brief session with photographers, the thirty-third President of the United States abandoned all restraint in private. His purple language echoed through the transom of the hotel suite, and a very pale Lyndon Johnson stationed me in the hallway to make certain no newsmen came close enough to overhear. The unexpurgated Truman message to John Kennedy was unprintable.

As soon as we were airborne again, disturbing news came. Flying weather over the eastern half of the United States was only marginal and deteriorating. At best, the majority leader would arrive well past the originally scheduled time of arrival. Furthermore, because of weather, an unscheduled refueling stop would be necessary at Cleveland.

Democratic Mayor Anthony J. Celebrezze sped to the airport to welcome his unscheduled visitor. At the mayor's urging, the senator left the plane for a visit to the VIP suite on the upper floors of the terminal. The hurried refueling was soon completed and minutes were passing, but Senator Johnson did not return. Members of the staff dutifully set off to retrieve him from the visit with the mayor. But the area around the terminal's elevator entrances was chaos. Airport personnel, workmen, and emergency squads were frantically trying to extricate mayor and senator from a jammed elevator. "Well," Senator Johnson declared philosophically when he finally returned to the waiting plane, "at least I can tell Jack I spent the afternoon with an important northern mayor."

The weather worsened as the Viscount sped through the darkening clouds. One hour out, the pilot advised that there would be fuel for only one pass at the closed-in runway on Otis Air Force Base, near the Kennedy home. If that failed, the flight would have to be rerouted to New Hampshire or Maine for the night. "No, fellas, you can't do this to me," the senator announced as he burst into the cockpit. "I got screwed last month in front of God and everybody. Please, please, don't do it to me again." It was a deadly earnest plea. He understood the derision that would be forthcoming in political circles if he missed the meeting with Senator Kennedy.

Crewmen responded valiantly. Told that Otis Air Force Base was closing down because of a low cloud ceiling and fog, the pilots insisted on holding course, gambling that a momentary opening in the weather might permit a landing. The approach was incredibly rough; even seasoned air travelers aboard became ill, and the tension in the cabin mounted. Lyndon Johnson, always a fatalist, betrayed no visible concern. But when the dim outline of treetops began appearing off the wingtips of the still airborne craft, he turned from the window and ran his eyes over the staff nearby. "Damn," he said seriously, "I didn't bring a Catholic—we need one to do the praying for this show up here."

The white-winged Viscount rode Protestant prayers safely to the runway, and Senator Johnson himself led the spontaneous burst of relieved applause from the passenger cabin. His spirits soared, and his humor returned. As he waited impatiently at the front of the craft for the ramp to be lowered, he carefully checked his tie, hair, and hat in a mirror; then he turned to George Reedy and myself. "So far, everything that could go wrong has gone wrong," he said. "Tell me, boys, is my fly open now?"

Appearing confident and smiling broadly, he went bouncing down the steps. One newspaper account described him as looking "like a Martian in a ten gallon hat." Only a sparse line of onlookers stood by disinterestedly, but the newly arrived visitor was now too buoyant to be concerned about crowd size. Sweeping one arm expansively toward the terminal, the majority leader startled the spectators by calling out loudly, "I have come to see my leader." But his leader was not present. An Air Force colonel stepped forward with unexpected news. Informed that a landing at Otis would be impossible, Senator Kennedy had sped away by automobile. He was, presumably, now hurrying across the rain-swept Cape toward Boston's Logan International Airport.

Until now, the transcontinental misadventures of the long day had encouraged a mood of relaxed jollity among Johnson aides. Near disasters seemed always to stalk the man's best intentions. The picket line at Kansas City, Harry Truman's sulfurous rage, the crippled elevator in Cleveland, and the marginal landing at Otis Air Force Base all fit into such a familiar pattern that one could only laugh. But now the laughing stopped.

In politics, as in diplomacy, it is the agony of participants to search for large significance in small events. We did not know that the northeastern seaboard was being lashed by an approaching Atlantic hurricane, or that our landing was a near miracle: only seconds before the pilot was to be ordered to abort the descent, a passing break in clouds and fog permitted the touchdown. Standing in the storm, we knew only that Senator Kennedy had departed, and no familiar figures of his organization were on hand. The long Johnson face fell. "Goddam it," he whispered glumly. "We kept him and Jackie waiting past their dinnertime." But in the confusion of the moment, more concerns came into play than the senator's customary anxiousness to please his peers, and a tenseness began to rise among us.

While we tried to keep it out of mind, we recognized that the journey to Hyannis Port could end happily or it could end in humiliation. Uniquely in national campaign history, the Kennedy-Johnson ticket was an alliance of adversaries, compounded in its contradictions by unnatural reversals of roles: the party leader now was the led; the senior member now held the junior role; and in the presence of the man who had vanquished him, the most powerful legislative figure in the nation would be powerless. Since Los Angeles, there had been no reassurances. The two senators had not talked; communications from the Kennedy staff about the visit itself tended to be curt and bristling with contempt. For our part, Johnson's intimates remained convinced that the members of the Massachusetts cabal, most of whom we did not know, were arrogant, rude, and ruthless.

The mutual antipathies were kept aflame by intermediaries reporting hostile statements from one camp to the other. On the night before the departure from Austin, a prominent Washington lawyer had telephoned from Boston alleging that he had just returned from "the compound." "You Texas boys," he told one of the staff, "are accustomed to all that southern bowing and scraping, but they play the game by different rules in Boston." He continued with a warning: "When you fellows get to the Cape, it'll be elbows in the ribs and knees in the crotch."

Lyndon Johnson reacted to such messages with lofty, and exasperating, disdain. He reminded us that Boston was a center of culture and enlightenment. "Jack's people" beat "his people," he chose to believe, not because of their training in the south wards but because of their learning at Harvard. "They beat the hell out of us," he explained, in a statement he repeated many times, "because they have superior educations." Nonetheless, he took the precaution of asking a longtime Washington friend, James Rowe, to be on hand at Hyannis Port. An old pro in national politics, Rowe had worked with the Irish Catholic politicians of the East for every Democratic presidential candidate since FDR; and as Senator Johnson explained, "Jim speaks the language." After our arrival at the air base, the senator added another precaution: he asked George Reedy and me to accompany him to the Kennedy residence. "I think everything's going to be all right," he said, "but I only think it, I don't know it. You fellas stay close, because I might need some witnesses." He added a typical Johnsonian admonition: "Remember, you may meet Mrs. Kennedy, so be sure to clean your fingernails and pull your tie knots tight."

Almost an hour after our arrival on Cape Cod, the two senators met at the entrance to John Kennedy's residence. As always when uncertain of what a meeting might hold, the majority leader seized the first moment and did not release it until he was sure of the next moment. In apparent high glee, he poured out a jumbled recital of the journey, including an expertly laundered version of former president Truman's remarks. "He's all fired up, and he thinks of you a lot." The Johnson voice swelled as he went along; arms pumped, hands clapped against forehead, eyes turned heavenward, and in one sudden gesture, the senator flung his arms out like airplane wings, banked steeply until his palm rested on Senator Kennedy's shoelaces, and then righted his imaginary craft, clapping his hands above his head. With uncontrolled hilarity, he retold the episode at Otis Air Force Base. "I came down the steps, and I saw these people, and I said, 'Take me to my leader,'" he related, "but they looked at me, and then at each other, and some poor little colonel comes over and whispers, 'Senator, your leader has fled.'"

The act came naturally. All the while he spoke and gestured so exuberantly, Lyndon Johnson's eyes and mind were not missing a nuance on the Kennedy features. He would not let the conversation begin until he knew how it would end. Satisfied with what he saw, he subsided abruptly, acknowledging none too comfortably Mrs. Johnson's reproachful stare from across the room.

As one does in such a situation, I watched John F. Kennedy closely myself. There was a lightness, even a fragility, about his manner that seemed incongruous in the world of political men. The grandson of the Boston pols watched the torrent of Johnson vitality with bemusement, smiling gently until the rich improbability of the final punch line evoked a hearty laugh. One impression was especially vivid. The young Massachusetts senator exuded self-assurance; unlike other public figures whom I had observed in such a conversation with Senator Johnson, Senator Kennedy was far too secure to feel threatened by the man who towered over him. He understood his guest, perhaps even better than his guest understood him, and because of that understanding, John Kennedy enjoyed Lyndon Johnson in an uncomplicated, unbothered way. What this communicated to the majority leader, I could not know, but I noted—as did George Reedy—that amid all his gesturing, Senator Johnson never once laid his hand or his arm on John Kennedy's shoulders, as he invariably did with other men.

The plan for the evening called for the Kennedys and the Johnsons to dine together at the residence, with the conference to come later. Reedy and I were dispatched to a nearby restaurant with the Kennedy press secretary, Pierre Salinger. He proved to be disappointing: instead of elbows, the amiable Salinger was a considerate, comfortable host. But before we could begin talking politics,

Senator Johnson personally telephoned to request our presence in the Kennedy living room.

The two senators were seated facing each other before the window opening onto the dark Nantucket night. Jim Rowe sat at Senator Johnson's side, passing him memoranda about details of campaign arrangements—speech coordination, transportation, itineraries, fund-raising. Beside Senator Kennedy was one of his brain trusters, Myer Feldman, a brilliant, incisive lawyer from Washington. The significance was not lost on any of us. Some years earlier, before meeting Senator Kennedy, Feldman had worked for and with the majority leader on the staff of a Senate subcommittee; of all the Kennedy entourage, he was the best and most favorably known to Senator Johnson. It struck me as an act of unusual thoughtfulness on Senator Kennedy's part to have selected as his assistant for the occasion someone with whom his senior colleague could be wholly at ease.

Conversation between the two men went along casually and easily, almost too easily. Senator Kennedy commented quickly and quietly on each agenda item, making it clear that the majority leader was to be entirely free to conduct his own campaign. For example, the presidential nominee vetoed a suggestion for having Johnson speeches read and approved in advance by members of the Kennedy staff. "You know what to say as well as I do, Lyndon," he commented. Senator Johnson obviously had not anticipated the ease of the conversation; he became repetitious, returning to points already settled and, at times, talking far too long. Kennedy's calm continued. He listened patiently, a finger resting on his lips, and occasionally he interrupted adroitly to move the discussion along. The wistfulness of the young senator continued to surprise and, in a sense, haunt me; he fitted no image which I brought to the meeting. When, the following day, Senator Johnson asked, "What did you think of him?" I replied, to the senator's bafflement, "Kennedy is a poet."

As the evening wore on uneventfully, Senator Kennedy's environment became more intriguing than the man himself. Unlike the homes of the wealthy in the Southwest, the Kennedy residence bespoke nothing of the owner's station in life: the furnishings were frugal, little of the bric-a-brac collected by public men was in evidence, and my Protestant eyes noted the conspicuous absence of religious symbols so often found in Catholic homes. My principal interest, however, began to focus on a white-coated, darkly hand-some older man coming and going during the conference whom I assumed to be the family butler.

The man entered the room after Reedy and I settled into place in chairs near the door. He emptied ashtrays, moved objects about on the tables, picked lint from the rug in usual butler fashion, disappearing for long periods into the kitchen. But he would return, picking up memoranda the senators had laid aside and studying them or, on occasion, drawing a chair close to sit and listen attentively to the discussion. Then he would be up and about on his rounds again. I became thirsty and decided, when this busy butler passed me again, I would ask for a glass of water. As he approached, however, my eyes happened to fall on his shoes: they were European cut, black patent slippers adorned with ornate bows. While this might be the fashion among servants of the rich, I was intimidated by a sudden doubt. I decided to endure my thirst awhile longer.

Soon the conference ended. The only problem had been the lack of problems. Relieved and stimulated, Senator Johnson led his new leader outside for a "surprise." Following an old Texas custom, the senator had brought with him as a gift a typical white Texas hat like his own—much nearer two-quart size than ten gallon. Proudly, he showed off the gift, related the tradition behind it, and handed it over to his host. Senator Kennedy glanced inside and held the hat at his side.

"You are supposed to put it on," Senator Johnson said.

The Kennedy grin flashed. "I can't put it on. It's not my size."

Flustered, the Texas senator looked himself to check the size. "It's seven and three-eighths—that's what your staff told us."

Senator Kennedy shook his head. "I wear a half."

The first cultural barrier of the evening rose between the men. "A half" came out, in Kennedy accents, as something akin to "ahave." The Johnson features wrinkled quizzically, and Senator Kennedy repeated, more loudly, "Ahave, ahave."

It might have been another language to the ears of the donor. Thoroughly confused and anxious, Senator Johnson leaned close to me and whispered, "What's he trying to say?" Senator Kennedy led the laughter—in which a deeply embarrassed Senator Johnson did not join—as I interpreted between Northeast and Southwest.

The rains had ceased, and the group began to stroll the narrow street out front, exchanging some pungent banter with friendly hecklers in a passing automobile. Two newsmen, Hugh Sidey of *Life* and Robert Novak of *The Wall Street Journal,* joined us. Sidey questioned me about the meeting, asking for details of where the two senators sat, what they drank, whether there were any "nibbles" on the table. In passing, I mentioned the remarkable butler with the fancy shoes. Sidey bent double with laughter. "That was no butler," he finally explained. "That was the Kennedys' brother-in-law, Prince Radziwill."

Once during the evening, we glimpsed Mrs. Kennedy. Wearing a white robe, she came partway down the stairs into the living room and called out to her husband, "John." We all rose, except Senator Kennedy himself, who listened politely while she urged him not to be up too late.

He then excused himself from our group, explaining with a smile that Jackie thought he should get more sleep. But Senator Johnson wanted to talk. Pierre Salinger drove us to a seaside hotel where we were to spend the night, and together we talked far past midnight. The strain was gone from Senator Johnson's face. In his view, "everything would be all right." For the first time since Los Angeles, he allowed himself to talk about the events preceding the convention, specifically his one serious campaign swing through the Northwest during the month of May. "I thought I gave you a little scare then," he said to Salinger, who acknowledged that the majority leader's campaigning had been effective: "It took a lot of steak and martinis to get the press who had been out with you back in line." Johnson seemed immensely pleased.

Mary Margaret Wiley, Senator Johnson's secretary, interrupted our long, amicable session with a telephone call. She reported that the two newsmen, Sidey and Novak, were under our windows, industriously transcribing the conversation. We hurried outside to catch them in the act, but Senator Johnson only marveled. "Even the Kennedy press," he said, "is smarter than mine."

One more detail remained for the visit. A press conference would be held the following morning after breakfast. "It is my judgment," Senator Johnson said, "that I ought to have some of those little, light lines like Kennedy uses in his speeches. If I get up there and sound too serious, the press is going to say I'm unhappy about the convention." Rapier wit was not a strong Johnson suit, but the following morning, in the living room of Ambassador Joe Kennedy's home, he amused the press and delighted his running mate by opening his remarks with the announcement, "The principal difference for the Republicans between 1860 and 1960 is Lincoln."

Kennedy told the assembled press, predominantly those who had accompanied Johnson from Texas, that he thought the Democratic Party was "fortunate" his Senate colleague was "willing to run for the office of the vice presidency.

"I don't say that from the point of view of any political strength that he might have in the election," Kennedy added. "What I mean is that if we are successful, we will be fortunate to have his assistance in carrying out all the programs to which the Democratic Party has committed itself. And I must say that if we are successful in November, that Senator Johnson, when elected, can play a role as vice president greater, more influential, more significant, and with greater benefit to the public interest than any vice president in recent times."

During the questions and answers, a familiar face appeared at the back of the room: it was Bobby Kennedy. Attired in a bulky gray sweater, his hair hanging over his forehead, and smiling a broad and toothy grin, the young brother seemed a very different person from the one I had encountered on the campaign trail: more youthful than I remembered, happier, very vulnerable, no longer a cornered animal. Senator Johnson sought him out after the news conference concluded, bear hugging him and tousling his hair as he called to the Texas press: "Here's the man who really did it to us." Bobby looked shy, embarrassed, and deeply pained.

At this moment I stood with a group of Texas editors watching the proceedings from an entrance off the broad porch. My position, at the front of the cluster, blocked the passageway. Suddenly the group behind me began to part, but before I could turn or move aside, a woman pushed beside me and without a word delivered a hard touch-football hip block. It caught me off balance, and in a graceless plunge I went over the top of a sofa before me and sprawled across its cushions. I recognized my feminine assailant as a Kennedy sister, Mrs. Eunice Shriver; unaware of what she had done, she entered the room and stood, hands on hips, surveying the crowd. The next President of the United States, standing close by, offered me a hand as I tried to scramble to my feet. Grinning, he said, "That's my sister."

The next Vice President of the United States, however, only saw my legs-above-head posture on the sofa. Face flushed, he drew me aside and pressed his nose close to mine. "Good God, son, what are you trying to do to me?" he whispered menacingly. "You want the Kennedys to think I run around with drunks?"

Hurricane rains were falling as the time came to go and our party made its way to the waiting bus. Senator Kennedy followed, hatless and coatless, through the rising storm. Aboard the bus he thanked the Texas contingent for coming to "God's country." The majority leader led the applause and told the editors, "Fellas, I have good news. If we win in November, Jack has promised that someday while they're in the White House, he'll bring Jackie with him and spend the night at the ranch." There was more applause, and we left.

Soon after our Viscount climbed over the dark clouds and leveled off for the return flight to Texas, one of the reporters aboard, Allen Duckworth, the influential but very conservative political editor of *The Dallas Morning News*, called me to his seat. A typewriter was on his lap. Duckworth showed me the lead for his story in the Sunday editions. "In an historic ceremony at Hyannis Port today," it read, "Senator John F. Kennedy accepted the surrender of Senator Lyndon B. Johnson of Texas and told him, 'The men may keep their horses for spring plowing.'"

10

THE LAST ROUNDUP

The trip to Hyannis Port had ended well. Whatever antipathies smoldered among those around, Senator John F. Kennedy himself was much too mature, too realistic about the politics of victory in 1960, and too innately decent to play small games with the man he had asked to be his running mate on the Democratic ticket. Lyndon Johnson had his new leader's trust; what the majority leader did with this first opportunity in national politics would be entirely up to him and his own organization. That presented the most difficult challenge yet in this difficult year.

In the sense that American politicians understand the term, the senior senator from Texas had no organization, either in his home state or nationally. A single part-time staff member, Cliff Carter, devoted attention to keeping Texas fences mended during the 1950s with his own warm handshake and patiently conciliatory manner; but Carter, a small-town 7UP bottler, made no pretense of being a political power or boss. The structure of designated county managers, in most but not all of the state's 254 counties, could only be described as flimsy. Most of the managers gave more of their time to other political figures, and the majority leader could pass many of these "Johnson men" on the streets without recognizing them.

The senator's fitful spurts of political activity before Los Angeles had yielded no lasting organizational gains. Throughout that period, he resisted attempts to form an adequate campaign staff. When efforts were made to build regional or state structures outside the Southwest, he artfully sabotaged them himself: on several occasions he simply refused to see individuals who had agreed to become campaign managers in major states. He resented and developed towering dislikes for several Texans who voluntarily put together citizen committees on his behalf. While he might appear the consummate politician in Washington, Senator Johnson, fully as much as the younger Congressman Johnson, still despised politics; he wanted no part of the big-city Democratic machines, and he felt that Texas support only advertised the geography he sought to escape. When he returned home from Massachusetts, facing his most important political challenge, he had no personal organization to support him in the national campaign.

His response was predictable. Once more, he turned back to those he remembered as "my boys," the young men who had served on his staff in the House of Representatives. The reaction, however, was not what he expected. Almost to a man, Lyndon Johnson's "boys" pulled back. Those who were active members of his staff—Walter Jenkins, George Reedy, and Cliff Carter—continued loyally at their tasks. Others, though, demurred: they had gone this far with him, but they chose to go no farther.

John Connally, as always, set the pattern. On the flight back from his meeting with Senator Kennedy, the vice presidential nominee confidently outlined his organizational plan: Connally would be the campaign manager at Washington headquarters; others of his past assistants and allies would become regional overseers; he even specified that I was to set up a speechwriting staff and be its director. Connally's reply, however, was blunt, firm, and final: "No." With less bluntness but equal finality, others, including myself, gave the same answer.

The reaction was not easily explained. Campaigning for Lyndon Johnson under the unexpected circumstances necessarily meant campaigning for John Kennedy; yet that presented no significant complications. In politics, you play the cards as they are dealt. If we had reservations about the Massachusetts senator as president, they were inconsequential against our questions about the Republican nominee, Vice President Richard Nixon. Our view of him was essentially that of the congressional elders: that he had fluked into his prominence without being fully tested; that he remained now, as when he came to Congress fourteen years earlier, very much a loner, a man nobody knew; that the steel essential for the presidency still was not forged in him. Connally offered the rationale all of us accepted when he said, "I'm for Kennedy because, whatever else, if it came down to protecting the vital interests of the United States, I'm certain he could be absolutely ruthless in making his choice." We wanted Senator Kennedy to win in November, and in actual fact, every "Johnson man" in Texas took active, aggressive, and effective roles in the subsequent campaign to deliver the Texas electoral votes to him.

Our collective hesitation related to Lyndon Johnson. Each of us had shared closely parallel experiences. On the basis of our campus attainments at the University of Texas, he chose us for his staff; none of us chose him. We went to Washington expecting two or three years of learning from him before beginning our own quests for careers; yet he proved to be an all-enveloping experience from which one never quite escaped. Harsh words, bitter quarrels, long, sulking estrangements, did not keep him away; when he confronted a new challenge, he came back to those who knew him best, and something about the relationship caused you to yield, to give your best to his career "one more time." Now his career was changing; whether the ticket won or lost—and we thought it sure to win— Lyndon Johnson would begin a new career in 1961. We had had enough of the anxieties of power, enough of the national stage, enough of subordinating our own lives to the career of another man. While we wished him well, it was time for Lyndon Johnson to find himself some "new boys."

The senator was deeply hurt. When I came to tell him my own negative decision about joining the campaign, he read my answer in my eyes before I spoke. For three memorable hours of mono-logue, during which I spoke hardly a word, he discoursed on the virtues of loyalty, faithfulness, and honor, mixing in affectionate and extravagant praise for each of "my boys." Several times he repeated, "This is the last go-round for us, the last time I'll have reason to ask." I was not unmoved, but my decision remained unchanged.

If Connally would not accept the campaign managership, Senator Johnson wanted the man whose political judgment he respected almost as much: Jim Rowe, the Washington attorney for the Hyannis Port conferences. Big, bluff, and engaging, this wise westerner knew his way around eastern politics as no Johnson associate had ever been permitted to learn; and Johnson welcomed his unexpected acceptance of the chief campaign role. It closed a circle: in the 1930s, Jim Rowe was FDR's youngest assistant at the White House and Lyndon Johnson's best friend in the New Deal palace guard.

But the 1960 arrangement did not last. Rowe's professionalism could tolerate only so much of the senator's political naïveté. Within three weeks the two old friends exploded at each other and Rowe stalked out with this advice, slightly expurgated: "Get yourself another boy." The second most powerful man in Washington faced the largest challenge of his political life very much alone.

It had been this way throughout the tormented year. Under the pressure of national politics, Lyndon Johnson's private world was not holding together. He was a man in serious trouble.

Yet the old conditioning began to have effect. Without being asked, the senator's "boys" started to relent. Connally still would accept no active part in the campaign; however, he persuaded one of the old pros of Texas campaigns, Jim Blundell of Dallas, to serve as liaison with the Kennedy staff at the Democratic National Committee. Others followed the same lead: if not willing to join the campaign themselves, they recruited able replacements. The majority leader called me to Washington, related what they were doing, and pulled out a typical Johnsonism. "We're heading for the last roundup," he said, long-faced and forlorn, "and there's an empty saddle in the old corral." I relented, too, and began writing the first of more than 120 speeches for the fall campaign. All of us understood—no one more clearly than Lyndon Johnson himself—that this was, indeed, the last time around for those who, in the words of the campaign slogan, had gone "All the Way with LBJ."

— 11 —

A FRIDAY AFTERNOON IN BRUSSELS

On Friday morning, November 8, 1963, I returned to Vice President Lyndon B. Johnson's suite at the Hotel Westbury in Brussels shortly before ten o'clock. As when I had departed after midnight the night before, the rooms were neat and orderly, and the new oil paintings had been removed from sight. But the quarters were no longer still and quiet.

Mrs. Juanita Roberts, the vice president's gracious secretary, presided cheerfully over the coffee service. Sam Gammon and Lee Stulman, the two young Foreign Service officers who served as policy aides, busily made a last-minute check of the papers they would carry to the vice president's morning talks with the Belgians. Colonel William Jackson, the military aide, was present, along with First Lieutenant Richard Nelson, a bright young Princeton graduate recently assigned to the staff to assist with speechwriting. Neither officer was in uniform; the vice president firmly forbade any "show of military" in his travel party, and both aides wore street clothes, which Dick Nelson impishly described as "our civilian disguise." Ambassador Douglas MacArthur III had returned; he and Mrs. MacArthur stood before the broad living room windows, pointing out landmarks of the Belgian capital to Mrs. Johnson and her secretary, Mrs. Bess Abell. The vice president, however, had not made an appearance, and I found him still in the bedroom.

Lyndon Johnson was fully dressed and ready to go, but he sat quietly on the edge of the bed, contemplating the walls. When I stepped through the doorway, I saw what was occupying him.

During the morning hours after my departure, the vice president had apparently padded around the royal suite gathering the paintings which he had purchased the previous evening; he had placed them carefully along three walls of the bedroom and was now engaged in thoughtful study of his new acquisitions.

The vice president did not speak, nor did I. It was not necessary; he knew the time, and as the Secret Service put it, he "knew the drill" for his morning schedule. I took a chair behind him and waited. He considered each of his paintings carefully and admiringly. Once he rose from the bed and moved close to one canvas, bending low to examine some detail and run his fingers over the brushwork. "Nice, isn't it," he said, smiling and resuming his seat on the bed. Otherwise the silence continued unbroken. I could not see his face and had no reading on his mood or thoughts.

On schedule, at one minute before ten, his wristwatch alarm sounded. Immediately the vice president started for the door, and I followed after him. He opened the door, looked into the living room, where Ambassador MacArthur and the others waited, and then he turned toward me, closing the door once more.

"Buzz," he said quietly, "I've changed my mind. You better stay here at the hotel and see if you can cancel the things on my schedule after lunch." Once again, as he had done on his written messages throughout the week, he added: "I need the afternoon for myself."

That was all. He opened the door again and strode briskly into the next room, booming his usual expansive, hail-fellow-well-met greeting to the ambassador, kissing Mrs. Johnson, and greeting Lieutenant Nelson with a cheery question: "All quiet on the Western Front this morning, General?" Then he was gone down the hallway.

I followed him to the elevator. The vice president, as always, entered first. While others crowded in around him, he looked out at me and held one hand over his head, moving the fingers in a smoothing gesture. His lips soundlessly formed the words of his instructions: "Handle it nice."

The schedule changes presented no problem. American Embassy officers telephoned their Belgian counterparts and spoke politely about the day's adverse weather; the Belgians obligingly anticipated the purpose of the calls and themselves suggested cancellation of the minor ceremonial functions scheduled for the afternoon. It was handled quickly and "nicely," and I returned to my own suite on the floor below to begin the long wait for the vice president's return at two-thirty.

What did it all mean? For the first time, I was confident that the vice president's behavior during the week represented no mere caprice. During my midnight hours with him, he had been too much himself, the way I most often saw him through his private hours on these missions abroad; no melancholy had been weighing on him as he conducted his cleanup of the suite, made his abortive attempt to escape the Secret Service, or delivered the speech he "would like to make" before the imaginary audience in his bedroom. The decision that I should remain behind to clear his afternoon schedule was clearly calculated.

At two o'clock in the morning, having one of his "own people" with him for the Belgian talks mattered greatly; by ten o'clock, though, something else mattered more. Something must be happening, somewhere, to influence his decision. Almost certainly it could not be anything associated with the Benelux mission; virtually all information about the trip reached the vice president through me, and I knew nothing was occurring which would prompt his unaccustomed desire for privacy each afternoon. Whatever concerned him so deeply must be happening back home, almost certainly in Washington. If that was so, I might have to wait until our return to the United States on Saturday before learning more about the matter.

The morning hours passed slowly. Since Monday in Luxembourg, the Benelux weather had been bright and beautiful, but today the sun was gone. Clouds shrouded the Belgian capital, and the city lay dim and damp under the cold of Europe's approaching winter. I remained in my room, reading and waiting by the telephone.

Around noon, there was a knock at the door, and Sergeant Paul Glynn entered. Since early in 1962, the sergeant had served as the vice president's personal aide, a military euphemism for valet. He proved to be one of the more valuable perquisites of the new office.

Serving as valet to Lyndon Johnson was not the Air Force's easiest assignment. In 1961 a succession of senior enlisted men tried it and promptly quit. Lyndon Johnson was wholly unaccustomed to the constant ministrations of body servants, waking him each morning, laying out his clothes, and hovering silently around the bedroom while he shaved, dressed, and talked on the telephone. Unceasingly suspicious of things military anyway, he darkly suspected these impassive, closemouthed attendants of being "Pentagon spies," and purposely made their working lives miserable until they resigned. Paul Glynn, however, proved a happy exception: resilient, good-humored, and loquacious, he handled the vice presidential temperament adroitly and won a vital place in the Johnson world.

True to his trade, Sergeant Glynn and his assistant, Sergeant Ken Gaddis, operated an exceptional intelligence network. Very little occurred within the travel entourage abroad of which they were not promptly aware. From experience, I suspected this must be the purpose of the sergeant's visit. Confirmation was not long coming.

"The boys," Sergeant Glynn said casually, using his customary reference to the Secret Service agents, "tell me you were with the Man half the night." I verified his information, and he drew up a chair, asking earnestly: "Did you learn anything about the mood?"

Sergeant Glynn, it developed, was as mystified as everyone else by the vice president's subdued and isolated week. He had attended to his regular duties in the suite each day, but there had been little conversation. "The Man's mind," he observed of the vice president, "seems to be a thousand miles away when he's alone." I asked if cables or other messages were reaching the quarters from any source other than myself; the answer was negative. "Who's he been talking to?" I pressed. "Nobody," Glynn replied. "He hasn't used the radio all week." Since his first mission to Africa, Lyndon Johnson had become a frequent user of the security radio apparatus which maintained continuous voice contact with the White House; sometimes he talked to the family residence in Washington to check up on the Johnson daughters, but more often he used the radio to contact his assistant, Walter Jenkins, and catch up on the office news. Paul Glynn's information, which I knew must be accurate, seemed to nullify my conjecture that something might be occurring in Washington to affect the vice president's spirits.

The topic was soon drained and wearisome. Our casual conversation turned to livelier discussions of what lay ahead. Knowing the vice president as he did, Sergeant Glynn looked forward to preparations for President and Mrs. Kennedy's forthcoming visit to the LBJ Ranch with a mixture of good-natured amusement and dread. This attitude was universal among those on the Johnson staff.

There were, of course, many Lyndon Johnsons. None was more formidable, however, than Lyndon Johnson the Host. On the occasions when he had entertained visiting heads of state at his ranch home, the vice president's staff, ranch hands, and neighbors had barely survived his frenetic and exacting preparations. One tale, popular in Austin at the time of German chancellor Konrad Adenauer's visit in 1961, had it that a ranch worker quit his job in an angry huff. "Goddam it, Lyndon," he supposedly said, "I didn't mind using silver polish on the barbed wire, but I'll be damned if I'm gonna run ahead of you and Adenauer spraying deodorant on the horse manure." The episode never happened, but the vice president's friends retold the story appreciatively: it aptly captured the insatiable perfectionism of Lyndon Johnson when important guests were coming to his home.

The perfectionism would be working overtime for November 22, not so much to satisfy John F. Kennedy, who had once visited the ranch before becoming president, as to please and impress "little Mrs. Kennedy."

At the White House, the young First Lady had been unusually attentive and considerate toward the vice president. She regularly included the Johnsons as guests at her small private parties and dances; she offered warm and sometimes effusive compliments on the vice president's public activities; at several public occasions, she flattered him by asking to be seated next to him. Mrs. Kennedy's nonpolitical social friends sometimes baffled the vice president; at one of the White House dances, he spent a pained evening trying to make table conversation with a lovely young New York socialite who did not understand the meaning of the term "appropriations." But "little Mrs. Kennedy" was the model First Lady, in the vice president's view, and he made no attempt to conceal his delight or contain his pride over her attentions.

When she asked his assistance in securing an ornate chandelier from the Capitol for her redecoration of the White House, he literally did not sleep until he obtained it for her. When she asked him to be the speaker at an occasion honoring André Malraux, the

French literary and political figure, he called for translations of all Malraux's writings and bravely tried to read through them. Mrs. Kennedy's presence as an overnight guest at the LBJ Ranch would require the best—and the most—from everyone.

Since Monday, when news of Mrs. Kennedy's decision to make the Texas trip had arrived, a running joke had developed among members of the travel party. Mrs. Johnson's secretary, Bess Abell, would bear the brunt of preparations for the visit. Other staff members, Secret Service agents, even the usually reserved State Department officers in the party, took to kidding Mrs. Abell about what she could expect the next two weeks. The favored tactic of the jokesters was to approach her and suddenly pretend to be placing a typically urgent Johnson-style telephone call from the LBJ Ranch.

In my room at the Westbury, Paul Glynn and I began passing the time repeating some of the better variations of this joke. Sample: "Hello, Neiman Marcus? This is Lyndon Johnson. Listen, little Mrs. Kennedy is coming down here and we don't have anything for her to eat off here. Our best plates are some reject crockery Lady Bird picked up at a bargain from the Casparis cafe in Johnson City. Now, I was wondering: could you loan me a couple barrels of your best china—a little gold around the edges, you know—and I'll send you back what's left of it on Monday?" Sample: "Tiffany's? Look, we've got a crisis on the ranch. Little Mrs. Kennedy's coming, and all we have for drinking glasses are some old peanut butter jars. I need a crate of your best crystal, monogrammed. What? Why LBJ, of course, you dimwit." Exaggerated as such lighthearted jests might be, they caught the flavor of Lyndon Johnson the Host and what the next two weeks would be like at the LBJ Ranch.

The humor finally subsided. Sergeant Glynn inquired about what the vice president had said during our nighttime conversation concerning the Kennedy visit. The subject, of course, had not been mentioned. I realized, as a matter of fact, that the vice president had not commented all week on the president's trip to Texas. We on the staff had learned of Mrs. Kennedy's plans only through Bess Abell, who had been told by Mrs. Johnson. Paul Glynn felt, and I agreed, that the vice president must be disciplining himself, permitting no word of the Texas affair to be mentioned while his official mission abroad was still in progress. That would most likely change on the Atlantic crossing Saturday afternoon. Glynn decided he should return to the royal suite to lay out pajamas in the event the vice president wanted to spend the afternoon resting. As he departed from my room, he sighed. "I wish November were already behind us."

At two-thirty, the telephone beside my chair rang. It was a Secret Service agent. "Volunteer has departed," he announced. "ETA ten minutes."

As always, the electronic network of security was watching closely, even in the streets of a foreign capital. "Volunteer" served as the Secret Service code word for the vice president. The message meant that he had departed from the site of his luncheon meeting and was now being driven to the Hotel Westbury; the estimated time of arrival at the entrance was ten minutes away. I collected the memoranda and messages that he should see and took the elevator to the lobby.

The limousine pulled to the curb on schedule, and I knew almost immediately that the morning talks must have gone well. The vice president's hands were pumping up and down as he spoke animatedly with Ambassador MacArthur, and he continued with the lively conversation after the limousine stopped. These were reliable signs of a buoyant mood.

Vice President Johnson prolonged his talk for almost ten minutes while a small crowd of spectators gathered on the sidewalk. When he finally emerged, the smiling audience applauded politely. Surprised, the vice president waved happily and shook the hands extended toward him. At this point, there was a loud whoop from the doorway, and a distinctly New Yorkish voice shouted: "Godamighty, if it isn't old Lyndon himself." The vice president's face froze, and he carefully kept his eyes on the crowd; in unison with the Secret Service agents, however, I turned to see a short, beaming American traveler pushing through the spectators, one hand extended while the other fished in his vest pocket for a business calling card. It was the kind of encounter which set Lyndon Johnson on edge, and the agents moved skillfully to block the tourist's approach, but the American only made matters worse.

Unaware that he was pinioned in a four-man square of Secret Service agents, the man began trying to hand his business card to the vice president, but he could not reach over the tall shoulders in front of him. "Lyndon, Lyndon," he called out loudly. "Godamighty, Lyndon, it's Harry Plunkett"—I've changed his name, of course—"Long Island Democrats, finance committee, 1960." Now jumping up and down, he shouted: "Raised lots of dough for you and Jack, yessir, lots of the old moola."

For a man who had spent his adult life in politics, Lyndon Johnson had an unaccountable and, at times, unreasoning dislike for campaign contributors; as a class, he seemed to feel, they were up to no worthy purpose. At the words "dough" and "moola," the vice president's face went white; he broke off from his hand shaking and hurried through the door being held for him by an agent. Realizing that "Harry Plunkett" had no idea of what he had done—or what had happened to him—I took his card and shook hands while his Secret Service escort crowded him toward the curb. "Mr. Plunkett" was too excited to be aware: he held out his hand to some spectators and cried, "Godamighty, I shook hands with ol' Lyndon himself."

The vice president had crossed the hotel lobby and was sulking out of sight in the waiting elevator when I finally caught up with him. He did not think the episode amusing. "Goddam loudmouth," he muttered. Then he turned to Special Agent Rufus Youngblood and asked earnestly: "Rufus, how're we ever going to lead the world with idiots like that running loose?" The elevator doors closed, and we rode in silence to the royal suite.

At the entrance to his quarters, the vice president looked at his watch. Immediately he seemed hurried. He took the message envelope from my hand, asked if I had anything to tell him, and when I did not moved quickly through the door, seemingly anxious to be alone once more. I exchanged shrugs with the Secret Service agents and went down the stairs to my room.

Another long wait was beginning. I considered leaving to spend the afternoon seeing Brussels, but the day had darkened and a storm was rising. Soon, an angry wind began howling against the hotel's upper floors, sheets of rain drove hard across the windows, and night seemed very near. It was no time to think of going out. I stood by the window, watching the light die in the ancient streets below and wondering when the storm would pass. Unexpectedly, the telephone rang again.

"Mr. Busby, I have a message from Volunteer." It was the same Secret Service agent who had called to alert me to the vice president's arrival. "If you are not too busy," the agent said crisply, "Volunteer would like to see you in his quarters as soon as possible."

None of the messages which I had handed the vice president required response or comment. I assumed that the storm must have awakened him from his nap. Most likely I would find him in his bed, grumbling about the disturbance and waiting to offer some just-remembered instruction about his evening schedule.

When I reached the bedroom, though, the vice president had not retired. His pajamas lay unused on the bed. Coat off and tie loosened, he sat facing the darkened windows with one hand resting on a telephone beside his chair. He acknowledged my entrance, but for several silent minutes he continued to stare into the darkness.

"Buzz," he said finally, "what do you want to do when this is all over?"

His tone and manner surprised me as much as his words. The vice president spoke brightly, a note of merriment in his voice, and after he had spoken, he bounded from the chair, standing over me and smiling broadly.

I was uncertain about the question. "This" had two connotations: he might mean the Benelux mission, which would be ending on Saturday, or on the basis of past usages of the term, he might be speaking of the vice presidency. I began replying in terms of the trip, relating my plans for Sunday in Washington.

He interrupted. "No, no," he said. "I mean what do you really want to do when I'm through with this job and we're all free again? What do you want to do then?"

It was not necessary to answer his question. The plans for the future were already taking shape.

"I'll tell you what we'll do," he said, beginning to pace the room. "We'll all go back down to Texas and I'll buy us a newspaper. You can be the editor and I'll be the publisher, and maybe I'll write something for you one day a week." He paused reflectively and then laughed. "I guess I've always wanted to be a big fat-ass publisher someday." Obviously pleased and even a bit excited by his imaginings, he quickened his back-and-forth striding, and his arms moved in wide gestures as he spoke. "We'll turn that state upside down," he declared with emphasis. "We'll take on the oil crowd, and the utilities, and the TMA,[1] and all the fat cats." He clapped his hands and made a strong shoving gesture. "We'll run 'em out of Austin, and we'll keep the bastards running across the Red River all the way to Kansas."

The Texas power structure that he was describing no longer monopolized state affairs at Austin. Other conservative interests—insurance, real estate, truckers, highway contractors—had long since emerged as dominant influences on Texas public policy. But he was remembering the battles he had fought and the enemies he had made in the Texas of the 1930s, and he punched the air with schoolboy zest, savoring a return to the old wars.

Once we had "driven the money changers from the temple," he continued, quoting as he so often did from the unforgotten passages of Franklin D. Roosevelt, there would be work to do "for the people." We would "pass an education bill, a water program, a measure to improve the small cities, and of course, we'll give 'em a little civil rights, too."

The poll tax, he announced, would be abolished—a goal for which he had actively campaigned several times since World War II. State universities and colleges would be integrated fully. A commission would be established to prevent employment discrimination among Texas firms selling to the state government. Something would be done about the "wetbacks," the cheap migratory labor from across the Rio Grande in Mexico, and "the Latins," Texas vernacular for Mexican-Americans, would have "their place in the sun." But he returned to his first interest, education. Oil company taxes should be doubled, he decreed, or maybe tripled, so Texas public schools would be "second to none." He meant, also, to expand appropriations for higher education. More money would be provided for "your university," he said, a reference to my alma mater, the University of Texas at Austin; but always the partisan of the small state schools

1. A reference that could mean either the Texas Manufacturers Association or the Texas Medical Association, both of which historically disliked him and opposed him politically.—S.B.

Lyndon Johnson relaxes poolside at LBJ Ranch with friends and family: (left to right) Abe Feinberg, Arthur Krim, Lyndon Nugent (grandson), Luci Johnson (back to camera), LBJ, Mathilde Krim, Robert Benjamin, unidentified woman.

Johnson and Lady Bird at a White House reception.

Johnson speaks with Horace Busby (left) and Marvin Watson at LBJ Ranch.

Johnson confers with advisers aboard Air Force One: *(clockwise from left) Bill Moyers, LBJ, Busby, John Connor (at table), Luther Hodges, Donald Hosnig, Kermit Gordon, George Reedy (far right), Stu Udall (seated, back to camera).*

Briefing on Air Force One*: (left to right) Harry McPherson (standing), Busby, Charlie Maguire and George Christian (against back wall), unidentified man (back to camera), LBJ, Charles Engelhard (behind LBJ).*

Busby makes a point in his White House office.

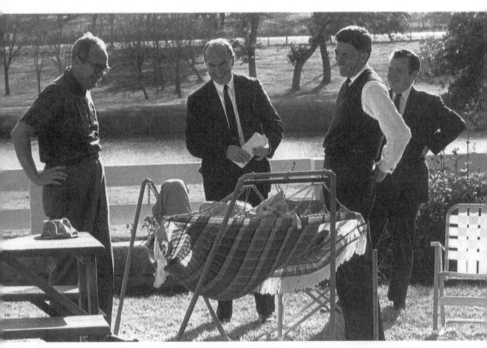

Lyndon Johnson holds court in hammock at LBJ Ranch with (left to right) Kermit Gordon, Donald Hornig, Najeeb Halaby, and Busby.

Johnson meets with Robert McNamara in the Cabinet Room with other advisers: (left to right) LBJ, McNamara, Busby, McGeorge Bundy (back to camera), Bill Moyers.

Johnson watches television with family and advisers in the White House: (left to right) Pat Nugent (Luci Johnson's husband), Clark Clifford, Busby, Lady Bird, Luci Johnson, LBJ.

Johnson consults with Busby.

Johnson and Lady Bird visit Busby and his secretaries in their White House office.

Partygoers laugh with the president in the Yellow Oval Room on the second floor of the White House: (left to right) Jane Wirtz, Dean Rusk, Bess Abell, Busby, Jane Freeman and Trudy Fowler (behind Busby), Bill Wirtz, rest unidentified.

Johnson strategizes with cabinet members and advisers at LBJ Ranch: (left to right) Kermit Gordon, Busby (in background), John Connor, LBJ, Bill Wirtz, Luther Hodges, Donald Hornig, Bill Moyers.

Johnson and Busby review documents in the Oval Office.

Johnson's temper flares with Busby on the tarmac.

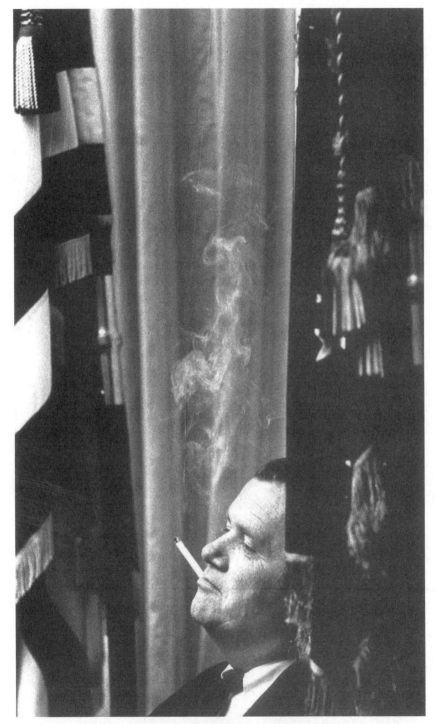

Busby observes a Cabinet meeting in the White House.

from which he graduated, Lyndon Johnson leveled a warning finger in my direction. "I'll be watching," he declared, "to make sure you bunch leave some money for my little schools, too."

Newspapers, in the mind of the vice president, were powerful instruments. The dream of what he could accomplish with one of his own was old, a dream he had spun many times in my hearing; yet as he spoke on and on, I thought his mood must be forced. He had not summoned me to his suite on this stormy afternoon to talk about so distant a future. I watched while the spirit slowly ebbed and a sadness returned to his long face.

"Buzz," he said at last, "I want to ask you a question."

I moved to a chair, and he stretched across the bed, propping himself on one elbow.

"Let's suppose," he began, "that you wanted to tell a fellow some bad news, and you had a choice. You could either pack up your wife, all your bags and baggage, all your people, fly fifteen hundred miles, spend the night in a strange bed in a strange house, and get up in the morning and tell the fellow the bad news in his own living room while his wife and kids were running in and out. Or you could stay at home, punch a button, call the fellow over across the street, give it to him in five minutes, and never miss a wink of sleep. Now which would you do?"

The question was long and became involved in its own words, but I looked up sharply at him. His meaning was entirely clear. No names were mentioned in the hypothetical circumstance, but I understood that he must be thinking of himself and President Kennedy.

On the eve of our departure from Washington, a story had begun making the rounds: as explanation for the president's overnight stay at the LBJ Ranch, the rumor suggested that he intended to advise Lyndon Johnson there would be no place for him on the Democratic ticket in 1964. Such a story was hardly credible.

President Kennedy's purpose in Texas was political: to win popular support in the state, which he had carried only narrowly in 1960, and to attract major contributions for the next campaign. Abrupt dismissal of the vice president, at this time and under these circumstances, would be highly impolitic and helpful to the Republicans. In fact, one of the sources busily spouting the story was the Republican Party's national chairman, Senator Thruston Morton of Kentucky. Only a few days earlier, Senator Morton had advised a Republican gathering that Lyndon Johnson was to be "purged," and this brightened GOP chances of winning Texas and the South in 1964. Furthermore, for just the reasons that the vice president described in his question, such a message, if it were to be delivered, would not likely be passed on face-to-face by the president himself. Other vice presidents had been "dumped" in the past, but such deeds were usually perpetrated by political hatchet men. Technically, vice presidents were elected by the people, too, and no president was in a position to summon his vice president and summarily announce: "You're fired."

The vice president sometimes dwelled overly much on stories such as this. I thought the rumor had been dismissed as idle talk of Washington's dull season, and was surprised at the vice president's lingering preoccupation with it. My face, I suppose, betrayed some of my irritation at this seemingly unnecessary emphasis. Challenged, Lyndon Johnson sighed heavily and nodded toward the telephone; he was, I sensed, about to tell me the whole story.

"I just talked to Walter Jenkins in Washington," he said quietly, adding significantly: "I've been talking to him on the phone every day this week as soon as he's gotten to the office." This instantly explained much. With European time six hours ahead of Washington, Lyndon Johnson's seclusion each afternoon had come at about the time Jenkins and others on the staff were reporting to work for the day in Washington. Because of the nature of the transatlantic conversations—which I still had to learn—the calls had been placed through regular channels rather than the White House radio.

A mirthless smile played across the vice president's lips, and he seemed almost apologetic. "You may not believe what's been happening, but you may as well know." Then he began relating what he had been learning from Walter Jenkins.

On Monday, as the vice president arrived in Luxembourg, teams of newsmen from major national publications began arriving almost simultaneously in Austin and Johnson City, as well as the major metropolitan centers of Texas. None of the reporters were known figures of the Washington press corps, but upward of forty correspondents thus far had been identified in different parts of the state. At first, when the newsmen began making their presence known, it was assumed that they were arriving to do advance stories on President Kennedy's visit. One of the senior figures, however, quickly revealed the true purpose. Talking with an attorney whom he mistakenly believed to be a Johnson enemy, the newsman said: "We're here to do a job on Lyndon Johnson. When we get through with the sonofabitch, Kennedy won't be able to touch him with a ten-foot pole in 1964."

It appeared to be a dragnet operation. The investigative teams were spreading out over the state, talking with attorneys, bankers, businessmen, and known political enemies of the vice president. Four or five publications were represented, but many questions from the different teams were almost identical. Evidently someone had compiled and distributed a master dossier on the vice president's twenty-six-year career in rough-and-tumble Texas politics; some questions, for example, involved campaign charges dating back to before World War II. "Whoever's behind it," the vice president conceded, "has done one hell of a thorough job."

Lyndon Johnson related the information passed on from Jenkins with professional detachment. In his Washington years, he had seen their enemies "do a job" on many public figures, discrediting them to prevent their reelection or advancement. On his own climb up the political ladder, he had been subjected to this same rite of power politics many times, but only within Texas. National headlines now would, he knew, give new national life and meaning to charges long settled and forgotten in his home state.

For anyone familiar with the ugly underside of power, the scenario was clearly foreseeable. One after another, sensationalized exposé-style articles would command national attention. There would be outcries for investigations. Speculation would begin among political writers about whether the vice president would help or hurt the Democratic ticket in the 1964 campaigns. Critics and opponents within the party itself—of whom Lyndon Johnson had an ample supply—would demand a "new face" for the number two position. Proponents of the change would soon coalesce their support around another candidate as an alternative. There would be a chorus of demands for an open convention to allow delegates to decide. At the last minute, pressure would build on President

Kennedy to avert an ugly floor fight by requesting his vice president to stand aside.

"It's pretty, very pretty," the vice president said, his tone neutral and clinical. "They know the president wouldn't dump me, so they're coming at him this way—at their own time, in their own way, they're going to present him with a fait accompli."

This was an old and popular game of power in Washington. "Dumping the vice president" began with Hannibal Hamlin, Abraham Lincoln's first vice president, who was removed from the Republican ticket in 1864 largely because of President Lincoln's own petulance and jealousy. Most vice presidents since had experienced the threat. During his own career in Washington, Lyndon Johnson had seen FDR's first two vice presidents, John Nance Garner and Henry A. Wallace, "dumped" at Democratic conventions, and he had empathized with Vice President Richard M. Nixon in 1956, when a White House cabal had almost succeeded in persuading President Dwight Eisenhower to select a new running mate for the second term.

In those cases, the patterns were strikingly similar. Attacks against the incumbents came from within the "palace guard" at the White House or from among the power brokers in control of the party; in each instance, the objective was to control the line of succession—to dictate who would take over the party and perhaps the White House upon completion of the incumbent president's term. The stakes had never been the vice presidency—that was virtually an irrelevancy—but, rather, the presidency itself.

When the vice president paused in his monologue, I asked the obvious question. The simultaneous arrival of the various teams of newsmen, the similarity of their dossiers and of their questions, the commonality of their revealed purposes—these things were not coincidence. "Who," I asked, "is orchestrating this?"

Lyndon Johnson made a face. He tucked his chin down, frowned, and shook his head reprovingly, as though dealing with a youngster. "Buzz," he said, pretending to be surprised, "you've been around too long to have to ask a question like that."

Of course I was not asking from ignorance or innocence. At any level of politics, one always knows the adversaries; at the level of the vice presidency, involved as that office is with the intrigues of the reigning court, sensitivity rises far higher. But my question was purposeful. For three years, since the election in November 1960, Lyndon Johnson had sealed his lips; even in the most private and confidential conversation, he would not permit himself to acknowledge that he had critics, detractors, or adversaries anywhere within the new administration. The principle might be commendable. "Nothing and nobody," he explained, "is ever going to divide the president and me, and I'm not going to say anything to anybody, not even my wife, that might get back to the president and cause him a moment's concern." The discipline was exacting and inflexible, but it irritated some of us close to the vice president: he carried it, we thought, to the point of unreality. I wanted to draw him out.

"You mean—" I began, but he did not permit me to finish my question.

"I don't mean anybody," he snapped. "You can guess the answer, dammit, but I'm not about to start naming names."

I tried from another direction. "President Kennedy's still for you."

On October 31, only three days before our departure for the Benelux, Washington's rumors and Senator Morton's public charge about a "purge" had prompted a press conference question to President Kennedy about the vice president's position in 1964. The president spoke firmly: Lyndon Johnson would be his running mate on the Democratic Party's national ticket in 1964. At my reference to the president, the vice president's eyes warmed and he smiled, but he answered with a question of his own. "Buzz," he asked, "how many friends do I have across the street?"

The reference, I knew, was to the White House in Washington, "across the street" from the vice presidential suite in the Executive Office Building. I gave him the answer which I knew he wanted. "One," I said.

"You're damn right," he fired back. "And who is that one?"

"The president," I replied.

"You're right again," he announced. "I've got one friend in that place—President John Fitzgerald Kennedy himself." Then he added quickly: "And, of course, little Mrs. Kennedy." After a moment's pause, he fell back on the pillows and looked at the ceiling. "In my job," he said softly, "that's all the friends a fellow has to have."

For a brief moment, he played with thoughts of what he could do under the circumstances. "I just might beat them to the punch," he said. "Before the president comes down home I could announce my candidacy for the Senate next year and campaign the state with him on that basis while he's there." But that avenue was not open to him, and he let it pass.

The vice president had told his story, and now he closed the book. He raised up from the bed, stepped to the windows, and stood nervously jingling the change in his pockets. The storm had quieted, and the Brussels streets were lighted and busy. After a few moments, he said, "This looks like an interesting city. I wish I could get to see it."

The wish fathered a thought. Grinning slyly, he came alive and hurried out to the entrance foyer. I followed and watched while he went through his familiar routine. Slowly and soundlessly, he opened the door and peeked into the corridor, checking once more on the presence of the Secret Service agents.

This time he turned back to me beaming. "There are only two of 'em," he whispered happily.

We retreated to the bedroom, and he outlined his plans. "You go out there and negotiate with 'em," he directed. "If we'll agree to stay out of dark alleys and not speak to strange women, see if they'll agree to let us go out for just a little walk, right around the hotel, without them following us."

I sought out Stuart Knight, the head of the detail, and his deputy, Rufus Youngblood, who was to assume command two weeks from today in Texas. Stu and Rufus were understanding. They agreed that the vice president could go for his early evening walk with only one agent visible to him; they made no promises about how many other agents might be nearby.

The vice president was enthusiastic. Quickly he straightened his tie, donned his coat and hat, and hurried to the elevator. At the lobby, while he remained out of sight, I was sent on a tour to see if "the loudmouth" might be present. The area was empty, though, and on my signal the vice president tiptoed gingerly across the carpet and out a side door. With Agent Jerry Kivett following, his walkie-talkie radio muffled underneath his coat, we disappeared into the darkness.

Wherever he went, Lyndon Johnson was insatiably curious about how people lived, where they bought "groceries," where they sent their children to school, and other such details. We made for the nearest residential block, and he passed the old row houses, peering unabashedly inside at the Belgian families gathered for dinner. "You know," he observed, "optometrists must make a mint in Europe, the lights over here are so damn dim."

At the edge of the business district near the hotel, skyscrapers were under construction, providing office space for the city's growing role as the capital of Europe's new unity. I pointed to the upper floors of one structure where workmen were still laboring by electric illumination. "Pride, that's what it is," the vice president commented. "These people in these countries have pride in getting a job done. If we don't get off our tails, they're going off and leaving us."

For perhaps half an hour, the walk continued aimlessly, with the vice president stopping to satisfy his curiosity at markers and memorials and cornerstones, speaking frequently about the age of Europe as contrasted with the youth of the United States. But the liveliness waned. He fell silent and began walking with long, determined strides that I found difficult to match. We circled past the Westbury again, but he chose not to enter: instead, we strode purposefully on to the corner and turned down a slope toward the central business district.

As we passed the darkness of an ancient cathedral, he stopped abruptly, pushed his hat far back on his head, and turned toward me. "Buzz," he said, "I've had a good run of it. I've done a lot more and come a lot farther than anybody who came from where I come from ever had any right to expect." Agent Kivett had approached closely, checking whether some assistance might be needed. The vice president turned and glowered until he moved on out of earshot, then Lyndon Johnson leaned in very close, until his face almost touched mine, and his clenched fists began pumping up and down.

"If they want me to go, all they have to do is say so and I'll be gone in five minutes." His voice fell to a hoarse and confidential whisper. "I don't care about that, it's their business. What I do care about, my friend, is one thing." He stopped and stood erect, turning to look in all directions. The street and sidewalk were empty except for the two of us and Jerry Kivett, now half a block away. The vice president leaned in close again. Lips set tight, he spoke firmly. "I care about the exit line."

That was all. The thoughts building up inside him were released, and he meant to say no more. Quickly, he pulled his hat down on his forehead and proceeded down the slope. The storm was resuming, and rain began to fall. With no question as to how it happened to be waiting so conveniently, the vice president stopped at the black limousine which had preceded us to the next intersection, opened the door, and told the Secret Service agents to take us back to the Westbury. No further mention was made of the afternoon.

On Saturday, the vice president left the hotel late in the day for the Brussels airport. Ambassador MacArthur and his wife accompanied the Johnsons. Mrs. MacArthur sat on the rear seat, between Mrs. Johnson and the vice president, while the ambassador and I straddled the limousine's jump seat. Mrs. MacArthur was a daughter of the former vice president Alben Barkley. Majority leader of Senate Democrats under both FDR and Harry Truman, the jovial old Kentuckian had been selected in 1948 by President Truman to be his running mate; he served loyally and ably throughout the term. At the Chicago Democratic convention in 1952, Truman sought to reward that loyalty by selecting Barkley as his successor, but the powers of the party wanted someone else. At a session that angered many Democratic senators, the party leaders met with the aging vice president and curtly told him he could not have the nomination: a younger man and newer face was needed. Alben Barkley, it was said, wept.

On the long drive to the airport, Lyndon Johnson began recalling to Mrs. MacArthur these events involving her father in 1952. "The rewards of loyalty in a job like this," he said rather tersely, "are a fist in the face." Neither Mrs. MacArthur nor the ambassador understood the sudden force of the statement or its import. When neither commented, the vice president called out to me: "Isn't that right, Buzz?" Without looking back, I nodded my head affirmatively.

The westward crossing over the Atlantic went quickly. The vice president slept in his cabin most of the way. When we reached Washington late Saturday night, I found that I could not sleep; for one of the few times in my association with him, I spent most of the night writing a diary of Lyndon Johnson's unusual week.

On Sunday afternoon, Mrs. Johnson telephoned, inviting my wife, Mary V., and me to dinner at The Elms, the Johnson residence in Washington's Spring Valley section. The only other guests were the Texas congressman Jack Brooks and his beautiful wife, Charlotte. Our evening was wholly relaxed. Lyndon Johnson took his favorite chair in a small sitting room off the handsome entrance hall of the large, comfortable home; he talked happily of his conferences in the Benelux and once more proudly exhibited the paintings he had acquired. At eleven o'clock, the Brookses departed, but the vice president followed Mary V. and me to our automobile on the circular drive.

The Washington sky was overcast and a mist had begun to fall, but Lyndon Johnson's thoughts were running ahead to Texas. He began to talk of the ranch, fondly and wistfully: the stars would be out there tonight, he reminded us, and tomorrow when he landed on the airstrip the sun would be shining bright. It would be good, he told us, to be home again, much better than being in Washington. I had the feeling he was wondering what might have happened to him by the time he returned again from the ranch to The Elms. Finally, he said good night and went back to the entrance.

On the steps, though, he turned and shouted one last word. "Buzz, I may stay on for a few days after the president leaves," he said, "and see if I can find that newspaper for us."

As we drove away, Mary V. asked, "What was that all about?"

"Nothing," I assured her. "The vice president is just thinking about changing jobs."

FOREBODINGS

Forebodings filled the middle weeks of November 1963. In Texas, the rancorous feud between partisans of Senator Ralph Yarborough and Governor John B. Connally burned hotter and hotter as the time for President Kennedy's visit neared. Arguments flamed over trivialities: who would stand where in receiving lines; who should sit next to whom at banquet tables; who would ride in which automobile in the parades at Houston, San Antonio, and Dallas. Neither side would consider concessions, even for the sake of appearances.

Since 1952, Ralph Yarborough—corporation lawyer, old-family Texan, American Legionnaire, orthodox Democrat—had been the maligned establishmentarian; ostracized, ridiculed, and exiled by his own kind, and none too warmly welcomed by the leaders of the labor forces with whom he sought sanctuary. In retreat, he thrived on suspicion of the power structure which rejected him. John Connally epitomized that power structure; in fact, on two occasions before he entered public life, Connally had taken time off from his legal work to help mastermind campaigns against Yarborough. But Connally, too, was an unforgiving, unyielding man. His conflicts had come in old clashes with organized labor: a farm boy populist beneath his sophisticated exterior, the hot-tempered Irishman throbbed with rural suspicions of labor's leadership and their purposes. His years with Lyndon Johnson had affected the governor, too: he harbored a passionate revulsion against compromise with political enemies.

Both men and their partisans were beyond the influence of reason, persuasion, or the Vice President of the United States.

Lyndon Johnson did not really understand the origins or depths of the conflict in his home state. During the 1950s, when the vendetta was developing, he had been occupied on the national stage as majority leader of the United States Senate, far above the battle. Now the governor and the senator held power, and the vice president held none, but it was the vice president's political life that was at stake.

The feud took its most ominous twist in regard to the main purpose of the Kennedy trip. Both sides were holding back on purchase of tickets to the fund-raising dinner in Austin on the final night of President Kennedy's tour. Unless that banquet was a financial success, Republicans nationally would be emboldened, President Kennedy would be embarrassed and hurt, and the vice president would be seriously humiliated and, quite possibly, politically ruined. At the ranch, he labored day and night, trying to sell hundred-dollar-a-plate tickets, and even took to calling Washington for help on this difficult chore.

"You must know some fat cat somewhere in Texas who will help us out," he told me plaintively. But I did not know any Texas "fat cats." Eight telephone calls to friends in Dallas and Fort Worth yielded the sale of exactly one ticket to the Austin dinner.

In Washington, where I had remained, rumors ran amuck. Each day newsmen were calling George Reedy or Walter Jenkins or myself to check out stories—always on "good authority"—that President Kennedy's purpose in planning to spend the night at the LBJ Ranch was to break the news that Lyndon Johnson would not be on the ticket in 1964. When we traced these stories back to their sources, the origins lay not at the White House or among Kennedy intimates but among Texans in Washington friendly to Senator Yarborough. Repetition, nonetheless, had its effect, intensifying tensions, magnifying worries, expanding our imagination of what might go wrong on the Texas journey.

One night during this period, I came home to find my wife reading through an accumulated stack of recent editions of *The Dallas Morning News*. Apart from its parochial politics and its indefensibly serious publicizing of the right-wing propagandists clustering near Dallas money, the fine Dallas newspaper afforded the best coverage of state affairs, and we subscribed to it as our link with home. Mary V. handed me the front page of a recent issue. "Read this," she said. "Someone has lost their mind." It was a story announcing that, on his visit to Dallas, President Kennedy would ride in an open-car motorcade from Love Field to the site of his luncheon address.

"I can't imagine your friends in the Secret Service letting the president do that," she said. I agreed with her. The thought of physical danger to the president did not occur. Our memories were still fresh, though, of 1960, when the vice president and Mrs. Johnson were mobbed in a Dallas hotel lobby. An ugliness had crept into Dallas politics which perplexed many Texans. Only a few weeks earlier there had been a nasty attack on Ambassador Adlai Stevenson when he spoke there. An open-car motorcade was an obvious invitation for more episodes—ugly signs, jeering chants, or perhaps an egg tossed at the presidential limousine.

The next day I voiced my concern to Walter Jenkins and learned that he shared it. In fact, he told me, Governor Connally, Cliff Carter, and all the Johnson men participating in plans for the Kennedy visit were counseling against the Dallas motorcade. But our interests and the interests of the Kennedy people were hopelessly at odds. We were thinking, selfishly perhaps, of avoiding street incidents which would acutely embarrass Vice President Johnson. The Kennedy advance men in charge of the visit were considering a far larger picture. It would be of considerable political value nationally to turn out a friendly parade route crowd for the president in the city which had been most hostile to him at the polls in 1960. The politics of John F. Kennedy overruled the politics of Lyndon B. Johnson in the decision to send the young president through the streets of downtown Dallas.

On Friday, all those concerns would come together—the president's ride through Dallas, the ticket sales for the fund-raising dinner at Austin, the climax at the LBJ Ranch after the politicking was done. November 22 was a day we all faced with dread.

On Thursday, November 21, I lunched with Leonard Marks at a club frequented by Washington's television and radio reporters. Since my conversation with the vice president in Brussels, I had come to the gloomy but inescapable conclusion that Lyndon John-son's days in that office were numbered; if the end did not come the following day in Texas, ugly times were clearly ahead for us all in Washington. I did not want to be around; the toll of peripheral involvement in palace politics was too great. With Marks, I explored prospects for moving on to work elsewhere, perhaps abroad. My conversation was neither angry nor bitter. I had simply had my fill of national politics, of the struggles for power, of the machinations on the national stage. It was time to begin something else.

I started Friday, the twenty-second of November 1963, doing a silly thing. Dressing for the morning drive to my office on Connecticut Avenue, I decided not to wear my usual business suit; instead, I rummaged through the closet to find the loudest plaid sports jacket, a gift from my wife on our second wedding anniversary. Once I had worn it to Lyndon Johnson's office in the Senate; he thought it looked like the jacket of a "racetrack character," and I had never worn it on a working day since. But on this day, the jacket matched my mood: the drama unfolding in Texas almost surely could not end well, and by nightfall much that I had counted on could be in shambles. Gaiety prevailed. I might as well be jaunty while there was time.

Friday was publication day for the *American Businessman*, my newsletter to corporate clients. Through this morning, however, my efforts to put the newsletter together went slowly. President Kennedy, Vice President Johnson, and all the accompanying reti-nue had spent the night in my hometown, Fort Worth, and I kept close watch on the UPI news ticker in our offices for an account of the visit there. Fort Worth, I thought, would give the president a warm welcome; in fact, in writing introductory remarks for the vice president to use at the Hotel Texas breakfast, I had pandered to the old Fort Worth disdain for its neighbor, "Big D." "When the president asked me what was the difference between Fort Worth and Dallas," one of the lines for the vice president read, "I told him, Fort Worth is the friendly city." That would draw laughter and applause from a Fort Worth audience.

By noontime I found myself far behind schedule and canceled plans for lunch. Others in the office went out to eat, shop, and soak up the warm Indian summer sun in Farragut Square across the street; with my secretary, Patty Scott, I remained at the office, buckling down to meet the early evening deadline for my copy. Patty had recently come to Washington from Dallas; she shared my concern over President Kennedy's reception in the city. As the time neared for the presidential party to arrive at Love Field, she began an almost continuous vigil over the Teletype machine. We kidded each other about our Texas paranoia, but Patty remained anxious. "You never know what those kooks are going to do," she said.

Then it came: the longest, the most unreal, the most terrible minute I had ever known.

Thirty feet away, in the empty reception room, the bells of the Teletype machine began sounding, four short, rapid rings, repeating over and over. This is the least often heard signal on Teletypes, but anyone who has worked for a wire service knows what it means: a "flash," a terse, one-line report of a major news development. Only matters of earthshaking moment received the priority of a flash.

I looked up from my typewriter. Patty Scott already had reached the Teletype machine and was watching the message come in, typed out slowly by hand. Her face suddenly began to form a horrible white mask. "Oh, God," she said, turning toward me. "Kennedy has been shot." And then she added, her voice breaking, "In Dallas."

It could not have taken more than two or three seconds for me to reach her side and begin reading myself the incredible message. But in that dash across the office I had thoughts enough to crowd an hour. First, I did not believe the news; I was absolutely, positively, unquestionably certain that there must be some mistake—"shot at," the message should read, not "shot." The President of the United States could not be shot, not with the Secret Service, not with the security, the protection, the caution, I knew accompanied every presidential step. The reporter was confused, the machine wrong, the "bulletin" to follow would surely correct this error. But shot where? When? By whom?

My heart went to my throat. Whatever else, a president could not be shot—or shot at—in the streets; too many times, in too many places in the world, I had talked with Secret Service men about the theories and techniques of what they called "protection." Their whole concept of motorcades was meant to protect presidents or vice presidents against gunmen: all eyes forward, all watching for the assassin who would have to step out of the curbside crowd, stop in view of the motorcycle officers and the agents, take his position, aim at the oncoming limousine. The Secret Service had their marksmanship, their alertness, as clear advantages, and, too, they insisted upon speed. That was why no vehicles other than motorcycles were ever permitted in front of a presidential or vice presidential limousine—a sudden acceleration, a full-throttle get-away, would jolt the target and confound any pistol marksman. Always the danger on the streets would be in front, where it could be seen and responded to.

No, whatever had happened could not have happened on the streets of Dallas, and that was what struck the horror. If there had been a shooting, it must have occurred at the Exposition Hall, where President Kennedy, I knew, had been scheduled to speak. Always, in such buildings, dangers were greater. Assassins might lurk in the narrow passageways leading toward the dais or—and this seemed far more likely—an assassin might have been mingling in the crowd, with a reception committee, some group that would conceal him and permit a close, frontal approach. If this had happened at the Exposition Hall, then it meant the unthinkable: only the better people of Dallas would be present for the speech; a nondescript, unknown assassin type would be too obvious in such a group. Even I had learned to run my eyes over crowds, looking for faces and clothes and manners that did not fit with the others present.

If it had happened where I now thought it must have happened, then it meant that someone of prominence in the Dallas community had come unhinged, taken it upon himself to commit a dastardly deed. And this led logically to a thought which would not leave me for several hours: we were on the edge of a horrendous internal trauma in the United States, because if the deed had been done by someone of the profile I now imagined, that person almost certainly would be found to have some sort of connection, however remote and tenuous, with the former senator from Texas, the Vice President of the United States.

The bulletin, datelined Dallas, began coming in. The details partly contradicted my imaginings. Three shots had been fired at the presidential limousine as it went under the triple underpass, which

I knew very well. An assassin had made use of the parade route, which I had seen published in *The Dallas Morning News*. But, for one paragraph at least, nothing in the account indicated that the UPI reporter—it must have been Merriman Smith—actually knew that the president had been shot. This raised a hope—a hope I seized and held to: that, indeed, the president had only been "shot at."

At my side, Patty began trembling and crying convulsively. I had no words of comfort. But now I realized my hope was a delusion. The story obviously was being filed from Parkland Hospital. The motorcade would not have proceeded there unless someone had been injured.

I did not wait for more. Impulsively, I turned to the telephone and called George Reedy at his office on the West Front of the Capitol. From his calmness, I knew instantly that he was unaware of the news, and I did not bother to ask. "Quick," I said. "Read your ticker—Kennedy's shot." Reedy slammed down the phone without saying anything in response. Then I called Walter Jenkins. "I know," he said, without waiting for me to speak. "I'll call you back in a minute."

The Teletype ran full tilt, but the story came out slowly, paragraph by paragraph. John Connally had been struck by the gunfire also. A police officer on a motorcycle had sped up the slope, the beautiful slope, at the triple underpass. People were seen crouching on the green, sheltering their children. But the assassin was not known, not identified in the stories.

I continued reacting by instinct. Mary V., I realized, must be at The Elms, the Johnson family residence. In October, before the trip to the Benelux countries, the Johnsons had stopped by our house on a Sunday afternoon. Mrs. Johnson had admired a montage Mary V. had made for my library using passes, dinner invitations, and other memorabilia from our around-the-world trip in 1961 to decorate a map of that journey. Mrs. Johnson, and the vice president as well, expressed the wish that my wife would do the same for them, and since they were away from The Elms on this day, Mary V. had planned to go there early in the morning to go through their trip files and prepare a similar wall map for them; it would be our Christmas present to them. When I called, the telephone rang for a long time before she answered. "Turn on your television," I said, and gave her a quick account of what had happened. She did not believe it until the television warmed up and she saw Walter Cronkite delivering the bulletins from New York.

"Don't hang up," I told her. "If it hasn't started already, everybody will be trying to call The Elms, and we'll never get through to you again." As I spoke, the other lines on the Johnson telephone instruments began flashing.

By now other members of my staff were hurrying in from their lunch hour and gathering around the Teletype. I knew there was more to do. Under any circumstances, Dallas would be a point of crisis for the vice president that afternoon, and perhaps for days if the president was hospitalized. The vice president had made the trip to Texas with none of his Washington staff; inevitably a call would be coming—"Get on down here immediately." I could not arrive in Dallas, under the circumstances so readily imaginable there, attired in the outfit I had donned that morning. Rosemary MacBride, receptionist in the office, came through the doorway; immediately I turned her around, handed her a five-dollar bill, and gave her instructions to take a taxi to my residence, pack a bag for me, and bring a more appropriate suit for me to wear to Dallas.

The reports from Dallas continued. It had become apparent that President Kennedy's wounds were grave—and so were John Connally's. On the open line I read the Teletype bulletins to Mary V. She, by now, had no more conversation in her; like a woman obsessed, she began repeating, "He won't die, he won't die, I know he won't die, he can't die." Reedy called back, then Jenkins, then I called each of them again. The three of us were to pass the next hours reaching for one another, all of us sharing the same sense of horror and terror, for we each had one thought. I put it to Reedy bluntly: "If the president dies," I said, barely able to get out the words, "can the vice president govern?"

This exposed the raw edge of the afternoon. Whatever had happened, had happened in Texas, the home state of the vice president. Any responsible person, aware of the intensity of national feelings about Texas, could not avoid a sense of dread at the realization that first the world, then the nation, could—indeed, inevitably would—become consumed with the notion this was somehow, in some remote, unreasoned way, a conspiracy. It was unthinkable, unimaginable, yet horribly real. I could feel a terrible wind beginning to rise and blow about us.

Jenkins now called for the third time. He had been summoned to the White House by Ralph Dungan, one of President Kennedy's special assistants. The news from Dallas was becoming more grim by the minute. My wife, on the other telephone, kept up her litany, "He won't die, he won't die." But now Jenkins was saying, "God, dear God, I wish I weren't here right now." But then he delivered the message which had prompted the call: a plane would be leaving shortly for Dallas, carrying members of the White House staff, and I was to be aboard. The prospect of flying to Dallas with President Kennedy's closest assistants touched off a new sense of dread for me—and I must have prayed that Rosemary MacBride was hurrying on her mission.

But then the news came: Malcolm Kilduff, assistant press secretary at the White House, had just announced that President Kennedy was dead. That meant one thing: Lyndon Baines Johnson would now become President of the United States.

I had no coherent thought for minutes. I wanted to reach the man, to be there, to help him some way, somehow, but there was no way, no way to reach him, no way to reach out and touch anything real.

Jenkins called back, trying hard to control his voice. There would be no flight to Dallas. "Mr. Johnson," he said, still using his usual form of reference, would be flying back to Washington immediately. I repeated to Jenkins the question I had asked moments before of Reedy: "Could he govern?" Jenkins remained silent for a long moment. "I'm afraid the country may start coming apart."

The next hours of the afternoon were agony. *Air Force One* was speeding its way back toward Washington, bearing the thirty-sixth President of the United States and the body of the thirty-fifth President of the United States. I remember hoping that the military had ordered air cover for the flight. But the far greater concern was the question of the assassin.

The UPI account now established that the shots had been fired from the red-brick Texas School Book Depository, a building I had often seen, perched on the edge of the incline going down under the triple underpass. If the gunman had fired from an upper story of the building, it seemed impossible that he could have escaped, yet the news accounts left the implication that he had done so. This raised a new specter: that the assassin had by now fled the city and would never be caught. That would set off a wave of suspicion, hysteria, and retribution beyond imagining. I could not think, I could scarcely react. I stood by the Teletype machine as though somehow my presence would influence its messages and all that it had reported in the last two hours would prove to be unreal. Then the bulletin came in. Dallas police announced that they had arrested one Lee Harvey Oswald, and the identifying phrase named him as "a member of the Fair Play for Cuba Committee." In all my thoughts, it had not occurred that this might have been the doing of someone from the left instead of the right, someone reacting to Cuban policy instead of liberal policy. Almost immediately, another shock came. It was mentioned that Oswald had lived in the Soviet Union. This detail injected an ominous new cause for worry.

The events of the afternoon had been too overwhelming, too vicious, too incomprehensible. For the first time, I walked away from the omnipotent Teletype machine and stood in my office, looking out across the crowds on Connecticut Avenue. Even if one had known nothing about the news, the view of the citizens along the avenue would have been evidence that something dreadful had occurred. Someone reminded me that the newsletter was not complete. I hated it, I hated the task that I knew would not wait. More for release than for any other reason, I sat at the typewriter and within the hour wrote as rapidly as I could—more than two thousand words trying to summarize the presidency of John F. Kennedy and the prospects for the presidency of Lyndon B. Johnson.

At intervals I stopped to talk again with my wife, who was still holding open the telephone line into The Elms. As I had anticipated, the other lines were now ringing without interruption, but she remained alone in the house. Gradually, however, she saw as no one else did that day the cold passing of power. First came the Secret Service and the police, quietly and dispassionately taking up stations around the house, around the surrounding fence, and in the street. Then came the telephone men, hurrying to install the communications required for a president, not required for a vice president. Then came the Johnsons' tearful younger daughter, Luci, swept out of her class at the National Cathedral School and hurried to the shelter of the home. Assured that her father and mother were alright, Luci reached impulsively for her sister, Lynda, at the University of Texas in Austin. Lynda, it developed, had reacted by hurrying to the Governor's Mansion to comfort the Connally children while word was awaited from Dallas about their gravely wounded father. Mary V. decided she would wait at the house until Mrs. Johnson arrived; then she intended to return to our home.

Soon after six o'clock, a black night descended on Washington. Connecticut Avenue, outside my window, was hushed. Most of the offices in the area had closed. The usual afternoon traffic jam did not develop. Shocked, stunned, helpless, Washington had gone to its hearth sides to share a national tragedy. The radio in the office reported the arrival of *Air Force One* at Andrews Air Force Base. I listened as Lyndon Johnson spoke his first public words as president, raising his voice to make himself heard above the whining engines.

An hour passed as I waited, for I knew not what. Then the telephone rang. It was the new president himself.

Since I had first met him at his office in Washington, I had been with Lyndon Johnson on each day that his public title had changed, from Congressman to Senator, from Senator to Vice President. Now, he was the President of the United States. But I could not bring myself to use the proper salutation. When I spoke, I did not say "Mr. President," I said only "Sir."

He made no reference to Dallas or the day. "I'm going to be leaving here soon," he said. "I'll come by and pick you up. We will call when I leave, and we will come by and pick you up—you wait at the curb." This did not seem right to me, nor did it seem advisable. At that raw nerve moment, every move this man made would be chronicled, reported, spread around the world. I did not know what he should do, but I knew he should not stop on Connecticut Avenue and pick me up. Carefully, I suggested to him that this would attract too much attention and that I should perhaps go on to The Elms in my own automobile. "What's the matter?" he asked very slowly. "Are you running from the press?"

I did not answer. He then suggested that I call Mary V. and ask her to stay at The Elms. When I arrived, a large crowd already had formed around the gate, but they were being held far back by the police. Nearer the gate was a cluster of men and women, most of whom I recognized as members of the press. I halted and rolled down the window for the identifying procedure with the Secret Service. At that instant, brilliant lights burst upon me from the blackness. I could hear the voice of a woman reporter calling out to one of the Johnson Secret Service agents, "Who's this one? What's his name? What does he do?" For no reason that I ever understood, I wanted at that moment to turn back.

— 13 —

THE PRESIDENT

Poison in the Power

I had known Lyndon Baines Johnson for almost sixteen years: as congressman, senator, majority leader, and vice president. Over that span, I had liked him and disliked him; respected him and disrespected him; at times thought his public performances magnificent and at other times thought his private preoccupations monumentally boring. I had traveled with him, campaigned with him, laughed with him, worried with him, shared with him moments both of the greatest consequence and of complete unimportance. I knew him better than I wanted to know any man. But on the night of November 22, 1963, waiting for him to arrive at The Elms, I was not waiting for any man I had ever known; I was waiting for the President of the United States.

The aura of the office preceded him. The handsome rooms of The Elms were hushed. Family friends who had waited for Mrs. Johnson's arrival gathered their coats and hats, and hurried away, to be gone before he came. The entryway and front hall remained conspicuously empty; when people crossed through it, they hurried their steps, not wanting to be in sight when he opened the door; yet whenever the door opened to admit a Secret Service agent or a telephone installer, faces appeared, peaking around doorframes to see if the sound meant that he had come. Mary V. and I sat in the sunroom, adjacent to the front hall; here we had last sat with him on the Sunday night, twelve days earlier, before he left for Texas. Dr. Willis Hurst of Atlanta, the brilliant young heart specialist who had saved his life after his heart attack in 1955, sat with us.

Nothing seemed appropriate to say. In the silence, a sort of dread grew of the meeting that was to come.

But then it came, and the meeting was easy. Mrs. Johnson, dressed in her robe, hurried down the curving stairway to greet him as he entered; they embraced and talked quietly for a moment. At the five doorways opening into the hall, I counted sixteen faces, including my own, watching. The Johnsons were not people anymore.

He glanced around impatiently, seeing the faces I had counted; I knew what he must be thinking. Quickly, with long strides, he stepped across the hall to the sunroom, seeking his solitude. Mary V. gave him a kiss. Dr. Hurst ran a practiced eye over his features and seemed to be visibly relieved. Lyndon Johnson was more controlled than calm. His words of greeting were barely audible. But after he bent to sit in his usual chair, he stood erect again, looking at the wall above the single television set. Hanging there was a portrait of Speaker Sam Rayburn, who had died just two years before. The old man's pupil raised his hand in a friendly salute. "How I wish you were here," he said, then settled into the chair. Outside the French doors, in the darkness, two Secret Service agents took up their positions.

"Turn on the television," he said to me. "I guess I am the only person in the United States who doesn't know what has happened today." I dialed the different channels, searching for a news broadcast. Commentators and guests were discussing the significance of the afternoon, but there was no news. He motioned me to his side. "Go find Chief Rowley of the Secret Service," he said. "I want to be sure Rufus Youngblood gets the highest award that he can receive for what he did today." Youngblood, one of the first agents we met on a trip to Africa in 1961, had been riding in the front seat of the vice presidential convertible at Dallas; with the sound of the first shot from the assassin's gun, Youngblood had vaulted into the rear of the automobile, pushed the man he was to protect onto the floorboard, and covered the vice president's body with his own. Chief James Rowley was not far away; I found him sitting in the next room, and with him sat Rufus Youngblood. I delivered the message, and when I had finished, I shook Youngblood's hand.

Back in the sunroom, the television program had changed. A network now was showing a long documentary on the Kennedy presidency. The first scenes were of the Los Angeles convention, speeches during the 1960 campaign, and the inaugural address; then the film clips began to portray John F. Kennedy as father, walking with his daughter, Caroline. Involuntarily, Lyndon Johnson's hand went up between his eyes and the television screen. "No, no," he said. "Turn it off, turn it off. It's all too fresh."

My wife leaned forward and patted him on the arm. Her eyes brimmed with tears.

"I wanted to find out about John Connally," he said. There still had been no news on the television screen. The White House operators soon reached Nellie Connally at Parkland Hospital in Dallas. I talked with her briefly, then handed the phone to Lyndon Johnson. He listened to her full report on her husband's condition: it was critical, more so than the available news reports had indicated. He shook his head as Nellie spoke, seeming not to want to believe what he heard. When she concluded, he said heavily, "Take care of Johnny. I need him now."

A report came in from Dallas: an indictment was being drawn there against Lee Harvey Oswald, stating that the accused assassin had acted as part of a Communist conspiracy. Much of the language was inflammatory. Lyndon Johnson came quickly to attention, sitting forward in his chair. "No," he said, "we must not have that. We must not start making accusations without evidence. It could tear this country apart." He asked me then to call Waggoner Carr, the attorney general of Texas. "Tell him the country needs the most responsible, the most thorough investigation, and I seem to remember that there is some law in Texas permitting the attorney general to take over in a situation like this." Carr, when I reached him, confirmed that he did have powers to establish a "court of inquiry," and he agreed to proceed immediately. It was a sobering reminder that under the many layers of government in our country, the murder of a president still was not a federal offense; jurisdiction rested with local and state authorities.

That night will never be described easily or adequately. We sat in the sunroom—Mary V., myself, Dr. Hurst, the president, and, intermittently, Lady Bird. His composure and coolheadedness were precisely what I anticipated. His mellowness and gentleness were not. I had said, over and over, Lyndon Johnson was qualified for only one job—the presidency. Short of that, he was always a man making important the unimportant to occupy his vast energies and abilities. That night, he was in every subtle sense The President.

What do you say in such a situation? Very little. Nothing of the day or of the morrow. I can only describe it as a night—and a room—almost unbearably alive with quiet and stillness.

An hour and a half passed before the new president finally had seen a news broadcast of the events of the day. He watched intently as films were shown of the triple underpass in Dallas, Parkland Hospital, and the Texas School Book Depository, from where the shots were fired. Then he turned off the picture and said good night. Very little had been said in the room since he entered, but as I followed Mary V. across the hall, he asked if I would stay behind. Of course, I did.

For more than an hour, around midnight, I sat in the bedroom listening when he wanted to speak. The silences were long. His thoughts were of what he had now to do. Mostly, he emphasized the legislation which had been stalled in the Congress. He thought there was a chance that it could be gotten through early in the coming year. But as he went down a mental list of the pending measures, he paused to observe: "You know, almost all the issues now are just about the same as they were when I came here in Congress nearly thirty years ago."

I mentioned the thoughts that I had carried with me throughout the afternoon and evening: how much had changed since our conversation only two weeks earlier in Brussels. "Yes," he said, with an air of sadness, "I guess we won't be going home for a while." At this, Mrs. Johnson, reading in bed beside him, began counting on her fingers. "Well, at least," she said, "it's only for nine months." She had counted the time until the next convention, when, she was thinking, someone else would be nominated; realizing the term would not end then, however, she counted off the additional months until January 1965. "No," she corrected herself, "I guess it will be for fourteen months."

"Mrs. Johnson," I said, "it won't be nine months—it is more likely to be nine years."

Her eyes fixed on me incredulously from across the room. With unexpected force she said sternly: "No."

Lyndon Johnson patted her arm reassuringly. "I'm afraid Buzz is right," he said. "At least, it may be for five years."

Thirteen months before, I had sat at The Elms in eerie similarity—during the Cuban crisis. The news that night in 1962 was bad—and it grew worse. Just before dawn, I left to drive the few blocks to our house through lifeless streets—thinking, as no mind could ever forget—that by late that afternoon, these houses and the people sleeping in them would almost surely be destroyed and dead. It was an awesome and agonizing memory, made all the more unforgettable by arriving at home, seeing the children asleep, finding Mary V. awake, and searching my eyes for what I could not tell her. This time, on November 22, Mary V. and I were together as we drove those same blocks through the late still night. How different the feeling—certainly, no less awesome—to sense the responsibility toward all those people asleep so hopefully in those same homes we passed.

There was one considerable difference. In October 1962, I went home and slept—there seemed nothing else to do. This time, I believe it may have been Wednesday before I went to bed again.

Saturday and Sunday were blurs. Chiefly, I remember being with President Eisenhower—and then with President Truman—talking with them while President Johnson made telephone calls and received intelligence briefings. Late that night, as he was to do again each night until Thanksgiving, the president called for me to come at bedtime and asked explicitly that I remain at the bedside until he was asleep. This, I might explain, I had done before, especially abroad—we called it "hand holding," or, sometimes, "gentling down," as with a thoroughbred racehorse. The president, I might add, was never a heavy sleeper, but pity poor Lady Bird—hands over eyes and arms over ears. In the darkness of the bedroom, I am sure the scene would have brought smiles—if not laughter—as I, after suitably long silences, would rise and tiptoe toward the door, only to be snapped back just as I was slipping through the exit. "Buzz, are you still there?"

On Monday, November 25, they buried John Fitzgerald Kennedy beneath the green of Arlington, on the slope across the Potomac. The sun shone brightly, and the drums beat slowly, as tens of millions the world round watched the thirty-fifth President of the United States be laid to rest. On Wednesday, November 27, at noon, the thirty-sixth President of the United States stood in the chamber of the House of Representatives before a joint session of Congress. "All I have," he began, "I would have given gladly not to be standing here today." Then he went on: "On the twentieth day of January of 1961, John F. Kennedy told his countrymen that our national work would not be finished 'in the first thousand days nor in the life of this Administration, nor even perhaps in our lifetime on this planet. But,' he said, 'let us begin.' Today, in this moment of new resolve, I would say to all my fellow Americans, let us continue." The applause was strong and ran long. On Thursday, November 28, a stunned and sorrowing nation paused to observe Thanksgiving Day. At twilight, in the Oval Office of the West Wing of the White House, the new president sat at his desk and spoke to his fellow countrymen.

"All of us have lived through seven days that none of us will ever forget," he said. "A great leader is dead; a great nation must move on. Yesterday is not ours to recover, but tomorrow is ours to win or to lose. I am resolved that we shall win the tomorrows before us." He had first arrived in Washington thirty-two years ago on the previous day, he recalled, and in that span he had seen "five presidents fill this awesome office. . . . I have known them well and I have counted them all as friends—President Herbert Hoover, President Franklin Roosevelt, President Harry Truman, President Dwight Eisenhower, and President John Kennedy."

"In each administration," he said, "the greatest burden that the president had to bear had been the burden of his own countrymen's unthinking and unreasoning hate and division. In these days, the fate of this office is the fate of us all. I would ask all Americans on this day of prayer and reverence to think on these things. Let all who speak and all who teach and all who preach and all who publish and all who broadcast and all who read or listen—let them reflect upon their responsibilities to bind our wounds, to heal our sores, to make our society well and whole for the tasks ahead of us. It is this work that I most want us to do: to banish rancor from our words and malice from our hearts; to close down the poison spring of hatred and intolerance and fanaticism; to perfect our unity North and South, East and West; to hasten the day when bias of race, religion, and region is no more; and to bring the day when our great energies and decencies and spirit will be free of the burdens that we have borne too long."

The power had passed. A nation so close to the abyss one week before now stood again on solid ground. The system had functioned as it was designed and intended to function. On Thanksgiving Day, 1963, America had more than it knew to be thankful for.

The power had passed, but there was poison in the power. The taste of it was to run through all the days of Lyndon Johnson's presidency. The first tastes began during those initial seven days.

The first day—Saturday, November 23—was free of it. In Washington throughout that day, even the elements seemed to mourn. The clouds hung low, the streets were dark, and the skies wept over the White House. Standing at a window on the east face of the gray old Executive Office Building, looking across at the White House, I felt that one could sense the tragedy unifying Americans. Telegrams by the hundreds were arriving every few minutes, some from men of prominence, most from Americans who wanted only to pledge their support. To read those messages, as I was doing, was to be reminded of the sanity and civility and decency of the American people in a time of trial.

Early that morning, I had been called to the vice presidential offices for another purpose. The thirty-fourth President of the United States, General Dwight D. Eisenhower, was on his way to offer his support, cooperation, and counsel. Would I come, the new president asked, and be with the general during his stay? Of course, I was delighted with the assignment.

General Eisenhower was a pleasure. Every impulse of the man was to cooperate. Modest, undemanding, attempting to be unobtrusive, he labored over memoranda offering suggestions to the new president. When his work was done, he began pacing through the rooms of the spacious suite. I saw him glancing at the ceilings, stopping in the doorways, and looking quizzically back over the rooms through which he had just passed. Suddenly his face lighted, and he broke into his famous grin. "By golly," he said excitedly.

"This was General Pershing's office. This is where I worked as his aide after the First World War." Eagerly, he called me over to see where his old desk had stood, and it was clear that his visit of the morning meant very much for him.

After attending a prayer service at St. John's, across Lafayette Square, and going with Mrs. Johnson to call on Mrs. Kennedy, the new president returned to the suite, conferred at length with General Eisenhower, then retreated to the smallest room among the offices. There he worked through the afternoon, making his own plans, even placing his own telephone calls. Once, while I was sitting beside his desk, he called the office of Senator Everett Dirksen. The telephone girl asked who was calling. "Lyndon Johnson." There was a pause, then he said: "Yes, *that* Lyndon Johnson." As he talked, he handed me a report transmitted from the Department of State.

It was from the government of the Soviet Union: a dossier of all the information the Soviets had on Lee Harvey Oswald and his movements and activities during his period of residence in the Soviet Union. The Russian ambassador had presented it less than twenty-four hours after Oswald's arrest in Dallas. When I finished looking through the remarkably complete and detailed information, Lyndon Johnson turned an old Texas expression into a question: "Me no Alamo?" "That's right," I replied, "me no Alamo."[1] Clearly the Soviet government recognized the ominous potential of American suspicions about Oswald's stay in Russia and was cooperating to the fullest to dispel any question of their culpability. Other documents on the desk, however, were far less reassuring. Intelligence agencies were feeding in undigested—and largely unverified—reports and rumors about Oswald's contacts during his curious journeys around the United States and Mexico during the weeks before Dallas. Steady and sober as America appeared to be on this solemn Saturday, its new president appreciated fully how irrational public opinion might become if an objective investigation into the assassination were not immediately undertaken.

Not everyone, however, believed that the nation was on an even keel. On Friday night, when *Air Force One* returned from Dallas, the

---

1. In 1836, Mexican troops overrun by Sam Houston's Republic of Texas army pleaded for mercy by saying "Me no Alamo," a reference to the battle cry of Houston's troops: "Remember the Alamo."—S.B.

nation had watched on television as the coffin of President Kennedy was lowered from the plane and driven away in an ambulance; then, amid the whir of motors and all the other sounds of a military air base, Lyndon Johnson had stepped to a waiting battery of microphones and made a simple fifty-six-word statement to the nation. He had to speak loudly to be heard; his voice seemed strident and harsh; already, he believed that it had been a mistake. Since then, he had been determined not to speak publicly again—and not to enter the presidential office—until his predecessor was buried. However, during the afternoon, Secretary of State Dean Rusk spoke for himself and other cabinet officers to express a deep concern: the nation, they felt, was seriously unsettled and needed to see and hear the man who had become its president.

Reluctantly, Lyndon Johnson went before the television cameras to read a proclamation eulogizing President Kennedy and declaring Monday a national day of mourning. I asked whether the text of the proclamation was appropriate to the objective; "Now don't question it," he said sharply. "Schlesinger and Sorensen probably wrote it, and Kennedy's people want it done just this way."

That night, at The Elms, I heard more of this. After dinner, the new president called me upstairs. He obviously had good news that he wanted to share: "I talked with each of the cabinet officers this afternoon," he said, "and they are all going to stay on." It was his assessment, with which I entirely concurred, that passage of the long-pending legislation in Congress had first priority; but valuable time would be lost, perhaps fatally, if the first months of the new year were devoted to wholesale changes in the top command of the executive branch. His antennae, finely tuned by the long years on Capitol Hill, told Lyndon Johnson the importance of keeping the cabinet intact. Now he beamed. "I think we have a chance to make it with our bills." But this was not all the good news. Almost playfully, he smiled and began urging me to guess what else had been accomplished before he left the office. When my first effort was wide of the mark, he announced proudly: "All the Kennedy men are staying right on. I told them that I needed them more than Jack did. Not a one of them hesitated. Isn't that wonderful?" I could not quite believe this. "Even Arthur Schlesinger?" I asked. "Yes sir, Schlesinger is staying, too," he said. "I told him that I had never had any success building a really good staff like President Kennedy's. When I told him I needed him more than Jack did, he seemed to be moved, and he is staying with us."

His request to the cabinet—and the response of the members— did not surprise me. However, I had not thought about the White House staff. On the one hand, I suppose I took it for granted that none of the men so long associated with John F. Kennedy would want to remain longer than a few days. On the other hand, it was difficult to think of anyone other than Walter Jenkins and George Reedy on whom President Johnson might call to serve as his staff at the White House. The loss of John Connally, now fighting for his life at Parkland Hospital, struck home: as in the past, Lyndon Johnson would very much need Connally to staff a Johnson White House with Johnson men. But John Connally could not participate now or for months to come. The new president had moved very fast during the late hours of Saturday afternoon. I hoped that he had moved in the right direction.

On Sunday, November 24, the taste of poison appeared in the new power.

That morning—for the first time in history—tens of millions of Americans sat in their homes and watched a man murdered before their eyes on television. No one could ever evaluate the impact upon the American psyche of the incredible scene when Jack Ruby stepped from the crowd in Dallas and fired his revolver at the chest of Lee Harvey Oswald. A weekend of somber tragedy became in an instant a time of stark trauma. In the minds of even the most reasonable men, reality began slipping away. A choking panic seemed to take command. What was happening to America? Where would the madness end?

My personal perspective on this was, necessarily, small; still, it was revealing. During the afternoon, I drove downtown to my office on Connecticut Avenue. There were memoranda I wanted to write and, I suppose, thoughts I wanted to think alone. But there was no quiet. Telephone calls began coming, first from Washington, then from people and places around the nation; in most instances, I had never met—or even heard of—the callers. The individuals involved wanted to communicate with someone close to the new president; my name, along with a number of others, had, of course, appeared in weekend news stories about the new president's associates. I assumed that the callers were simply casting about at random and I happened to be accessible by telephone during the afternoon.

The calls took two lines. First, the callers were concerned for the safety of the new president at the funeral ceremonies on Monday. It was known that the late president's widow and brothers would lead a march through the streets of Washington, from the White House to St. Matthew's Cathedral; walking with them would be the visiting heads of state and, it was presumed, President Johnson. The Ruby-Oswald episode, following the events of Friday, had touched off a sort of hysteria. "You must not let President Johnson go on the streets tomorrow," the early callers said. But as the afternoon progressed, the callers became more and more strident: some screamed into the telephone, several wept, a few were virtually incoherent.

Their words mattered less than their tone. In my small universe of the afternoon, it seemed painfully evident that a precariously balanced nation was beginning to sway; what might be brought on by another provocation, I did not know, but the signs were alarming. Years of association with Lyndon Johnson—and with others of the politicians who had served during the divisive times of the 1930s—had conditioned my mind to think, at times like this, of whether the country could hold together. Or would it come apart? The balance is always delicate; under the stress of the two events of this weekend, that balance, I thought, could easily be crumpling. But along with the calls on this theme, there came another line of messages, not nearly so numerous but far more unnerving.

After having seen the horror of the second Dallas murder that morning, the nation watched Sunday afternoon the haunting ritual in Washington as President Kennedy's body was borne to the Rotunda of the Capitol; there, in one of the most heartrending scenes ever witnessed, the beautiful young widow knelt beside the flag-draped coffin and then kissed it. No one could watch without being deeply affected. But the effects were not all sympathetic. The second line taken by the callers who reached me was venomous, directed against Mrs. Kennedy, Robert Kennedy, all the Kennedys. I was not prepared for it, I could not comprehend it, and I am sure I did not cope well with it.

Profane, vulgar, gratingly harsh, the words were, in many instances, alarming. But the most memorable of such calls came near nightfall. The caller identified himself carefully and precisely; he was an upstate New York industrialist of some national standing in the business community, and he took an active interest in politics. With the identification out of the way, he proceeded to his blunt message: "I just want to say that you poor, dumb Texas sons of bitches are letting them take it away from you." He proceeded with an explicit denunciation of the new president for going into hiding, and of the Kennedys for playing on the national emotions with "a royal funeral." "Mark my words," he ended bitterly, "you Texans will look like the bottom of a birdcage by the time this is over." I had never heard from the man before, and I never heard from him again.

I was not the only member of the Johnson world receiving such calls. Early in the evening, his executive assistant Liz Carpenter telephoned. She, too, had been besieged by calls specifically about the president's participation in the funeral march the following day. Unlike mine, however, her instinct had been to go to The Elms, where President and Mrs. Johnson were spending the day; from her visit there, however, she had another and still more disturbing story to report. "It's started happening," she said with obvious anger. "They are slicing at him." Who are "they"? I wanted to know. "Bobby, Bobby's people," Liz replied tersely.

On Friday afternoon, amid the confused reports from Dallas, I had felt a flash of anger when, alone among the news agencies, the Voice of America—a part, I could only think at the time, of the Kennedy administration—put out the report that Lyndon Johnson had suffered a heart attack. It was entirely without factual foundation or corroboration; for the government's own news agency to broadcast this around the world seemed to me inexcusable. But now this same old theme—which we had heard so much in 1960—was being replayed. Word had come from within the circle of Kennedy family friends arranging the funeral events on Monday that the attorney general and the widow fully understood the new president's health problem. Accordingly, they were planning for him to ride in his limousine rather than walk in the procession with members of the family and visiting heads of state. Liz Carpenter, like myself, had been influenced by the influx of telephone calls; we both thought that he should not be exposed on the streets. But I knew before Liz told me what his reaction would be now. "There is not a chance in the world that he will ride tomorrow," she said. The poison had begun to flow.

On Monday morning, the Johnsons received ten tickets of admission to President Kennedy's funeral at St. Matthew's Cathedral in Washington. Mrs. Johnson selected several close associates, including myself, to attend. When I went to The Elms to pick up the ticket, Liz Carpenter was there again, also planning to attend, and asked if I would accompany her. A Secret Service agent advised that access to that area of the cathedral would be difficult unless we were riding in an official car. Liz requested a White House automobile, and this led to a sharp and ugly dispute: the White House cars, someone advised, were for the Kennedys. At the funeral itself, nerves continued to be jangled. We sat, huddled together it seemed, in a corner of the cathedral. At no time in my life did I ever feel quite so out of place, or quite so miserable: the inadvertent encounters with members of the Kennedy world were unpleasant in a way one tries for years to put out of mind.

Late in the afternoon, after the funeral, the new president himself called. He said nothing about the day. His thoughts were of the meetings which had been planned at the Department of State between himself and the visiting heads of state. But his principal question was revealing. "Is it your judgment," he asked, "that it would be all right for me to go into the presidential office in the West Wing tonight?"

14

AFTERNOON AT GETTYSBURG, 1967

A storm was coming, blowing hard at Lyndon B. Johnson, but neither his public actions nor his private moods presented any clue as to when he might begin making his moves for the election year ahead. As November neared its end, I was expecting—or perhaps hoping—to be hearing soon. It was no surprise, then, when in the last week of the month my day began with a call from the White House.

"Are you crowded on your schedule for today?" the president asked, and I answered him, of course, that I was not. "Good," he said. "If you have a few hours this afternoon, there is something personal I need you to do for me."

The president wanted me to go to Gettysburg. Former president and Mrs. Eisenhower were leaving their farm home in the historic Pennsylvania village on the following day for their annual journey to Palm Springs, California. Before departing, however, General Eisenhower wanted to conclude a pending transaction with the United States government. It had been his decision some years earlier to transfer his farm and home near the Gettysburg battlegrounds to the government for preservation as a historic monument; while the transfer would not occur until six months after his death, the general was anxious to hand over the final papers before leaving for the West.

"I've asked Stu Udall," President Johnson said, referring to the secretary of the interior, "to fly up there in a helicopter this afternoon to receive the deed, and I want you to go along."

The assignment was very welcome, but I did not understand why my presence would matter, or what my role might be.

"It's all cut and dried, I know," the president said, "but I know there's more to it than may appear on the surface. A man doesn't hand over a deed to a place he loves, and his wife loves, without choking up inside. It's going to be an emotional thing for Ike and Mamie, and I want you there for me and Lady Bird, so the general won't feel it's just a bureaucratic thing."

The president started to say more, but he stopped; then, after a pause, he added, "You never know when Lady Bird and I may be doing the same thing ourselves."

After lunch, I met Secretary Udall at his office, and we drove over Memorial Bridge, and past Arlington Cemetery, to the Pentagon, where the helicopter waited. It was an Indian summer afternoon, clear and cool, as the craft rose above the glistening waters of the Potomac and hurried north toward the Maryland hills. Stu Udall lost himself in a silent muse, as he usually did, and I sat at the window watching the unspoiled valley pass below. When the last of Washington faded from sight, the world seemed unperturbed and strong. The crops were harvested, the fields plowed, the leaves gone from the trees; neat now, the fine old land which had served so many Americans so long and so well waited patiently for its winter sleep to begin.

The hour passed quickly, but the shadows were longer and the wind blew stiff and chill from the north when the helicopter touched down at the Eisenhower farm. The gracious old house, freshly painted and carefully kept, stood strong and solid in the afternoon. An aide hurried to greet us. The general, he explained, must remain inside to avoid exposure to the cold. As we talked, a friendly shout carried above the biting gale, and we turned to see General Eisenhower standing on the doorstep, waving heartily, his face lighted by the familiar smile.

One could sense, even from afar, the eagerness with which the general awaited our arrival. The aide called for him to return indoors and urged us to hurry up the long drive, but the general could restrain himself no longer. Hand outstretched, he came hurrying toward us. "I know I am not supposed to do this," he said apologetically to the aide, "but I am so grateful to these gentlemen for their courtesy in coming, I just must greet them myself."

He had a warm handclasp for each member of the party, including the helicopter crew. "Busby? Busby?" He puzzled over my name. "By George, are you related to my classmate at West Point?" We established that I must not be, but when he learned the purpose of my presence, he put his arm around me and we walked together to the house.

At the entrance, the general hurried in ahead of us. "Mamie," he called, "Mamie, the gentlemen are here."

Secretary Udall and I waited in the front hall, glancing into the adjacent living room—long and spacious, filled with memorabilia of a crowded lifetime, but dim and gray now with the curtains drawn and no lamps burning. Stu's impassive Arizona face softened. "I feel," he whispered, "like we're the bastards from the bank foreclosing on the homestead."

It became evident before long that, as President Johnson had anticipated, Mrs. Eisenhower felt much the same way. The general beckoned us to the glassed-in sunporch at the rear of the farmhouse; there his wife laid down the cards from her game of solitaire and smiled a greeting. "He and I were observing our quiet hour," she explained. "That means I play this, as best I can, and"—she nodded toward an easel and canvas at the opposite end of the room—"he does his painting." Her eyes misted over, and she turned her head away.

General Eisenhower's own spirits were effervescent. With an eager, almost youthful enthusiasm, he stood at the windows, pointing out features of the broad pasturelands surrounding the residence; it pleased him enormously, as it also pleased Secretary Udall's conservationist heart, that these acres were to "belong to the people" and would remain as he had known them. After she had composed herself, Mrs. Eisenhower joined us to admire the autumn view, and the general explained to her that I had come to represent the president and Mrs. Johnson.

"No one has ever been nicer to me or to us than your president," General Eisenhower said. Putting his arm around his wife, he gave a husbandly laugh. "President Johnson is always after us to use *Air*

Force One whenever we have a trip to make, but this little lady says no, she has done all the flying she ever intends to do." That was why, he explained, they would be traveling by private railroad car when they departed the following afternoon for California.

Mrs. Eisenhower invited us to be seated. Secretary Udall drew his chair up to talk with the general, and I sat on the sofa with her.

"I so appreciate your coming," she said. "Ike has been very firm about this. He refuses to leave for California until the deed to this place is signed, sealed, and delivered." She touched a handkerchief to her eyes, apologizing. "I'm sorry, I can't help the way I feel, but this is the first home we have ever owned. I know it is ours as long as Ike lives, but I can't feel about it the way he does. To me, signing the deed only means I am back to living in"—her voice choked and she closed her eyes, thinking back over a long trail of posts—"the government house again."

From across the porch, General Eisenhower followed his wife's quietly emotional conversation with me, and he sought to brighten the mood. "Mamie," he called, "tell them about the night we came here to buy this place." The memory evoked a hearty laugh from both of them, and she related the story with fine humor.

During the general's service as president of Columbia University, the Eisenhowers began house-hunting on weekends, seeking a small-town retreat to which they expected to retire before the 1950s ended. One Friday afternoon, they departed from Morning-side Heights with an old Eisenhower friend, George Allen, and his wife, bound for Gettysburg. When they arrived near midnight, the hotels and motels were fully occupied; after some searching, they located a tourist home with two vacant rooms. But the owner had his standards: he looked over the general of the Army and his companion, sniffed suspiciously, and peered out through the darkness at the two women waiting in the automobiles. Sorry, the owner told the future president, but he and his wife did not run that kind of establishment. "We only rent rooms to married couples."

Remembrance of the episode lightened Mrs. Eisenhower's spirits, and she recalled many of the joys which Gettysburg had brought them. But her thoughts that afternoon went back further. Learning that my Texas home was Austin, she related that during her family's residence in nearby San Antonio, she frequently attended

University of Texas football games. After one game, she and her companions returned to San Antonio much later than anticipated, and she found her anxious father valiantly entertaining her waiting blind date for the evening, a young lieutenant from the Army post, Dwight Eisenhower.

The mists returned once more, but she glanced across the porch and said, "Life has been very good to us ever since."

General Eisenhower, for his part, displayed none of his wife's melancholy. Our coming brought some sort of release for him. He talked freely of many things, his voice still firm and strong; he spoke of old friends and of men whom he especially admired. All of the subjects, I noticed, were civilians, mostly men of business whom he had come to know after his return from the Great Crusade in Europe; all received what seemed to be his highest accolade as "a good American"; and all were gone. Only occasionally—when his long, thin fingers twisted nervously around the arm of his chair or when, after flashing his warm and ready smile, his face sagged and showed the whiteness on his cheeks—did one realize that Dwight Eisenhower was seventy-seven years old. But the realization weighed heavily on his wife.

While the general spoke, Mrs. Eisenhower turned to me and, with no apparent relation to the conversation in progress, asked, "You do know, don't you, that we lost our first son?" She seemed to be speaking of a contemporary event. Yet I knew that the death of their firstborn had occurred more than forty years earlier. After I nodded, she shifted to the edge of the sofa cushion, turning her back toward her husband; a smile lighted her friendly face, and she spoke with animation. "A few years ago," she said, "I went out all alone, and I had the body of our son reburied in Kansas, on the grounds of the chapel at Ike's library in Abilene." Now, on the train trip west, "Ike has agreed that we can go by Abilene to visit the grave, and we can see where we are all going to be." The tears came again, but they ran down over a contented smile.

Secretary Udall rose to leave. General Eisenhower made certain that we had the deed with us, and after we told Mrs. Eisenhower good-bye, he followed us out into the cold to say farewell at the helicopter's side. On the ride back toward Washington, I began writing an account of the afternoon for President Johnson. I realized that I had seen a man at peace, his life in order, his thoughts of the future serene, and I wondered, as I wrote, whether the man who now occupied the White House would ever know a time like this in his life ahead. But knowing President Johnson's abiding concern for the health of both his living predecessors, General Eisenhower and President Truman, I wrote very frankly: Mrs. Eisenhower's worry, I felt, was less for the transfer of the house than for whether her husband would ever return to the Gettysburg farm again. Her premonitions were to prove correct.

Secretary Udall and I had shared General Eisenhower's last afternoon on the Gettysburg farm, in the only house he and Mamie ever owned.

15

STATE OF THE UNION

Sunday, January 14, 1968, was a day to spend by the fire. Cold and wet, the day grew dark by noon, and only the logs burning on a country hearth could dispel the winter gloom. Three weeks had passed since the end of the trip around the world, and I had not seen or talked with President Lyndon B. Johnson.[1] Over the holidays he had entertained Israel's prime minister, Levi Eshkol, at the LBJ Ranch, and he had returned to Washington only the previous day to begin the labors of what would be his thirtieth full year in the public life of the nation's capital. With the Sunday *New York Times* spread before me, I sat on the floor of our old Maryland farmhouse reading about the politics of this national election year.

The conversation aboard *Air Force One*, somewhere over Iran, already was a fading memory. It was washed from my mind entirely under the flood of newspaper words. Although challenged within his own party by Senator Eugene McCarthy, and beset by protests against the war in Vietnam, President Johnson nonetheless emerged from the news analysis as still the commanding political figure he had been since 1964; neither his nomination nor his reelection was seriously in question, and the idea of him withdrawing from

---

1. Busby, who was no longer on the White House staff by December 1967, was asked by the president to accompany him on this around-the-world trip, the secret purpose of which was to visit the American troops in Vietnam. *Air Force One* departed from Andrews Air Force Base on December 19, 1967, stopping in Honolulu, Hawaii; Melbourne, Australia; Cam Ranh Bay, Vietnam; Karachi, Pakistan; Rome, Italy; and Lajesfield, Azores, before returning to Andrews on December 24, 1967.—S.B.

politics seemed too unreal to deserve even fleeting consideration. Instead, my thoughts on this long, dismal afternoon played idly with speculations about what he would say on Wednesday night, when he appeared before a joint session of Congress to deliver his fifth State of the Union message.

The address would present a demanding challenge. Whatever he might say, the president's words would be taken as the opening of his campaign for reelection in November. Critics, inside and outside Congress, would be attuned to every nuance, listening for false notes that might betray hesitancy, uncertainty, or weakness; listening especially for subtle signals which might reveal a telling unease about their criticisms. Yet the challenge was an opportunity. If the Lyndon Johnson who appeared on the nation's television screens at midweek was a confident leader, strengthened rather than crippled by the besieging of his presidency, that would be enough. His image as an all-but-invincible politician held more sway over his enemies than over his friends; only an intimation of invulnerability would silence the baying at his heels and turn the cautious men of politics to thoughts of 1972.

On this second Sunday of the new year, I knew that the calendar required the president to be working over drafts of the address that could control the challenging year, and I hoped that he was going about the task with the determination, originality, and political shrewdness of which he was uniquely capable. When the telephone rang, however, the words as well as the voice were all too familiar. "This goddam draft they've given me wouldn't make chickens cackle if you waved it at 'em in the dark," the president said. "It's too long, too dull, too flat, too bureaucratic—every little two-bit bureau in the government has managed to get at least one line in on their pet project."

There was no humor in his tone, only the fitful grimness which he brought to his perpetual war with the bureaucracy.

"I get the best minds in Washington together," he went on angrily, "and what do they come up with? Vomit. Fifty pages of vomit."

He cut off his caustic comments abruptly. Could I, he asked with a characteristic touch, "give up your nap for your country and help your president?" I agreed to come immediately to the White House. "Understand," he said apologetically, "I wouldn't bother you if I didn't need a little Churchill in this thing." After twenty years, he still aspired to the standard which eluded him.

It is common among public men never to ask only one person to undertake an assignment if three or four others can be found to perform the same duty. When I reached the White House, I was not surprised to find other friends already gathered on the second floor of the Executive Mansion, at work on the same assignment. There were not enough copies of the draft to go around, so I settled back to await my turn. My good friend George Reedy labored intently over the pages, penciling suggested changes into the lines. "Is it bad?" I asked. "Not too bad," he replied without looking up, "but it needs work."

Sergeant Paul Glynn, the president's personal aide, appeared at the doorway and looked over the room. Then he beckoned me to the corridor. I had been told that the president was sleeping, but Sergeant Glynn whispered, "He wants to see you."

One learned at the White House that Sergeant Glynn was the most accurate authority on the temper of the man he served. Loyal and tight-lipped, the sergeant nonetheless would provide expert judgments to his own friends if he thought they might need forewarning.

As we hurried toward the tall, dark-stained double doors opening into the president's bedroom, I asked the usual question about the presidential mood. Holding the door for me, Sergeant Glynn answered with a silent hand signal: thumbs down.

The president was in bed, in his pajamas and under the covers, but very much awake. Around him were strewn newspapers, clippings, and typewritten memoranda. Impatiently, before I could greet him, he snapped: "What did you think of the speech?" I had not read it, of course, but I trusted Reedy's opinion. "Not too bad," I replied, "but it needs some work." The president snorted. "Hell, don't quote George Reedy to me," he grumbled. "You haven't read it."

The detail did not bother him. He motioned me to a small chair beside the medicine stand at the head of his canopied bed. After I was seated, he started to speak but took one look at me, sighed disgustedly, and turned back the covers. I continued to sit while the President of the United States slipped out of bed, padded barefoot across the room, and returned in a moment, silently handing me a notepad and pencil. Back under the covers, propped upright against his thick pillows, the president came immediately to the point.

"I didn't get you down here to waste your time on the State of the Union."

I looked up, surprised. His dark eyes, intent and piercing, were fixed on mine.

"I have made up my mind," he declared, with sudden force. "I can't get peace in Vietnam and be president, too."

The portent of his words did not register. I had come into the room thinking politically, of campaign, conventions, elections, and all that lay ahead during the year. His first remark simply had no relevant meaning. But he leaned toward me, and his words came through tightly set lips.

"Those other fellows over there"—he swung a long arm in what I took to be the general direction of Southeast Asia—"won't let me have both, and"—now he jerked a contemptuous thumb over his shoulder toward Capitol Hill—"that bunch up there doesn't want me to have either."

He had decided on his course. On Wednesday night, when he spoke before the joint session of the House and Senate, he would read through to the end of his long text on the state of the union. While the members of Congress were applauding the concluding lines, he intended to reach into the inside pocket of his coat— abruptly he sat forward on the bed and began demonstrating each gesture with obvious relish—take out a two-page supplemental statement, and unfold it on the lectern. When the great chamber where his career began was quiet once more, he would read from the paper in his hand.

"And so, my friends of many years, my colleagues, my fellow coun- trymen in your homes tonight"—he tilted his head upward, threw out his chin, and spoke with the cadence of the public platform, living the moment before the hushed and wondering Congress—"I have come before you to announce that in this year of nineteen and sixty-eight, I will not, under any circumstances, be a candidate for reelection as President of the United States." A smile played across his face, and he raised one hand as if gesturing to the assemblage. Then he turned toward me, still intent and unsmiling, but with a deep satisfaction showing on his face.

"That," he said, "ought to surprise the living hell out of them."

He waited for my comment, but I had not bargained for this turn of events. I kept my eyes closely on the tablet, saying nothing. In truth, the living hell had just been surprised out of me. After a moment, he leaned back against the pillows and spoke quietly. I had been summoned to draft the withdrawal announcement which he would have in his coat pocket because I was no longer a part of the White House world. "A secret won't keep ten minutes around this place," he said. If word of his intentions got out, however, "this town would be a jungle." He trusted me now, as in the past, to keep his confidence, but as a further precaution, I was henceforth to avoid all contact with my former colleagues on the staff. "One of them might read your mind," he warned. Then he lowered his voice to whisper earnestly and confidentially. "There are some damn smart sonsabitches around here, you know." With the ground rules established, he began going through the points he wanted to make supporting his decision.

It had been late in the dreary winter afternoon when I entered the presidential bedroom; now, as he spoke, the gray light coming through the thick glass of the bulletproof windows failed rapidly. In a short while, night closed in around us, and only the small reading lamp above his head glowed against the darkness. The setting was not real, and instinctively I remained wary. Did he mean this? Was I there, truly, to write the words ending his political life? Or was I there only to be some part of an exercise in presidential therapy, listening until the emotion spent itself and then forgetting what I had heard?

Public men, climbing the long and tiring ladder of American political life, often talk of quitting, of giving up their offices, of retiring to other pursuits. Over the years I had known him, Lyndon Johnson had engaged in such talk more often than most, as congressman, as senator, as vice president, even in his early months as president. But whereas in other times I might have been responding to his words—debating, arguing, cajoling—now I made no attempt to intervene. It was possible, I realized, that his question to me on the flight around the world had been in the nature of a poll: he had learned then my spontaneous and unconsidered answer, where I stood, and now he was sharing his most personal confidence. But

I thought it best only to listen; he seemed to be talking more to himself than to me, and in any event, he was the President of the United States. On this decision, only he could counsel himself.

Whenever he outlined a speech, the president dictated, much in the manner of a classroom teacher following a well-prepared outline. He had no notes, of course, but his outline came out in proper order, and however long the pauses in his discourse, he resumed each time in correct sequence: "Point One: Civil Rights," "Point Two: The Economy and Jobs," "Point Three: Social Legislation," and under that topic "A. Education," "B. Health Care," "C. Cities." With the sure instincts of a master of the political craft, he was reciting the record, listing in the fine detail which politicians cherish the number of new programs, the amount of funding, the measurable results through his four years, one month, and twenty-two days in the presidency. As defenses of records go, his case was strong and the quantity of accomplishments impressive, but nothing said yet explained his decision not to seek reelection.

"Point Six"—this one on housing—was completed. Then he began: "Point Seven: The War."

The president recoiled, as if he wished he had not heard his own voice. He fell back against the pillows, touched his forehead with the fingers of both hands, and closed his eyes. "This war," he said, the words barely audible. "This goddam war."

The silence that followed was long and painful, and I looked away. But he never returned to the thought.

In a moment, he lifted up one of the newspapers and pointed to the latest Gallup poll. He made no reference to the figures showing his overall popularity still holding up after the late summer decline. Instead, he thumped the page and said, "It shows that a majority of Democrats still approve the job I'm doing, and still approve the conduct of the war." But he raised his hand before I could comment. "The name of this game is to quit while you're ahead," he said quietly. "I've always prayed I'd have sense enough to get out when the time came, before they had to carry me out."

The paper was laid aside. As though unaware of my presence, he began scanning the memoranda spread around him, conducting some sort of count. His survey complete, he explained, "I've got the nomination, too. Somebody may try, but they can't take it away. I've got my votes already."

He appeared pleased, but the conversation took an unexpected turn, and I felt myself tensing. A different man seemed to have entered the room, a man whom I knew too well, a man whom I did not like to have speak for the President of the United States. The same one-two-three style continued, but now Lyndon Johnson was listing—and painfully elaborating upon—the reasons why he should not be president. He was too personal, too intimate, too abject. His accent was wrong, his education wrong, his style wrong. I frowned disapprovingly and laid down the pencil; this had no place in any public speech a president might make. But he saw the reaction and only argued more strongly and more harshly, raising the specter of his oldest demon: geography. "I do not believe," he said, "that a man born in my section can lead, or will be permitted to lead, this nation in these times." I shook my head impatiently and closed the tablet to emphasize that I was not transcribing his words.

"All right, all right," he said petulantly, "have it your way." Then he leaned to the edge of the bed, a sudden fire burning in his eyes. "But give me this one," he said. "Get this one down."

I reopened the tablet, and he spoke very slowly so that I could write each word in longhand.

"On that day in November, so long ago, when I came before you for the first time as president, to speak in a time of sorrow and sadness—no, make that, tragedy and trial—I said then, 'Let us continue.' We have continued. A thousand days have become two thousand, and two thousand soon will become three. We have done the work of the fallen hero whose place I have labored to fill. We have borne the burdens, we have carried the torch, we have kept the flame alive, and its light still shines. We of this generation have kept faith with ourselves, and we have kept the trust of John F. Kennedy. I say again tonight, as my last words to you and to the nation, let us continue.

"Now," he asked, his tone edged, "does that possibly, perhaps, maybe meet with your approval?"

I nodded that it did, and he appeared satisfied in some special, private way.

By now, he had spoken for well over one hour, and I had made no comment. But I knew he was done, and I rose to leave.

He called to me across the room. "Aren't you going to say anything?"

"Mr. President," I replied, "we'll have to think about this."

Those were to be the last words spoken between us on the matter for almost three months.

After I left the president's bedroom, I wrote out a statement for him. It came hard. Now that I faced it, I was none too sure of his decision or of its timing. When I read back through the jumble of notes, I found it difficult to establish a rationale for the action. He had argued personally, of course, contending that qualities about himself and his circumstances made accomplishment impossible: yet against this he had listed a record of accomplishment without postwar parallel. I could not conceal the contradiction satisfactorily in my words.

A further concern developed as I wrestled with this assignment. Perhaps great power should not be laid down except for great cause. No such cause existed. Yet if he removed himself from politics, the nation would be vulnerable abroad—and perhaps at home—to the inherent weaknesses of a lame-duck presidency. I wrote a brief note expressing this quandary to him, but I did not forget that the decision was his alone. "On a matter such as this," I said, "every man must step to his own drum." When I sent the statement to him the following day, there was no acknowledgment, and I could not know for sure that he had received it.

At midweek, he delivered the State of the Union message. The words were greatly improved over the first draft I'd read but still far from the quality he had aspired to for the occasion. I listened none too attentively, waiting anxiously for the close. When he reached the end of his text, I moved nearer the television screen. The applause swelled. The president nodded toward the audience without smiling. Members rose to their feet, cheers began, and he still stood over the lectern, perhaps hesitating, perhaps not. But his hand did not move to the coat pocket. He nodded again and closed the text. It was over, and he moved away.

I concluded then that my visit to the White House on the previous Sunday must have been for purposes of therapy.

— 16 —

A SUNDAY AT THE WHITE HOUSE

Sunday, March 31, 1968, began drably. The sunshine and spring-time of Saturday were gone. Overnight, winter had returned; sullen clouds sat low on the eastern horizon, shutting out the early sun, and the Maryland pastures lay gray and lifeless under the morning chill. My own mood matched the day.

At midnight, when the White House operator had called with the cryptic message from the president, there had been a moment of elation. The summons to the White House at nine this morning could only mean that after so many weeks of delay, there was to be a decision at least. The main purpose of the speech would be to announce the cessation of bombing in North Vietnam. Whether the president also chose to renounce a second term or whether he elected to make the campaign did not greatly matter; the important consideration, as I saw it, was that the choice would be deliberate—one which Lyndon Johnson had finally taken time to make for himself, rather than having it forced upon him by the chance of circumstance that had so dogged him in the office. Whatever the decision, if it was his own, the future would be better. For this I was grateful and, in a sense, happier than I had been in days, but the happiness did not last.

Just minutes after the midnight call, the telephone rang again. It was the White House once more, but this time the call came from Jim Jones, the young assistant who only recently had been placed in charge of the president's daily schedule. "I was just checking," he began. "Did you get the word that the president wants you here in the morning at nine?"

In my own term on the White House staff, when Jim Jones first came to work there, we had been friends. His cordiality and helpfulness had continued since, but when, out of old habit, I casually asked what the morning held, the friendliness froze out of Jones's distinctive Oklahoma voice, and he spoke evasively. I had to put my question pointedly. "Why does the president want to see me, Jim?"

Jones hesitated. There was no mistaking the sharpness when he finally replied. "It has to do with the speech," he said, "with the peroration."

The word seemed strangely stiff and formal. In my time around Lyndon Johnson, we called the ending for a speech what it was—"the end," not something so elegant as "the peroration." Both the tone and the vocabulary of my caller aroused a suspicion that Jones had something more to say than he had yet said. I pressed him again.

"But I sent the president a draft peroration late in the afternoon."

"Yes," he said coldly. "I know you did."

"Has he seen it yet?"

The answer was even colder. "Yes, he has seen it."

I realized the conversation was becoming a contest. We were sparring with each other over something Jones did not intend to tell me. Again from habit, I applied the old Lyndon Johnson dictum that "the most important thing a man has to tell you is nearly always what he tries to keep from telling you—if you're smart enough, and patient enough, you'll stay with him, until you make him say it." I became determined to stay with Jim Jones until he said whatever he seemed bent on holding back.

"What was his reaction?" I asked.

There was no acknowledgment of the question, only silence. I tried again.

"Was his reaction up or down?"

"Neither," Jones said tersely.

Trying a new tactic, I questioned Jones about himself. "Have you seen what I wrote?" Without hesitation he answered, speaking with a sudden and forceful intensity.

"Yes, I've seen it," he said, "and I think it's awful, just awful. The language is all right—don't get me wrong about that—but it's your idea that I don't like. It is terrible; in fact, it stinks." Jones had not intended to speak as he did or to say so much. Very abruptly he ended the conversation. But when the receiver clicked in my ear, I thought I knew what had happened and, perhaps, what lay ahead.

On Saturday nights, President Johnson very often worked late in the Oval Office. Usually before the long night ended, he called together several of his special assistants and passed the hours with high-spirited, good-humored accounts of the events and experiences of his week. Quite commonly, if he happened to have a speech draft on his desk, he entertained his audience by reading the text aloud, parodying himself as he interpolated comments which could be expected from critics in the press. In such a situation, the president must have been unable to contain his secret longer; with the draft of the withdrawal statement in hand, he had surprised Jim Jones and others on duty for the evening by reading it to them. I knew what their reactions must have been: to a man, they had expressed instant and heated disagreement. Furthermore, considering Jones's emphasis—in saying "it's *your* idea that I don't like"—I assumed that the president had played another of his favorite games. Wanting to draw out candid responses from those around him, he had undoubtedly presented the statement as my idea rather than his own. That was a familiar Lyndon Johnson tactic and, in situations such as this, a very useful one.

Almost certainly the outcome of any such session would have been negative. On Saturday the president's thoughts about withdrawing had been only tentative. Any articulate opposition from members of the staff whom he respected and trusted would have set in motion a search on his part for reasons and justifications to delay again the decision already delayed so long. Quite possibly the reason for my summons was typically Lyndon Johnson: he only wanted to tell me in person that his decision would have to wait, and with that he would ask me to "put a little Churchill" in his "peroration" for Sunday night's address.

After the conversation with Jim Jones, I hardly bothered with sleep. At six o'clock on Sunday morning I was in the kitchen at our home. Reading through the news of the day was not encouraging. On page one, *The Washington Post* headlined the announcement of the president's televised address, but nothing in the story hinted at the possibility of a withdrawal announcement. On the same page, a story was offered about the Reverend Martin Luther King, Jr.; he was to speak that morning from the pulpit at Washington's National Cathedral, outlining plans for the Poor People's March on the national capital later in the month. But the inside pages of the Sunday edition were especially interesting.

The Gallup poll appeared that day: it reported that the president's overall popularity remained relatively low but stable, as was to be expected. But I studied the fine print, which I knew was read with more care by the president himself: for the first time, fewer than 50 percent of the members of the president's own Democratic Party approved his handling of the war in Vietnam.

That, I thought, might be decisive. Like the opposition of Senator Eugene McCarthy and the new candidacy of Senator Robert Kennedy, this poll statistic only made it more difficult for the president to consider withdrawing from the politics of 1968. For many reasons, he had waited to make and announce his final decision, and now it was apparent that he had waited too long.

At eight o'clock, when I departed from our farmhouse at Sandy Spring, Maryland, I was thoroughly convinced of what awaited. I was to be involved in a long and interesting but futile day on the "Sunday shift" at the White House, seventeen miles away.

Washington still slept its usual late Sunday sleep. From the Maryland line into the center of the District of Columbia, Sixteenth Street stood empty except for the early buses carrying their passengers to the city's churches. I reached Lafayette Square at ten minutes before the hour and began following the usual winding route of White House drivers past the cluster of government buildings and art museums toward the Southwest Gate. At South Executive Avenue, which curves around the mansion's broad grounds, I stopped at the turn-through hidden among the flowers bordering the roadway. While checking for approaching traffic, I saw a White House policeman standing against the iron picket fence, watching intently to his left along the broad sidewalk, and I followed the direction of his stare.

Thirty yards away a short, hatless man, dressed in a bulky overcoat several sizes too large for his frame, stood motionless on the walk, his eyes fixed on the Executive Mansion. As the officer and I watched, the pedestrian reached into his coat pocket for a small book, which I took to be a Bible; then he made a sudden backward leap to the middle of the walk. Bible in hand, the man threw his arms heavenward, moving his lips rapidly and apparently beseeching some personal god to exorcise this house of power. As suddenly as the ritual began it stopped; satisfied, the passerby returned the Bible to his pocket and hurried on around the walk out of sight. The policeman, who had recognized me by now, opened his palms and shrugged. The White House has many meanings. I waved a greeting and turned toward the entrance.

The guardhouse at the Southwest Gate controls two entrances into the White House compound: the West Executive Avenue entrance, which is used by staff and others to reach the basement of the West Wing, and the South Grounds entrance, which opens into the circular drive to the diplomatic entrance of the mansion itself. A detail of four or five uniformed policemen is posted at the guardhouse to check the identities of arrivals against the daily gate list authorizing their admission. As I approached the gate from a block away, I flicked on the right turn indicator signaling that I was an arriving guest; one officer, carrying the gate list clipboard, moved out of the shelter to make the identification. He was not an officer I knew, and his face showed no recognition of me. When I pulled to a stop and lowered the car window, he said very coolly, "Yes, can I help you?"

There is always a likelihood that one's name will not be on the checklist as expected. I began to explain that the White House operator had called and said the president would be expecting me at nine o'clock, but the story sounded implausible even to me. The officer appeared unimpressed. "Your identification, please?"

I reached for my wallet, but a voice shouted from the guardhouse, "That's Mr. Busby." I looked up to see a welcome face: a stout and apple-cheeked officer who always had a smile and joke to start each day. Taking charge impressively, he motioned for the gate to be opened and hurried to my window. "We knew you were coming," he said, laughing at his own humor. "Shoulda baked a cake, huh?" He extended his hand and we shook vigorously.

Then he leaned closer through the window. "Big doings today, huh? Big doings." He rolled his eyes as he spoke, and I realized for the first time that White House police were all around the entrance. One officer patrolled the walk beneath the old stone face of the Executive Office Building to the left. Others were stationed beside the fence surrounding the grounds. Standing in the center of the street, in position to halt traffic coming around the curve, another officer waited with walkie-talkie in hand. The deployment could have meant only that the Southwest Gate was on the alert for important visitors, possibly the National Security Council or even the cabinet.

My jolly friend went on. "Bet there's gonna be a little speech-writing today." He chuckled.

Truthfully, I replied, "I don't know why I'm here."

That brought a big laugh. "Oh, that's rich." The officer chortled. "Big doings and you don't know why you are here." He thought it was only a play, the kind to which White House police are accustomed.

The gate was open, and I drove inside, slowing to the prescribed five-mile-an-hour speed limit. I passed the old and unused tennis court and the great fountain, which still had not begun operation. I turned the curve on the east side of the grounds.

The South Grounds of the White House were never lovelier. Impeccably trim and luxuriant, with the fragrance of new blossoms filling the air, the gracefully sloping acres of green lawn and greener trees formed as always a special and private world. The dense plantings along the fences shut out the sights and stifled the sounds of Washington's streets. The graceful mound, designed by Thomas Jefferson, long since overgrown with handsome trees and flowering shrubs, added to the solitude; and the faint streaks of ground fog, hovering just above the new-mown grass, seemed to shroud the history that is ever present around the home of the American president.

I parked my sedan at the end of the line of family automobiles waiting on the curving drive and began the walk toward the mansion. On ahead, I could see standing at the entrance a Lincoln Continental: the right rear door was open, and from the exhaust I knew the engine was running. This meant, I assumed, that the First Lady must be preparing to leave for a Sunday schedule on her own while the president labored over his address for the night. Since the long black limousines of officialdom were not in evidence yet, there would be time, at least briefly, for the president to discuss his personal decision before taking up consideration of the bombing halt again.

As I passed the line of empty automobiles, there was a rustle at my side, only a slight sound but enough to attract a glance. At my left, only inches away in a station wagon, sat six crew-cut young Secret Service agents. I knew none of them; yet if their training had been as complete as usual, all of them presumably recognized me. They did not nod or blink but only stared impassively. I knew all my assumptions about the morning had been wrong. This was Halfback, the code name for the Secret Service chase car that trails the president wherever he goes. Not Mrs. Johnson but the president himself was preparing to leave the White House. There would be no long discussion, no careful deliberation. The Saturday night debate must have settled the president's course: he would not be making his announcement, or even considering it further, on this last day of March. The only appropriate word to express my reaction was "Damn."

A White House butler waited at the entrance to the Diplomatic Reception Room, the lovely oval room on the ground floor of the Executive Mansion. In other times, there would have been no one there, but now I was very much a guest, an outsider; regulations required that someone escort me through the mansion to my destination. I followed the butler through the dark hall to the elevator, and we went in silence to the family floor. As the doors opened back, my guide motioned to his left. "The president," he said with a courtly flourish, "is expecting you in the bedroom."

Across the great center hall, which runs the length of the second floor, the heavy double doors to the presidential bedroom were closed. Outside the room, a lamp shone brightly over the small desk where Sergeant Glynn usually waited, but the sergeant was not there to signal thumbs up or thumbs down about the presidential mood. I opened the door slowly and quietly. As expected, I could hear the president speaking on the telephone, but I was not prepared for what I saw.

The president's bedroom was filled with people: family, friends, staff, valets, and even two physicians. Nearest the door, leaning against the wall of the closet alcove, stood the president's son-in-law Pat Nugent, Luci's husband. Around the corner from him, I could see one of the regular White House physicians; waiting with him was another physician in Navy uniform. Across the room, in a corner by the window, Sergeant Glynn and his assistant, Sergeant Ken Gaddis, were hurriedly laying out new suits, which apparently had just arrived from the tailor; the haste of their movements told me that they were preparing the clothes for a quick presidential inspection before he departed.

On the floor in the middle of the room was the Johnsons' daughter Luci, watching over her toddling son, "Little Lyn." Lyn was joyfully engaged in his own private game with his grandfather; raising his arms over his head, he would run toward the president, who stood beside the canopied bed cradling the telephone on his shoulder. When his grandson came close, the president bent forward, punching a long finger at the child's waist, and Lyn, squealing and laughing, toppled backward and threw his fat legs in the air. But the first person to realize I had entered the alcove was Jim Jones. He turned from his position at the foot of the bed and waved a silent salutation; then he grinned very broadly, too broadly, I thought—it must be a smile of triumph.

As I moved toward Jones, however, I became aware of another figure in the room: it was the president's good friend from New York, Arthur Krim. Lawyer, corporate executive, exceptionally wise counselor, Krim was a frequent visitor; now he sat in the bedroom's rocking chair, quietly reading the text of the president's speech for the night. When Krim saw me, he bounced out of the chair and hurried across the room. Beaming happily, leaning close, he whispered, "What do you think of the bombshell?"

I did not know why he was present. If the president was seeking counsel outside the White House circle on his decision to withdraw, Krim certainly would have been high on the list of those whose opinions would be most valued. Instinctively, though, I knew I should not take for granted that he had yet been made a confidant; there were, after all, two "bombshells" under consideration.

"I'm all for it," I replied, neutrally.

"Gee," Krim exclaimed boyishly, "I am too. This will make things so much better, so much better. I only wish it could have come earlier."

I still could not be sure of what he knew. Then I saw the president shoot a dark glance in my direction; still speaking on the telephone, he touched his fingers to his lips. Arthur Krim, I realized then, was commenting on the announcement of the bombing halt.

The president's conversation continued for another ten minutes or so. Then the two physicians stepped quickly to his side. The physician in uniform was introduced as an expert from the naval hospital at Bethesda, but without further conversation both of the medical men began examining one of the president's hands. For years Lyndon Johnson had been plagued with what we inexactly called "skin cancers," and periodic treatments were required. As the medical men went to work, scraping instruments across skin, the president passed out instructions to Jim Jones about other calls he wanted to make later in the day.

When the medical attention concluded, the president stepped to the window to look over the new clothes; he selected one suit for his television appearance that night, rejected the tie laid out with it, and chose another.

Then, finally, he turned to me. "Horace and I," he announced to the group, "have some private business to discuss." Moving to the door, he added, "It will take us about twenty minutes."

Not five times in the twenty years I had known him had Lyndon Johnson called me by my proper name, Horace. The formality about the name, the announcement that our discussion would require only twenty minutes, and the general bustle of the presidential morning all confirmed my expectations. The president must have called me to the White House for a brief but final announcement that he could not go forward with the idea we had discussed the day before.

I followed him out of the bedroom and down the center corridor to the sitting room area referred to by the family as the West Hall. Here a broad window, arched across its top, looks out over the West Wing toward the Executive Office Building. On many occasions, both at noon and in the evening, those of us on the staff sat here with the president and the First Lady and their guests, engaged in pleasant conversation before meals were served. The president took his usual wing-back chair, and I sat facing him at the other end of the sofa. Almost as soon as we were seated, he rose again, walked over to a table in the center of the area, and came back with a notepad and pencil, which he handed to me. "Here," he said. "Take notes."

The telephone at his fingertips rang. He picked it up, listened to the operator, agreed to take the call, but cautioned her, "Honey, now don't ring me again for a few minutes—I have a very important conference going."

It was almost ten o'clock, eleven hours before the national telecast, when the president at last began to discuss what he might say. He was sharp-eyed and alert. The lines seemed to have disappeared from his face, and the heaviness was gone from his shoulders. In other times those of us on the staff would have explained his appearance and his manner by saying that he was "organized." This was a very good sign.

The president reached into his pocket for a copy of the draft text I had sent him the previous day. Holding it aloft in one hand, he said, "There are many things to consider about this. There's the matter of health. I'll be sixty years old this year; my father and nearly all of the men on the Johnson side of my family have died in their sixtieth year. I don't know whether I would live out another four-year term here." I had heard this often, of course, and while I understood his feelings, I hoped he would not be making a decision on this basis. But he said no more on the subject.

"Then there's the war," he said, pausing and adding after a moment, "this damn war." He leaned forward, his eyes narrowing, and he spoke evenly. "I have done all I can to get it over with. After tonight, there's nothing else left, I suppose, that I can do. It's getting awfully close, too. The father of that baby"—he motioned back toward the bedroom, where Little Lyn was still playing—"is going over next month. The other daughter"—referring to Lynda—"came back this morning from California, where she had seen her man off to war, and she looked at me and her mother, and she said, 'Why, Daddy, why?'"

Time was short and I started to speak, but he raised his hand. He wanted no interruption. He continued, his words coming rapidly and with force as he listed other concerns, then dismissed them.

"But those are all personal matters," he said. "You must never forget that fellow out in Omaha or Indianapolis or Denver. He has a wife going into the hospital for a cancer operation, a daughter he's trying to put through school, a boy on his way to Vietnam, car payments to meet, insurance premiums due, a mortgage hanging over his head, and his mother needing to go into a nursing home. When that fellow looks at the White House, he thinks the man there has it made, has everything in the world—and he's right. All my troubles put together aren't as big for a president as that little fellow's troubles are for him. We have to remember that. We have to remember that here in this house"—he slapped his palm firmly against the arm of his chair—"no man who sits here can ever afford to think of himself first."

Taking notes rapidly, I turned the page of the tablet he had handed me, nodding my agreement with what he had just said. Those thoughts off his mind now, he leaned back in the chair and said, "All right, now let's look at these things objectively."

"First of all," he said, "I want to make one thing clear to you. You and I are the only two people who will ever believe that I won't know whether I'm going to do this or not until I get to the last line of my speech on the TelePrompTer." He looked out the window for a long moment. "These days," he said, "you never know what might happen somewhere in the world between now and tonight. I might not be able to do it even if I decide I want to." Then he assumed a crisp and direct, orderly manner.

"Point one." He held up one finger, still the classroom teacher, emphasizing his outline. "If I do this, the great question is, can I get my orders carried out?" I knew what he meant, but it came as a jolting thought. As he had done so many times since 1963, and most recently during the *Pueblo* crisis,[1] he was facing his old concern: could the commander in chief keep control of the forces he was supposed to direct? Now he expressed these thoughts explicitly. "If you have a lame-duck president sitting here, what's to keep some general from deciding he's going to have a little war of his

---

1. On January 23, 1968, North Korea captured the U.S. intelligence ship *Pueblo* off the coast of Wonsan. The humiliating loss of the vessel, viewed as a blow to the proud American naval tradition of not giving up the ship, created a crisis atmosphere in Washington and other Western capitals.—S.B.

own—with China or somebody else?" I wrote down his observations but made no attempt to reply.

Two fingers went up now. "Point two. Will this hurt or help in getting peace? Will Hanoi or Moscow or Peking—or Saigon for that matter—think we are collapsing over here?" He pursued this for a moment, then turned the question aside. "I suppose there's not really any way to know that answer in advance; it's just a risk you have to take.

"Point three—that's political." He leaned forward again; a brief smile crossed his face, but his eyes hardened. "They tell me it would cost about ten million dollars—can you imagine that, ten million dollars—for me to go through the primaries and win the nomination. The money is no problem. It seems to be coming in from everywhere. You wouldn't believe how this money works." His tone became confiding, and he leaned forward in his chair. "Let me tell you this, Buzz. When I came into this office, I didn't owe one sonofabitch in the United States anything. I wasn't obligated, I didn't have any big bunch of campaign contributors nudging me or trying to tell me what to do. That's the way a president ought to be, don't you agree?"

I readily agreed, nodding my head as I wrote. "If I go through with this and all this money comes in," he continued, "I'll never be a free man again. I don't know these people that the money comes from. They may be as honest as the day is long, or they may be crooks. With my luck, they will probably turn out to be crooks. But I'll tell you this: I don't want to know them. If a president has to spend ten million dollars to get the renomination of this party, then it's time for him and his party and everybody else to go some other way. I don't want to go that way."

Now he was leaning so far forward that he appeared about to leave his chair. "The biggest reason not to do it is just one thing." He almost hissed the words as he spoke. "I want out of this cage."

He swept his arms in all directions and pointed firmly out the window toward his office in the West Wing. "I've had a good life in Washington, a damned good life," he continued. "Anyone who came from where I came from and got even half this far ought to thank his God every night. I have no complaints." Now he punctuated his speech, slapping his palms together loudly. "But I don't want to spend the rest of my life with sixteen fellows, wearing big guns under their coats, following me everywhere I go. I don't want the whole damn world watching every time I move and listening every time I open my mouth. Sometime before I go, I want to be able to go down to that ranch and sit by that river and look out over the hills and be a human being."

He spoke with more passion than I had heard from him in a long time. But he straightened suddenly and sat back stiffly in his chair and looked at his watch. "Now," he said, "I would appreciate hearing your viewpoint on these matters."

I had not expected to be asked to say anything. But I looked down at the notes on my tablet and began to comment, point by point. First, under the climate developing in Washington, I thought that a withdrawal might actually help him in the matter of having his orders obeyed, not merely by the military but by the civil officers of government as well. "So many people are so convinced that you want power blindly that they are going to be doing all sorts of things to defy you," I said. "There will be more resignations and more talk of resignations every day." He nodded vigorous agreement. "This is confusing to the government and to the chain of command," I continued. "I know this action by you would surprise and stun many people, but I think it will permit them to see you in a new light and help to accomplish your objective."

He agreed again and interrupted to tell me he had talked with General William Westmoreland, commander of the U.S. forces in Vietnam, about the possible effect upon the troops in the field. "Westmoreland," he said, "thinks they'll take it all right."

I continued. The matter of the effect upon peace, I explained, seemed to me to be most compelling. Without the withdrawal statement, his order to stop the bombing would be regarded around the world, and certainly at home, as only a self-serving political gesture. It would be seen as an effort to affect the outcome in the Wisconsin primary on Tuesday, but when those returns came in negatively, the bombing halt itself would be discredited and dead as leverage for peace negotiations. Once again he agreed, even showing some enthusiasm. Time was running out, and I made only one more point.

"Everyone in the world thinks you would do anything to hang

on to power. That impression has colored the whole public reaction to your presidency. I personally feel that if you take this step it will help in the long term for people to see better all that you have accomplished in your administration."

"Yes," he said, "I think that's right. I think it is very compelling."

The president stood, indicating our talk had ended. The signals outside—the guards at the gate, the waiting automobile, the station wagon loaded with Secret Service—still meant that he must be departing. Yet until now there had been no specific assignment, no explanation for my summons.

As the president moved toward the elevator, he began to outline what he wanted. "I have promised Luci that I will go to church with her and Pat," he told me. "I rather like what you wrote in January better than what you wrote yesterday." This was his first direct reference to the earlier discussions. George Christian, he went on, had a copy of the first statement. "He has had it in his pocket every day since the State of the Union."

The president directed me to seclude myself in the Treaty Room on the family floor, call Christian, and have him read the January draft. "Then put together another draft," he said, "and I'll be back in about an hour and a half to read it." Then he added an admonition: "Don't call anyone other than George," he said. "Don't let a soul know you're over here."

At the elevator alcove I had one last question. "Mr. President," I said. "What do you think the chances are for going through with this?"

He stopped, rubbed his lips together, and looked for a long time down the dim corridor toward the Lincoln Bedroom, weighing the answer carefully. Then, as he liked to do, he posted the odds in percentages. "Eighty–twenty," he said, "against it."

The family floor had been vacant during the conversation. At least no one else was in sight. But I took no chance of encountering someone who might suspect my purposes and hurried to the Treaty Room, away from the living area. I drew up a chair to the long, rectangular conference table and pressed a button marked "Butler." I needed a larger tablet on which to write, but the White House staff also assumed I needed some coffee. The butler appeared with a handsome silver service and smiled wisely. "You've got a lot of work to do today," he said.

Shortly before eleven o'clock, ten hours before time for national broadcast, I telephoned George Christian. It was not easy to do. Until now, I had had no contact with anyone on the staff other than my unpromising conversation at midnight with Jim Jones. I had no idea what Christian's reactions would be, and I began the conversation hesitantly.

"I suppose you have some idea of why I am here at the White House."

"Yes," he replied noncommittally, "I have a general idea."

I recounted the chronology of the past twenty-four hours, making sure Christian understood that my labors were entirely at the president's initiative. My caution became conspicuous, and Christian finally began to laugh. "You don't have to defend yourself. You are among friends. I am for it, too."

George Christian had a chronology of his own to relate. Over the next few minutes I listened, with more relief than surprise, hearing for the first time a full account of the president's groping for a decision. It had been a longer struggle than I knew.

The previous October, during one of his quiet times alone in Texas, President Johnson first began thinking of his course. He called Christian to the ranch, reviewed his options, and tentatively mentioned the alternative of not seeking reelection. While he had not considered this possibility, Christian surprised himself—and, he thought, the president also—by agreeing immediately that this might be a desirable course. Encouraged, the president dispatched Christian to the Governor's Mansion in Austin to sound out John Connally.

The governor was weighing his own future. Before the end of the year, he had to decide whether he would seek reelection for a fourth term. The governor faced few of the problems besetting his mentor. Senator Ralph Yarborough's liberal Democratic partisans thoroughly detested Connally, brandishing the same epithets so often used against the president: "arrogant," "vain," "power hungry." Likewise the state's Republicans taunted him about his Johnson ties: a popular GOP bumper sticker played on this theme, translating the LBJ initials into "Lyndon's Boy John." For six years as governor, however, Connally had practiced the kind of tough-minded politics which he had so long advocated to Lyndon Johnson in vain. On small matters or large, he spurned compromise, yielding no quarter to his political enemies. Personable, supremely self-confident, savoring the images of power without apology, Connally held tighter political control over Texas than any other governor of recent years. Yet when Christian presented the president's options, Connally did not hesitate on his recommendation: relinquish the power.

Governor Connally and George Christian composed a suggested withdrawal statement. Mrs. Johnson read it and approved both the action and the statement. On visits to the ranch, Connally urged a prompt decision: whether it was to run again or to withdraw, the president should announce his choice before January; circumstances might overtake him once the election year began. But Lyndon Johnson hesitated. While the man wanted to announce his retirement, the president was bound by other considerations: the continuing war in Vietnam, increasingly well-organized protest at home, and political exploitation of dissent within his own party made it questionable whether he should or could yield the office of the presidency.

At Christmas, after his six-day journey around the world, the president once again closed himself off at the ranch, brooding over his choice. The trip, he thought, had been productive. Face-to-face conferences with Asian leaders at Prime Minister Harold Holt's funeral in Australia, meetings with American commanders in Vietnam, and a conversation with Pope Paul VI at the Vatican had reassured him on two points: first, he had delivered his warning about the "kamikaze" attack by the Vietcong which he "smelled coming," and now both Americans and their Asian allies would be ready if the attack came; second, he had "inched forward" toward new negotiating positions which might improve chances for the start of peace talks in 1968. If the likely attack could be absorbed and peace negotiations started, there would be no serious obstacles to his withdrawal.

Offsetting these positive results, however, was the deeply hurtful coverage of his mission in *Life* magazine. The account depicted his trip as unnecessary and overly spectacular, and it only confirmed the president's belief that, right or wrong, "they aren't going to let me win on anything." The criticism also led him to another conclusion: if he appeared to capitulate to his domestic critics, in the press or in politics, his position might cost him—and the nation—the chance to bring Hanoi to the peace table.

Pondering this dilemma, the president withdrew further over the holidays, saying little to indicate his thinking. When he had summoned me to the White House in January, upon his return from Texas, he had told no one of his decision to announce his withdrawal at the end of his State of the Union message to Congress.

Several hours before his annual visit to Capitol Hill, the president had shared with Mrs. Johnson the draft I had prepared. She took the copy to her hairdresser's appointment, read it over, and approved. But the president's intuitions held him back. Afterward he saw the humor of the family situation and spun out a story of the sort that appealed to his sense of high comedy. "I was up there reading, getting down to the end," he related to George Christian, "and I started feeling my pockets trying to find my little two-page statement; it wasn't in my inside pockets, it wasn't in my outside pockets, it wasn't in my ass pockets. I said to myself, 'This is a hell of a note. The President of the United States can't quit because his wife's got the papers in her purse.'"

Christian and I both laughed heartily but indulgently: we knew the man well enough to enjoy the characteristic story, poking fun at himself, but we knew him much too well to place credence in it. The president knew he could not withdraw that night. In Vietnam, the test still had not come, and there was still no movement toward the peace table. One week later, as John Connally had feared, events overtook the president's decision and appeared to bury it. After the *Pueblo* crisis and the Tet Offensive,[2] President Johnson could not consider such an announcement. Once March came, and the Vietnam situation stabilized, his interest revived.

---

2. On the night of January 31, 1968, an estimated seventy thousand North Vietnamese soldiers launched the Tet Offensive, violating the temporary truce they had pledged to observe around the lunar new year celebration, and attacked more than one hundred towns and cities, including Saigon. Caught off guard, American troops suffered heavy casualties. The offensive had a lasting effect on U.S. public opinion and has become widely viewed as the turning point in the war.—S.B.

He focused on the New Hampshire primary. President Harry S. Truman had announced his withdrawal at the end of March 1952, after being soundly trounced in the New Hampshire primary by his challenger, Senator Estes Kefauver of Tennessee. Sixteen years later the analogies were many: an unpopular war in Asia; widening protest both of American involvement and of restraints on the use of the nation's military power; increasing criticism of the draft; rising prices; soaring spending for defense while the needs of the nation's schools, welfare programs, highways, and cities went unsatisfied. But there was one major difference.

In Senator Eugene McCarthy, Lyndon Johnson faced what Washington regarded as a less than formidable opponent. The time to act would be right after the votes were counted. A decisive victory should refute criticism at home, and strengthen the president's hand for dealings with Hanoi. But the victory proved hollow: New Hampshire, a hawkish state, disturbed by the administration's continuing restraint after the *Pueblo* and Tet episodes, lashed out with a vote that gave Senator McCarthy new stature; and before the Minnesotan could return to Washington to receive his admiring welcome, Senator Robert Kennedy was taking the final step toward carrying out his long vendetta against Lyndon Johnson. In the face of these challenges, it did not appear that the president would be able to choose his own course; events had forced him to make—and, of course, to win—another race.

This was where the situation stood until Saturday, one day before the end of March. Politics, Christian related, had not been discussed during the intensive review of Vietnam policy; neither, he admitted, had the unfortunate political timing of the bombing halt announcement. When the decision—involving people from the State Department, Pentagon, National Security Council, and numerous elder statesmen whom the president drew into the deliberations—finally came together, there was only characteristic haste to arrange television time, draft a speech, and get the president before a national audience. On Saturday morning, with debates closed, conferences out of the way, and his bombing decision irrevocable, Lyndon Johnson once again was able to be alone with his private thoughts. No one at the White House, including George Christian, knew of the telephone call to me.

Late Saturday afternoon, a meeting began in the Cabinet Room. Secretary of State Dean Rusk, Secretary of Defense Clark Clifford, and his predecessor, Robert McNamara, along with key White House advisers, sat around the great table, "nit-picking"—the president's term—over the language of the Sunday night speech. A large brown envelope, marked "Personal," was handed to the president unopened. He read my new draft thoughtfully for several minutes, then slid it across the table to George Christian and winked. "That," he whispered, "may be the peroration."

The secret kept through the long drafting session. After dark, though, the president called together four assistants: Marvin Watson, who had taken over direction of campaign affairs; Jim Jones; Larry Temple; and Christian. As I had surmised after my midnight call from Jones, they met in the small, crowded anteroom off the Oval Office, and the president read the draft aloud. When I asked about the reaction, Christian laughed. "Larry wasn't too surprised, but Marvin and Jim went up in smoke."

As Christian related the long account, the pieces were fitting together in my mind. On that Saturday back in December, as *Air Force One* flew into the darkness over Iran, the president's question to me—"What would you do next year?"—was part of the typical polling operation. He knew already how Governor Connally, George Christian, and perhaps others felt; he had long known Mrs. Johnson's views. When I gave him my two-word answer—"Not run"—another piece locked into place; if he decided to withdraw, I could be called upon to write his public statement and he could preserve the essential secrecy about his intentions until the very last.

On this Sunday, though, he had begun to share the secret, and sides were forming in the palace guard. The common denominator struck me: those he consulted who had been most involved with politics and campaigns and the life of power at other levels as well as at the White House—Mrs. Johnson, Governor Connally, Christian, myself, and perhaps Larry Temple, until recently an assistant to Connally—were quick to accept and encourage his relinquishment of power; those whose experience centered mainly on Lyndon Johnson's White House, however, were taking the contrary view.

What were the chances, I asked Christian, for the announcement to be made? "Not good," he replied after a moment. "If word gets out to the cabinet, or even around more of the staff, I don't think he'll be able to do it."

"Maybe they're right and we're wrong," I suggested.

"It could be," Christian replied thoughtfully, "but I agree with what you said about him. He's done all he came here wanting to do, and if he has four more years, they're not going to let him do anything more."

Christian had other thoughts, though, and he continued. "But there's the country and the office to think of, too. If he has to fight it out with Bobby, the media, and all the rest, this country's going to be coming apart at the seams by November, and the office is going to suffer. And there's another thing that's not easy to talk about." He hesitated, seemingly reluctant to continue, but then he disclosed what gnawed at his mind. "I read the Secret Service reports and talk with their agents all the time. Buzz, there's no doubt about it: if the man makes the race, somebody's going to pick him off. They won't just try, they'll do it any way that's necessary. Bombs. Airplanes. Collisions. Anything. There are some wild people loose right now. Now, for God's sake, don't say a word to him about this. He knows all about it, but you know him, he'd just announce for reelection tonight.

"But," Christian went on solemnly, "like I say, you've got to think of the country. Two presidents in five years? I'm afraid the people couldn't take that."

Since leaving the White House, I had been little exposed to this kind of talk, so constantly on the minds of those who must go with presidents when they leave the relative security of 1600 Pennsylvania Avenue. It was ugly and jolting, all the more because it came from the calmest and least excitable member of the president's staff. I changed the subject.

"It's getting late," I suggested. "You'd better read me the January draft."

He had it in hand. I listened carefully and tried for a few moments to transcribe my earlier words. But Christian and I reached the same conclusion at the same time.

"You aren't going to use this," he said. "Why don't you just start fresh?"

The conversation came to an end. Before he left the telephone, however, George Christian had an admonition.

"I don't want to tell you how to run your business," he said, "and I know you are going to get god-awful tired staying up there by yourself. But I want to make this suggestion. I think it would be well-advised for you to stay put all day. Don't leave the second floor. You might not get back up there," he explained, then added with a laugh, "or somebody else might get in."

— 17 —

THE NINTH HOUR

Twelve o'clock, noon. Nine hours remained. I was writing on the last page of the draft when President Johnson came through the door. His spirits were unaccountably high. "Well, Judge"—he laughed, having conferred one of his friendlier titles on me—"how much do we have finished? One sentence or two?"

This was a standing joke between us. On most speeches I wrote slowly or, to be exact, rewrote again and again, often completing the text only minutes before it was to be read. Once, in fact, Lyndon Johnson began reading a speech to the Senate before I had completed the last pages. Needless to say, the practice was a source of monumental irritation. But when I handed over four pages of manuscript, much more than he had expected, the president threw up his hands. "Damn," he exclaimed. "You must really want to get me out of town."

He laid the pages side by side on the historic table in the center of the room, then stood over them reading. When he began jingling coins in his pocket, I took it as an indication that he must be relatively pleased. I continued writing hurriedly, and after he had completed the other pages, he stood looking over my shoulder as I finished the final lines.

"Good," he said when I wrote the last sentence. "This reads much better."

He clapped my shoulder and laughed heartily. "You may make it as a speechwriter yet." With that he gathered the pages, tapped them on the table until they were neatly in place, and departed, still offering no significant comments.

A quarter hour later the president returned. He sat in a chair near mine, placing one long leg across another chair, and looked squarely at me. I was astonished by his appearance.

The Lyndon Johnson I knew had always been a man of many faces, each accurately reflecting the mood stirring within. At the start of the morning, his face was firm, intent, bent on decision. When he had returned to the Treaty Room a few minutes before, he'd shown what might have been a mask: while he smiled and laughed, his eyes were evasive. But now his long face sagged: the firmness was gone, a deep melancholy filled his eyes, and he seemed impossibly tired.

"I went to see the vice president after church," he said quietly. "It got to him, I guess." The president ran a finger from each eye down his cheeks. I knew Vice President Hubert Humphrey to be an emotional man who seldom concealed his inner feelings. The president's gesture meant that tears had come when the vice president learned of the decision being contemplated.

I smiled understandingly, but the president did not. "He says he wishes I wouldn't do it, but that it's my decision."

He fell silent, staring awhile out the window and shuffling the pages of the statement, brooding over some thought he had brought from his meeting with Humphrey.

When he faced me again, the look in his eyes was that of a man trapped. "Humphrey says he can't take that fellow," he explained. "Two weeks, maybe three weeks, the other fellow will have it all sewed up. Humphrey doesn't know whether he even wants to try."

I winced. Until now, there had been no mention of Senator Robert Kennedy. But Hubert Humphrey had raised the one issue I most feared would enter the discussion: that the president could not withdraw because only he had the strength to keep the Democratic Party nomination from Senator Kennedy. The presidency already was battered and injured by just this level of fighting over it; it would not be true to Lyndon Johnson's devotion to the office to decide his personal course on such a basis. But I did not agree with the vice president's analysis of his own strength, and I decided to speak my piece.

"Mr. President," I said, "I disagree with Humphrey's view. Sure, Bobby will probably win all the primaries after Wisconsin, whether you are in or out. If you got out, though, there would be a flood running for Humphrey all across the country. People don't realize here in Washington that Bobby scares people. They don't understand him, they're not sure of him, and they're not going to let him have it, at least not this year." Humphrey, I suggested, was still intimidated by memories of the West Virginia primary in 1960, when Kennedy money and manpower—directed by Bobby on behalf of his brother Jack—had so crushed the Minnesotan. Now the situation was very different. "In two weeks," I argued, "Humphrey will have more money and more support than he ever thought possible because he'll be the man to stop Kennedy."

The president pondered this for a while. "Maybe there's something to that," he replied, but he did not seem persuaded. He stood and looked out the window, across the South Grounds toward the Washington Monument. Then he began walking around the room, eyes on the ceiling, saying nothing. After ten minutes or perhaps longer, he returned and sat at the table, reading the speech draft again.

When the president took a pen from his coat pocket and appeared ready to edit, I felt compelled to speak. Over recent years the White House style had been reduced to ten-word, staccato sentences. In composing the draft hastily during the morning, I had reverted to Lyndon Johnson's older style of longer, free-flowing sentences, and I mentioned this to him apologetically. "Oh, that's fine with me," he said. "You use lots of commas."

One phrase, however, received the president's special attention. In the climactic sentence of the announcement, I had written, "I shall not seek and will not accept the nomination of my party." The president used his pen to strike out the word "will."

"No sir," he said. "I won't say that. It's too presumptuous. They haven't offered me any nomination yet." He changed it to read "I would not accept."

I protested mildly. The sentence must be firm and unequivocal, with no ambiguities. Grammar aside, the use of "would" struck me as inviting questions, doubts, and possibly debate about the firmness of his intention. "The press," I reminded him, "will nitpick every word in that sentence, looking for an escape clause."

"Well, let 'em, dammit, let 'em," the president snapped. "I am still not going to reject something that hasn't been offered to me and that's final."

His editing complete, he folded the speech, stuffed it in his pocket, and started out of the room. But he stopped at the door and took the draft from his pocket again. "Here," he said. "You'd better keep this. I'm going over to the West Wing for a while and it might fall out of my pocket." His manner loosened again, and he winked. "I don't want this falling into the hands of the enemy," he said, and laughed.

Once again I found myself alone on the family floor of the White House. There were no voices, no doors opening and closing, no coming and going, only silence. My work, of course, seemed to be done. Although the president's decision had not yet been made, I did not anticipate more writing during the eight hours that now remained before his broadcast. Neither did I anticipate with any enthusiasm passing those hours concealing myself in the Treaty Room. For a while I occupied the minutes making notes of the day's conversations, but this became tiresome. I began to pace the floor, considering an excursion to the West Wing in search of company and conversation with my friends on the staff. But I remembered George Christian's admonition and decided that I should not leave the floor. Instead, I ventured no farther from my post in the Treaty Room than the room adjacent to the east, the Lincoln Bedroom.

All presidents since John Adams have resided at the White House, but the abiding presence within the family quarters is Abraham Lincoln. The structure itself is new—walls, floors, ceilings, were rebuilt during the Truman administration to prevent the imminent collapse of the elegant old mansion—but that is only a detail. The White House is Lincoln's home, and his spirit seems to hover on the second floor.

Nowhere is that presence more pervasive than in the bedroom that bears his name. A simple room, still furnished much as it was during his residence, the Lincoln Bedroom exerts a compelling influence on its visitors. Often when the Johnsons asked members of the staff to show visitors through the family quarters, it was striking how hushed and almost reverent guests became when they entered this room. The mystique of the presidency was nowhere so strong and real as in nearness to the president who had preserved the Union.

On occasion, the thirty-sixth President of the Union delighted in offering the room overnight to his most special guests. Early in his presidency, in fact, such an arrangement brought Lyndon Johnson one of his most gratifying moments. During the 1930s, the best-known and most controversial figure on the University of Texas campus at Austin was J. Frank Dobie. His many books · had won him national and international distinction as one of the West's great folklorists; in Texas, however, Professor Dobie was best known as a sharp-tongued, plainspoken Roosevelt liberal, given to freewheeling criticisms of the statehouse establishment. Very nearly the only Texas political figure who won J. Frank Dobie's approval and enthusiasm was the young Tenth District congressman, Lyndon Johnson. Even before World War II, Dobie told campus audiences that "Lyndon ought to be our president someday." When that came to pass, Lyndon Johnson did not forget.

Although "Pancho," as Dobie was affectionately known, had been retired almost twenty years, he remained alert and active, eyes twinkling beneath his white hair. The president ascertained through Mrs. Dobie that her husband was equal to a trip to Washington and a night at the White House. Late into the evening, the president sat listening to his guest; Dobie was a master storyteller, and he enthralled his audience that night. When it came time for the old man to retire, the president led him down the center hall and invited him to sleep in the Lincoln Bedroom.

Early the next morning, when the butler brought the president's coffee, J. Frank Dobie followed in through the door, still wearing his pajamas. The old man's eyes plainly showed he had not slept. "Mr. President," he called out emotionally, "I have been up all night. In there in that room, I couldn't sleep, I couldn't shut my eyes, I couldn't even lie down. I kept thinking where I was, and the spirit of the man was right in there with me."

The two men had their breakfast together. Subsequently, the president bestowed upon his old friend the Presidential Medal of Freedom, honoring his long career as folklorist of the West. When the Dobies returned to Austin, the old man entered the hospital, and in a matter of days his long and rich career came to an end. Mrs. Dobie assured the president that "the biggest thrill and deepest pleasure of Frank's life was the night in the Lincoln Bedroom."

While I walked about the room, studying the memorabilia, a butler entered and stood at the door waiting until I turned and saw him there.

"Mr. Busby," he said, "the First Lady wonders if you would care to join the family for lunch."

I followed him down the corridor toward the West Hall and turned in to the small family dining room overlooking Pennsylvania Avenue and Lafayette Square. The room was bright, fresh, and alive with the afternoon sun, and I slipped quietly into the chair which waited for me. Only after I had been present for several minutes did I realize that the atmosphere was electric.

Five others were present besides the president and the First Lady: Luci and her husband, Pat; Arthur Krim and his wife, Mathilde; and the president's secretary, Marie Fehmer. Over the next three quarters of an hour, who said what did not greatly matter, and I considered the conversations to be entirely private. But the flow of emotions and feelings mattered greatly to the course of the day.

On other Sundays since February, it developed, the president had apparently talked of announcing his withdrawal from politics. The conversations had not been taken seriously. On this last day of March, however, the matter was entirely different. Lyndon Johnson still had not revealed the decision he was considering, at least not the seriousness with which he was pursuing it; but his manner and the fact that he would be facing a television audience in only seven hours clearly suggested what might be on his mind. When my presence on the floor was disclosed—the president himself revealed it by suggesting I be invited to lunch—that added an entirely new dimension. I could be there for only one purpose, and this realization was just registering clearly when I entered the room.

Almost immediately the protests began. No one addressed the president directly; that somehow seemed improper and forbidden. The comments, instead, were directed at me. Hesitantly at first, and then with more force than I intended, I began to answer. Again and again, I cut my responses short. It was not my place to be speaking about this decision in the presence of the president. Each time, though, the president nodded his agreement with my response.

The intensity of the objections—and the electricity of the room—mounted. I tried not to answer. The president looked up from his plate and asked, "What about that, Buzz?" When I spoke, no one seemed to be listening more closely than Lyndon Johnson. The heat of the exchanges grew, and I wanted to leave, but the president left instead. He abruptly rose from his chair and stepped into the hall, allowing the conversation to rise and slowly fall before he returned.

Worlds were suddenly spinning, crazily and dizzyingly, on this Sunday afternoon, and the group grasped for what seemed steadying: delay. That was what he must do: the president must delay, think this over more carefully, discuss it more fully, give all those who would be affected some opportunity to be heard. The president pushed back his chair and left the room again. I felt that he must know that, if he delayed beyond today, the decision would never be his to make.

Food remained on the plates, barely touched. No one present cared about a meal. The waiters removed the main course and the salads, and brought the Sunday dessert. Once more the president returned, eating his own low-calorie pudding. Still he did not choose to speak. Abruptly the room was silent. Seven persons bent over their plates eating now and carefully avoiding any glance right or left. It was as memorable a moment as I had experienced inside the White House, and I came very near to praying for some chance to escape.

The president answered my wishes. When he finished his dessert, he rose and moved quickly toward the door. "Come on, Buzz," he said, "I need to see you for a minute." I was at his side in an instant.

He did not speak again until we were in his bedroom and the door had closed behind us. "Did any of that," he asked, "swerve you any?"

I started to present a discreet reply but then stopped and answered honestly, "No, sir, I still feel the same."

He grinned approvingly. "I thought you did rather well," he said. "In fact," he added, still parceling out his classroom grades, "I think you made an A minus, or maybe an A."

We stood together just inside the door, listening while voices passed in the center hall outside. When all was silent once more, he hurried to the elevator and departed. I returned once more to the quiet of the Treaty Room.

Now it was nearing three o'clock. The broadcast was six hours away. Still no decision had been firmly made.

I realized that I still had the draft of the announcement in my pocket. Since tossing it to me at one o'clock, the president had shown no further interest in the words. I sat down at the table again and began to read it. Almost immediately an old habit took hold. I set out to write the text anew.

Until now, I had been generally following the outline which the president had presented on that Sunday afternoon in January when I sat alone with him in his White House bedroom. The ideas were his, but the words were mine. I did not want it this way. Under the emotion of the encounter in the dining room, perhaps, I began to write once more, this time summoning up words and phrases from the president's own career—the words and phrases which were his own. I could not, of course, ask for reference volumes or call to the West Wing to check my memory with those of others on the staff. Out of my own long years in Lyndon Johnson's company, though, I reconstructed many of the thoughts—and many of the phrases—which he liked best.

When the president reappeared, I had the new draft ready.

He entered the room laughing to himself. "You better never go near the West Wing again," he said in good humor. "They're all against you, Buzz, all against you."

I knew he must only have been testing more reactions, still deliberating, still wanting to know what others thought before he decided finally what he thought. But I did not reply directly. I slid the new draft across the table toward him and offered no explanation. He began reading while still standing, but then it registered that the words were new and he settled into a chair. A smile formed on his lips, and his face began to beam. He looked up at me as if announcing an original discovery.

"Why," he said with amazement, "this is me."

Still holding the draft to complete his reading, he turned away from the table and bolted from the room. I heard the door close and the elevator descend. The president was on his way again to his office in the West Wing.

Almost immediately after the president's departure, I heard doors open and close in the corridor. I thought nothing of it at the moment. Several minutes later, however, the hall began to echo with a sound I never expected to hear in the White House: loud, pained sobs coming, I knew, from Lynda.

As the president had told me at the start of the day, Lynda had returned around five that morning from California. There, on the previous day, she had told her new husband, Major Charles Robb, good-bye as he departed with his Marine comrades for Vietnam. During the morning and through the lunch, Lynda had been sleeping in her bedroom, across the center hall from where I sat. Now, apparently, she had awakened and learned from her sister or her mother what her father was considering.

The wails came down the corridor toward where I waited. Remembering my experience in January, when Lynda and her husband had sought me out in this same room to discuss the State of the Union text, I thought she must be coming again to confront me about this stunning development. I steeled for an encounter which I did not know whether I could endure. Then a door slammed across the hall and silence returned.

I stayed very carefully out of sight for the next half hour.

The elevator stopped at the family floor again and the door opened. Once more the president entered the Treaty Room, this time accompanied by Marie Fehmer. He went over the draft again, making a few minor changes, and told me to get it into shape. "Marie is going to type it for me," he explained, and left the room.

Marie Fehmer sat in the chair beside me while I completed the task. She said nothing, but by her silence she could not have said more. I felt the chill and tried to make conversation.

"What do you think about it?" I asked.

"I'll type it," she replied.

"Are you for it?"

Marie took the copy from my hand and stood; then she answered firmly and coolly, "I am not," and left the room.

I needed some support by now. With four o'clock approaching and the speech only five hours away, I knew nothing of what had been happening in the West Wing or elsewhere on this long day. I asked the operator to locate George Christian.

Since early afternoon, Christian had been at his desk in the White House press office. Most of the special assistants were on duty, along with their assistants and secretaries. Over the last two hours, however, tensions had begun to grow.

On his frequent visits to the West Wing, the president's interest still focused on the main text, reviewing the situation in Vietnam; the speech remained too long in the president's judgment, and he was exhorting the staff both to shorten it and to enliven it. "The country," he repeated, "will be asleep before I get to the end." But suspicions were spreading that the president must be holding back, keeping some secret about the night. In their offices, Marvin Watson and Jim Jones were too visibly unhappy, Larry Temple and George Christian too guarded; something must be afoot, and those not yet privy to the president's thoughts were increasingly perturbed. "It's getting sticky," Christian reported with a mirthless laugh.

What, I asked, was the state of the president's thinking? Christian had no sure clues. A short while earlier, he reported, the president had asked him to call Governor Connally in Texas. "He wanted to know how John felt now," Christian explained, "but he did not commit himself." The governor's response had been blunt. "Tonight is better than tomorrow night," he had said, "and last night would have been better than tonight, because time is running out."

I was curious about one detail. Why had the president not telephoned John Connally himself? Christian laughed heartily. "Haven't you heard?" he asked. "Everything's normal between them—they're not speaking these days."

The point at issue between them did not surprise me. On March 22, after Senator Robert Kennedy's entry into the fight for the nomination, Lyndon Johnson had stunned and riled many of his associates and political friends by appointing the Kennedy brother-in-law Sargent Shriver as his ambassador to France. Shriver had served the president well as director of the Office of Economic Opportunity; of course, the president had never forgotten the first days of his administration, when Shriver had interceded, at some cost to himself, trying to placate Bobby Kennedy's hostility to Lyndon Johnson; nonetheless, among old Johnson friends, the gesture carried to new lengths the president's all too familiar philosophy of "Reward your enemies first." Although no overt break had occurred between Connally and the president, Lyndon Johnson knew how strongly his prize protégé felt about such matters and did not want to speak to him directly. George Christian, who had worked for both men and understood their temperaments, was serving as a bridge across a widening gap.

As our conversation ended, Christian once again urged me not to leave the family floor of the White House. "Stay put," he asked. "This thing may get right down to the last hour, and then somebody will walk in and try to change the president's mind."

Did that mean, I asked quickly, that the decision had been settled? No, Christian answered, but he thought the chances stood at "fifty-fifty." Since morning, the odds had improved, but the decisive hours still remained.

After the telephone conversation, I sat at the Treaty Room table, idling away the time. Unexpectedly Mrs. Johnson appeared in the doorway. "Mr. Buzz," she said, in her typical greeting, "our friend wants to see you in the bedroom."

The president lay on his bed beneath the covers. On afternoons before major television appearances, naps were prescribed to remove the tensions and tiredness from the presidential face, which 100 million Americans would be watching intently on their television screens. The bedroom lamps were out and curtains drawn, but the president had other things on his mind before he slept.

At five o'clock, he told me, Soviet Ambassador Anatoly Dobrynin would be coming to the White House. At that time the president intended to advise the ambassador of the bombing halt announcement so that the information could be relayed to Moscow in advance of the television speech. It was vital, the president emphasized, for the Kremlin to understand that this was a sincere effort to secure the start of peace negotiations with Hanoi; it was no less essential, he felt, that Moscow's leaders understand this decision had not been forced upon the president by the peace demonstrations or the war critics in the Senate. His meeting with Ambassador Dobrynin, he thought, would be "the most important thing I've done today."

But a new question had arisen about the president's personal political decision. While Mrs. Johnson stood behind me, in the rear of the darkened room, the president explained. "It has been suggested," he said, "that I should delay my announcement until later in the week." On Thursday night, he was scheduled to address an election-year fund-raising dinner for House and Senate Democrats; all the members of his party in Congress would be present for the occasion, and television time could be arranged to assure a national audience. "The thinking is," the president continued, "that such a context would be more appropriate if I am going to say anything about my political plans."

This was a complete surprise. Until now nothing had been mentioned about the Thursday night affair or the president's appearance there. Uncertain where this suggestion had originated, I hesitated to respond. The president read my thoughts. "It's my decision," he said. "Just give me your thoughts about the forums."

On this point the answer seemed obvious. If he made his announcement at the dinner, network television cameras were certain to focus on audience reaction; that meant the nation would witness not only the response of the president's supporters but also the applause of his principal political critics—Senator J. William Fulbright, Senator Wayne Morse, and of course, Senator Robert Kennedy. Such scenes, I suggested, might leave the impression that he was "capitulating" to opponents of his policy. Furthermore, whatever the impression at home, the appearance of a party leader abandoning power before his critics "would not be helpful with Hanoi."

The president's face remained impassive, and his comment revealed nothing. "Yes," he said, "I think that is to be considered."

Mrs. Johnson turned and left the room, and I followed her through the door as the president prepared for his short rest.

The Treaty Room, where I resumed my vigil, adjoins the lovely Yellow Oval Room at the center of the White House. Once called simply the "Ladies' Sitting Room," this broad and bright room has acquired a more formal purpose in modern times. Here presidents receive foreign heads of state and important diplomats amid a setting of Louis XVI furnishings, Cézanne paintings, and the capital's most majestic view: the handsome vista of the Washington Monument, the Tidal Basin, and the Jefferson Memorial in the distance. More than in any other of the family floor's rooms, the dignity and stature of the office of the presidency pervades the Yellow Oval Room and impresses itself upon all who enter.

At five-fifteen, I heard voices in the Yellow Oval Room. Words were not distinguishable, but I recognized the speech of Ambassador Dobrynin and the president's special assistant for national security affairs, Walt Rostow. In the usual fashion of diplomacy, the two men talked pleasantly, laughing frequently and admiring the view. Rostow, of course, was loyally occupying the time entertaining the visitor until the president could dress and join them.

The president entered at five-thirty. His greeting was cordial and strong, and immediately he began to read the announcement he would make three and a half hours later disclosing the historic change in American policy in Vietnam. The level of the voices fell, and the speech was muffled by the walls, but in his usual style, Lyndon Johnson was speaking firmly and earnestly, pressing his case.

There could be no failure now. In just over three hours, the president would take upon himself the responsibility of turning the policy of one of the world's great powers. This moment had a meaning unlike any others of this long Sunday on the family floor at 1600 Pennsylvania Avenue.

For the first time on this last day of March, the White House was the White House again and the president was the president. Feelings of family and friends, attitudes of staff and associates, implications of politics and elections—all those concerns which had been swirling around Lyndon Johnson the man—were of no consequence now. If the bombing halt was to have credence, if it was to be understood in the capitals of America's adversaries as well as those of America's allies, if it was to be productive in moving the world toward peace, then the president must succeed in conveying his meaning to the man who sat before him now, the ambassador from the Soviet Union. Yet one question overhung the conversation.

What would be the effect on world understanding of this last earnest effort for peace if, after the president spoke tonight, his own countrymen dismissed the public words as only an attempt by Lyndon Johnson to influence for his own benefit a political primary in this American election year? If the president was not to be misunderstood abroad, he must first be fully understood at home.

The thoughts were mine, but I had spent twenty years learning such thoughts about the office of the presidency from the man who now occupied it. I felt certain that they must be very much in his mind as he filled the presidency on his mission in the next room. I was anxious to see what his attitude might be when he emerged from the conference with Ambassador Dobrynin.

Twilight began to dim the afternoon as the conversation continued in the Gold Room and the clock moved toward six. That hour had a particular significance. For his television appearances, the president read his text from a moving roll of paper fed through a device known as a TelePrompTer. This permitted him to face the cameras directly without lowering his face and eyes to read from a manuscript on his desk. Typing the text on the long, continuous roll of TelePrompTer paper, however, was a cumbersome process, performed by an enlisted man assigned to the White House Communications Agency. For this task to be completed before the nine o'clock broadcast, the TelePrompTer crew had to receive the final text at six o'clock.

At the start of the morning, during his first talk with me, the president had referred to the TelePrompTer. Only the two of us, he said, could believe that he would not know until he reached the last line of his regular text on the TelePrompTer roll whether he would go ahead with the statement announcing his withdrawal. I still believed that. But the question was about to become academic. Unless some version of the withdrawal statement soon reached the TelePrompTer crew, there would be no additional text for the president to read when he reached the end of his message about Vietnam. Although he could, of course, simply read from a typewritten manuscript on his desk, that went against his nature: it would appear untidy and ill-considered, and he was unlikely to present any statement under such circumstances. If there was to be a withdrawal statement ready for his use, some decision had to be made at six o'clock.

The president and Ambassador Dobrynin ended their conversation at ten minutes before the hour. After a parting exchange in the center hall, the ambassador hurried away to transmit what he had just learned to Moscow, and the president retired to his bedroom.

Voices were drifting down the hallway from the family sitting room. Evidently guests were arriving and probably members of the staff. I did not know who might be present, however, and I remained carefully out of sight in the Treaty Room.

At precisely six o'clock I heard a familiar voice call out loudly. "All right, everybody, be quiet for a minute and listen to this." Then the president began to read aloud: "Finally, my fellow Americans, let me say this." These were the opening words of his withdrawal statement.

I moved to the doorway to listen more closely, but his voice boomed out: "Buzz, if you're down there, come here."

The president stood beside Sergeant Glynn's small desk, holding the draft announcement of his political future in one hand while he waved family and guests closer with the other. When I arrived at the circle, he hastily explained: "Some idiot's been editing my words, and we've got to straighten out some things." Then he began to read the full text to the assembled group.

For all those present other than myself, it was the first hearing of the proposed statement. Faces were taut, and emotional tears began welling up in several eyes. But the president himself seemed to be a changed man. As he had been at the start of the morning, he was "organized"—composed, poised, and confident—speaking with unusual authority. He was the president again. He did not seem to see any of those standing before him. At intervals he marked his words by raising a finger, pointing at me, and saying, "Question," then continuing without interruption. I took this to mean that he was noting the places where others had made editing suggestions that he wanted to question.

When the president concluded, there was a sort of gasp from the group, then a shocked silence. The vague possibility was suddenly becoming real and tangible and near. The president disregarded the reaction, quickly turning his back and motioning me to the desk to go over the text with him.

At one point early in the statement, I had included what I thought to be one of the most eloquent passages from President Kennedy's inaugural address in 1961. The full sentence read: "Yet, I believe that now, no less than when the decade began, this genera-tion of Americans is willing to"—and here the Kennedy quotation began—"'pay any price, bear any burden, meet any hardship, support any friend, oppose any foe to assure the survival and success of liberty.'" I could repeat the line from memory, but I had included it only after finding the words used in one of the earlier versions of the principal text for the night. Now the president questioned it.

"Abe Fortas," he said, referring to his longtime friend now on the Supreme Court, "cut that out yesterday. He said that when Bobby's running against us, we shouldn't dignify him by quoting his brother. What's your judgment?"

I differed with Fortas. Robert Kennedy's activities should not intrude on the president's respect for John F. Kennedy. If he liked the quotation, I thought he should use it. The president erased his question mark beside the sentence. "I sure as hell like the quote," he said, "and that's the way I feel too."

At another point in the text, I realized when I heard it read aloud that I had made a mistake. Counting the months and days back to November 22, 1963, I had incorrectly placed the total at "forty-nine months and ten days ago." I recognized that this, of course, was wrong. "I'm glad you caught that," the president said, "but how long have I been in this place?" Together, each of us using a pencil, we carefully recalculated and revised the text to read: "Fifty-two months and ten days ago." The president looked up, bemused. "Fifty-two months," he said. "That sounds like fifty years."

The next sentence drew his special wrath. Alluding to the start of his administration, I had written: "I asked then for your help and God's"—a reference to his first words on the night of November 22, 1963—"that we might continue America on its course"—a refrain from his first address to Congress as president—"binding up our wounds, healing our history"—words drawn from his many civil rights speeches—"moving forward in new unity, to clear the American agenda and to keep the American commitment for all of our people." The phrase "to clear the American agenda" had been deleted. Indignantly the president pointed his pencil at the offending editor's marks and leaned close to me, keeping his voice low so others would not overhear. "Some sonofabitch cut out the guts," he said. " 'Clearing the agenda'—why, that's been our main work, that's what we've been doing for all those fifty-two months and however many days—put it back in." I restored the phrase to the text.

One more question remained. The climactic sentence still read as the president had dictated it at noon: "Accordingly, I shall not seek, and I would not accept, the nomination of my party for another term as your president."

"Mr. President," I began, "I hate to bring it up—"

"But what?" he snapped. Then, seeing my pencil resting on the sentence, he remembered my earlier protest. "All right, all right," he said. "I guess you've earned something—change it to 'will not accept.'"

He raised up and handed the manuscript toward Jim Jones, who stood nearby. But he drew it back quickly and began searching through the words again.

"Somewhere in here," he said, "you have me saying I won't give an hour of my time to 'any partisan causes.'" I quickly found the place. "We better change that," he said, "to read 'any personal partisan causes.'" Then he smiled for the first time. "Unless you put that in"—he grinned—"I might not be able to go out and help Humphrey beat Nixon this fall."

The editing was complete, although the president still had not declared his final decision about using it. Appearing to relax, he turned and looked toward his family and friends, smiling happily. While the president and I had worked over the draft, however, the family and guests assembling on the second floor had moved on to the end of the hall; now they stood in a small cluster, grim faced and tense, whispering among themselves. The smile left the president's face.

"I think I'd better go over to the office," he announced, disappearing into the elevator.

I reacted to the gathering at the end of the corridor as the president had done. The group was becoming formidable. Recovering from the first shock of hearing the president's words, the members were beginning to raise their voices and pound fists together with sudden determination. I retreated to the seclusion of the Treaty Room.

Two and half hours remained before the television speech was to begin. Outward evidence of the decision meant nothing. Almost certainly during this time the president would begin calling key friends and associates, advising them of the decision under consideration and soliciting their reactions. Inevitably each reaction would be negative, and any one of the comments could be decisive in persuading him to delay. If the president did not resort to the telephone, however, there still was the likelihood of others intervening with him in these last hours. Someone—one of the staff in the West Wing, one of the guests in the center hall, perhaps even one of the family—would very likely be drawing in a cabinet officer, or someone of comparable stature, to make a last-minute appeal against the withdrawal course. As George Christian had suggested earlier, the last hour would be the most decisive of the day.

Time never moved more slowly as the clock crawled past seven, then seven-thirty, and on to seven-forty-five. Voices were rising in the hall outside the Treaty Room; doors opened and closed; several times the elevator ascended to the floor to discharge a passenger. But I stayed out of sight. My presence, I felt, could only be provocative, as it had been at lunch, and I wanted to say nothing more.

I had heard the president return about seven-thirty. Before television appearances, he usually had his hair trimmed, and the barber was waiting in the bedroom. But I could hear him speaking in the hallway occasionally, and I finally left my sanctuary to join the gathering. It was a mistake.

In the family sitting room area, Luci Nugent had taken command of the gathering. This year she would be old enough to vote for the first time. "If this happens," she said of the withdrawal announcement, "I'll never have a chance to vote for Daddy." While her mother watched, silent and anxious, Luci went from person to person, exhorting each of them to "do something." She soon saw me sitting in the corner trying to remain inconspicuous. Leveling her finger at me from across the room, Luci approached, speaking with what was for her a very unnatural fierceness. "Mr. Busby," she demanded, "why? Tell me why."

I waited for her further question as others approached to listen.

"Mr. Busby," she said, speaking evenly for a moment, "every person on this floor loves my father—they like him, admire him, understand him, or they wouldn't be here. That includes you. But why is it that out of all the people here you are the only one who wants him to give up this office?"

The silence seemed thunderous as the group awaited my answer. I wanted to deny what Luci had said. No one else, only her father, was making this decision; I was there at his request. But such clarification did not seem relevant. "Maybe," I said rather lamely, "it's because I'm the only one here who's not here all the time."

The answer was opaque, and Luci turned away, still searching for support and assistance. She settled on the president's friend Arthur Krim. As Luci began imploring him to intercede, the others gathered around, supporting her entreaties. When Krim anxiously protested that it was not his "place" to speak to the president on this decision, voices rose: he must speak. He must persuade the president to delay, to think this over, to get the opinions of others. Krim held back, but he was clearly outmanned and overmatched.

At this point the elevator doors opened unexpectedly. Marvin Watson emerged. Until now I had not seen or talked with Watson, but I knew the significance of his arrival. Although still relatively new to the president's service, Watson had won a special place in Lyndon Johnson's esteem: no one in the White House was more trusted and, I knew, no one in the White House was more opposed to withdrawal.

Watson saw me sitting a few feet away from the door to the president's bedroom. He paused and spoke with unaccustomed formality. "I see you have had a very good day." Then he entered the bedroom.

I knew what this meant. Marvin Watson would express himself clearly and unmistakably, but also with faultless propriety. Deeply opposed as he was to this course, Watson respected both the presidency and the president too much to press any views of his own; that was why he held Lyndon Johnson's extraordinary trust. Since morning, I had had more than my share of time alone with the president; Marvin Watson deserved time alone now. I made no move to follow.

I waited for the elevator door to open again. In a few minutes it did, and Walt Rostow emerged, accompanied by his wife, Elspeth. Mrs. Johnson earlier had invited them to the mansion to watch the television speech with her, but Walt's broad smile told me that he probably knew nothing of the developing decision.

It was 8:20 now, and Arthur Krim hurried past on his way to the president's presence. After what seemed hardly a minute, he returned. I stopped him before he could speak to the others. "He says," Krim reported, "that the decision has been made."

— 18 —

THE CLOSE

The thirty-first of March 1968 was a day of history. It was one of those very rare days, perhaps no more than five or ten in a generation, which all Americans share together and do not soon forget. What the people saw on their television screens that Sunday night would live long after in their minds and memories.

Since 1960, Americans had witnessed the removal of three presidents from the nation's highest office: one, the oldest of the chief executives, was removed by the orderly workings of the Constitution's limits upon presidential terms; another, the youngest man to lead the nation, was removed by the violence of an assassin's gun; and now still another, the man who had won the office by the largest vote in the Republic's history, removed himself by his own choice. Given the history and mystique of the office, and the mythology of power with which the 1960s enshrouded it, this last act was, in many ways, the most nearly inexplicable, and those who beheld it were left to wonder at what they had seen.

On Monday morning, after the climactic night at the White House, there was, of course, no way to know in Washington how the laying down of power was being received across the country. When a call came inviting me to accompany the president's party to Chicago, where he was to speak before noon, I readily accepted, hoping that the journey might afford some insight into the people's reaction. I did not anticipate what insight it might bring into President Lyndon B. Johnson himself.

The purpose of the trip was an appearance before the annual

conference of the nation's television and radio broadcasters. While the invitation had been received weeks before, the final decision on acceptance came only after the Sunday night appearance; public announcement was made only minutes before the president departed for Andrews Air Force Base to board *Air Force One* for the flight. In the realities of political arrangements, this meant there could be no great welcoming crowds lining Chicago's downtown streets. The people there were already in their offices, settling into the daily routine; most would not learn of the president's visit until after he had come and gone. It was not surprising, then, when the presidential motorcade pulled to the curb at the hotel where the broadcasters were assembled, to find the sidewalks deserted and the entrance clear except for photographers, police, and a handful of local dignitaries.

Overnight, *Air Force One* crewmen had somehow collected morning newspaper editions from more than two dozen cities: not only Washington, New York, and Baltimore but Cleveland, Detroit, Pittsburgh, Omaha, Atlanta, Miami, Boston, and other places. In the cabin the president became bemused, and not a little baffled, by these newspapers' accounts of local public reaction to his Sunday night announcement. His face registering wonderment and occasional disbelief, the president read aloud the stories telling of large crowds gathering in streets outside television studios to watch reruns of his speech, of public events being interrupted for announcements of the event, of telephone usage in several metropolitan areas reaching new peaks during the hour after the television appearance, and in some instances, of telephone company equipment breaking down under the overload. Entirely serious, he remarked to those sitting with him in the lounge of the big aircraft, "I didn't think there would be this much interest."

At the entrance to the convention hotel, there did not appear to be much Chicago interest. After the formalities of a few handshakes, the president hurried inside, turning to his left and following the Secret Service toward the wide stairway at the end of the lobby. Those of us in his travel party followed close behind, intent only on reaching the mezzanine convention hall; it did not occur to us to look over the lobby to the right. However, when the president mounted the first stairs and became visible among the surrounding screen of security men, a burst of applause began behind us. Experienced ears knew immediately that this was not the scattered hand clapping of casual onlookers. Before I could turn, someone in our group whistled in surprise. "Jesus," the voice said, "look at that."

The lobby was jammed from wall to wall. How many were present I could not guess, but the mood of the crowd was even more imposing than the numbers. No cheers, no shouts, no shoving, no hands reaching out; the audience stood respectfully, almost at attention, yet its applause somehow conveyed a rare quality of awe and respectfulness. Only twelve hours earlier, these Chicagoans had watched this man act out a drama none would forget. Until perhaps no more than an hour earlier, and in most instances less, they were still talking with their friends of what had been seen and heard; as far as they knew then, the president must be seven hundred miles away, going on with his duties at the White House. But here he was, passing before their eyes. The people stood transfixed.

The density of the throng obscured the view of the president when he first entered; only those in the front row knew that he had arrived. But with each step upward on the long flight of stairs, he came into sight of more of those waiting in the lobby, and the volume of the applause grew louder as he climbed. Hunched forward, hurrying on toward the speaking site, he appeared unaware of the swelling sound, and of the crowd, which he had not yet seen.

When he finally came into full view near the top of the stairs, the applause went reaching for him, thunderous and insistent. He hesitated, took another step, then stopped, and the security men stopped with him; but he did not turn. He seemed to be puzzling over the sound behind him, trying to identify it and comprehend it. A secretary from the White House press office, standing at my side, whispered the thought running in my own mind. "Poor man," she said, "he doesn't remember what a friendly crowd sounds like."

Lyndon Johnson glanced back over his shoulder very warily, still not turning, and saw the applauding audience for the first time. A surprised smile played uncertainly across his face. As members of his staff had learned to do whenever this man was thrust onto the public stage, I watched his revealing hands: they began moving hesitantly and nervously, touching along the edge of his coat, rising chest high, then falling back to his sides, where he held them stiffly, clenching and unclenching his fists uncomfortably. I yearned, as I am sure others in the entourage did too, for a walkie-talkie, so we could shout to the agents at his side: "Tell him to raise his arms and wave to the people—it's all his, it's all his."

The applause in this Chicago hotel lobby *was* all his. After tens of thousands of hours in their leadership, Lyndon Johnson had, in his one hour the night before, finally reached through to the people he sought to serve. But life had so conditioned him to the contentious that he could not now, graciously and naturally, accept the respect which the people were extending to him on this April morning. From the top of the stairs there came no broad and confident smile, no proud wave, not even the V-for-victory sign he had allowed himself to use as a congressman twenty years before. He could not, or dared not, communicate the gratitude he must have felt. His right arm darted out furtively, the fingers of his right hand moving stiffly in an awkward acknowledging gesture, and then he was gone, hunched forward and plunging away again, not to keep his appointment but to escape his unease.

At most, the moment may have lasted twenty seconds. To me, however, it told much of twenty years. I was glad that I had made the journey with him.

After Monday morning in Chicago, I was confident that Lyndon B. Johnson had begun the happiest week of his presidency and, possibly, of his public career. By the time *Air Force One* had returned to Washington, those expectations were being fulfilled.

At the White House, an unprecedented tide of messages flooded in from throughout the nation. Democrats and Republicans, friends and strangers, hawks and doves, suddenly saw the president, and even the presidency, in a new light; an impulse toward unity, nonpartisanship, and cooperation came welling up and swept toward the chief executive. A climate was forming again, as it had at the beginning of his presidency, in which Lyndon Johnson could function at his own best to make the political system function again at its best. Time was not too short. The most imposing achievements of his administration had been wrought in the first nine months of his elective term, and now nine full months were his to achieve much more for the future of the nation.

The president himself sensed the opportunity. Almost immediately after I arrived back at my office from Andrews Air Force Base, he was calling. He wanted to share with someone several of the messages waiting in his bedroom—warm and even effusive telegrams from prominent figures who had become severe critics. But beyond the unaccustomed and unexpected praise, his demeanor was that of a new man: his conversation began to quicken with talk of what could be achieved over the balance of the year. There was fresh excitement and an old bite in his tone as he declared, "We're going to get this show on the road again."

That evening and throughout the following day, the calls continued. I was only a listener, of course, but I had shared Sunday with him, and he wanted now to share its fruit with me. Over the telephone, he read friendly articles and editorials from many newspapers, letters from the public, handwritten notes from his cabinet. The man who worked best in a climate of broad unity and high purpose was getting it together again. At the White House, energies surged, vision soared, and the first week of April promised to be the best of all times.

On Wednesday, the promise welled beyond all expectations. A broadcast from Hanoi announced that, in view of President Johnson's Sunday night statement, the government of North Vietnam was willing to begin negotiations for ending the war. Lyndon Johnson's "roll of the dice" appeared to have won the high stakes. Washington became an electric place. Congress, the bureaucracy, even the media, pulsed with a new current of respect for the president. The old pro, battered and beleaguered, had come up off the floor to score a stunning victory. Public figures with whom he had virtually lost civil contact came by the Oval Office to offer its occupant their hands again. On Capitol Hill, the oldest critic of all, Senator William Fulbright, called a press conference. On Monday he, almost alone among public men, had expressed skepticism about the Johnson offer to negotiate; contrarily, he announced to the press that his wife told him he "talked too much."

When Thursday came, Lyndon Johnson left the White House, as he had done infrequently in recent months, flying to New York for the installation of Terence Cardinal Cooke as archbishop of the Roman Catholic diocese. No pickets were waiting when the limousine arrived at St. Patrick's Cathedral. Only the sounds of cheering followed him to the entrance. He stepped into the hushed cathedral and strode briskly down the center aisle toward the pew reserved at the front. As he moved past the rows of laymen and churchmen assembled for the occasion, the audience began to rise, and before he reached his seat, St. Patrick's echoed with applause. It was, for Lyndon Johnson, his brightest shining hour.

On Sunday, during the time of decision at the White House, President Johnson had hesitated once, late in the afternoon, considering postponement of his withdrawal until Thursday night. He had expected then to speak that evening at a fund-raising dinner for congressional Democrats, and he had been urged to consider that occasion as more appropriate for his personal political announcement. But the dinner was forgotten now. As soon as he returned from New York, the president intended to depart for Hawaii to confer with General William Westmoreland about the situation in Vietnam. Once more I had been invited to make the trip, and I looked forward to it as a happy ending to the happiest of weeks.

The president was anxious to be airborne before the start of the Thursday night dinner: he had begged off on the plea that he would be "out of town," and he was a stickler for observing that technicality. When the White House advised me of the earlier departure time, I hurried home to pack, listening on the drive to radio news broadcasts of the remarkable St. Patrick's ovation.

Only a week before nothing had been right, but in the early evening of April 4, it seemed that nothing could be wrong.

19

CONVULSION

At the house, I gathered summer sports clothes for the Pacific journey, hurrying to be ready before the White House driver arrived. I did not answer immediately when I heard our older daughter, Betsy, calling from her room on the third floor of the farmhouse. In a moment, she came running down the stairs.

"Dad," she said, her face very pale, "the radio just announced that Martin Luther King has been shot in Memphis."

The habits one forms on the periphery of public affairs are not easily lost. At news such as this, the mind leaves the moment behind and vaults ahead, imagining the meanings, projecting the consequences, grappling with the future even before it has begun. It required no imagination to know the meaning of what I had just heard.

On Sunday morning, as he had outlined the factors bearing on his decision, the president had spoken of the tensions in the cities. "They could go just like that," he said, snapping his fingers. It was a judgment with which I agreed. Over the seven months since the riots of the previous summer, I had gone several times into the black ghettos of New York, Chicago, and Detroit; anyone could sense that the rage was rising, not receding. It was impossible to conceive any event more provocative than what had happened in Memphis: the most prominent of Negro Americans gunned down by a white sniper in a southern city. On this April evening, the deadliest of venoms would be flowing through the nation's veins.

Could the convulsion be avoided? Or would the cities begin to go, like that?

I had no time to call the White House. The car was waiting in the driveway, and the driver thought we should leave immediately. I lingered only long enough to learn from the television news that Dr. King remained alive, under emergency room treatment in a Memphis hospital.

Darkness had come over the Maryland suburbs. Andrews Air Force Base lay forty miles away, on the opposite side of the District of Columbia. The White House driver, anxious about time, said little as he threaded the black Mercury sedan through the lanes of high-speed traffic on the Capital Beltway, over the Cabin John Bridge across the Potomac, and into the Virginia night. But as we sped past the exits to Dulles International Airport, the two-way radio came alive. I heard the military dispatcher at the garage call out his customary code. "Carpet to Nine-three."

My driver maneuvered toward the slow outside lane but said nothing. I wondered who of the White House staff might be riding in Car 93. The call repeated. This time, his maneuvering completed, the driver reached for the hand microphone and replied.

"Ninety-three to Carpet. Go ahead."

"Do you have your passenger, Ninety-three?"

"Affirmative."

"Stand by," the dispatcher directed. "We have a patch for him from Crown." That meant someone at the White House was placing a call to me, which would be relayed through the switchboard.

It was Jim Jones in the president's office.

"How far are you from Crown?" he asked. I checked with the driver and answered: "Twenty-five to thirty minutes."

"That may be too long," he said. He went off the line but returned again in a moment. "Volunteer"—that meant the president—"wants you to proceed to the White House. Tell the driver to make it as fast as possible."

I knew what the answer must be, but I asked anyway. "Is the news from Memphis bad?"

"Yes," Jones replied. "They are about to make the announcement."

I knew that the Reverend Martin Luther King, Jr., was dead.

The driver made his Beltway exit during my conversation. Grimly, we raced through the Virginia streets and across the Theodore Roosevelt Bridge into the District. Eighteen minutes after the radio call I reached the Oval Office. But it was too late. The president had already issued the public statement he had wanted me to draft.

"There won't be any flight to Hawaii tonight," he told me when I entered. "But you better stay around."

The exuberance of the week seemed to be draining from his long face as I watched him behind the desk. Solemnly, he directed the White House operators to reach the widow, Mrs. Coretta King, and the father, Martin Luther King, Sr., of whom President Johnson was very fond. Then he walked across the office to the French doors opening onto the garden. Without speaking, he stared out into the night while he waited for the calls.

Lyndon Johnson knew what was coming, and he knew he had little time. Tiredly, he went back to being president. His channels of communication were better—and his chain of command surer— to any foreign spot on the globe than to any of the cities within the nation. For this hour, he had no power, only persuasion, and he began using that: trying to save the cities, hoping to spare the nation—and particularly black Americans themselves—the grief and suffering that could flash across the land from Harlem to Watts.

I had rarely seen him so subdued or so alone within himself. He read the news Teletypes beside his desk, and his face tightened several times when messages were handed to him by Secret Service agents. But he did not engage his staff in conversation, or solicit views from others about what to do. He was on the telephone himself: calling mayors, calling governors, calling black leaders, calling officials in the federal government. Two themes ran through most of the conversations. First, he urged the leaders, both public and private, to go into the ghettos. "For God's sake," he said several times, "go see the people, let them see you, let them know you care, that we all care." Second, he dwelled on avoiding bloodshed. "Both sides," he warned one mayor, referring to police and blacks, "are going to be scared of the other. Don't, please, send your skinny little rookies out with great big guns all by themselves—if the shooting starts, it may never stop." But he put down the telephone discouraged.

"I'm not getting through," he said. "They're all holing up like generals in a dugout getting ready to watch a war."

The television set showed a picture of Vice President Hubert Humphrey, and the president turned up the sound. It was a scene filmed moments earlier at the fund-raising dinner for congressional Democrats. The vice president stepped to the lectern and announced Dr. King's death; after a minute of silent prayer, the dinner adjourned and the scheduled speeches were canceled. If the president had saved the announcement of his withdrawal for this occasion, it would not have been made.

New York and Chicago were the cities being watched most carefully as the shock began to spread. If a convulsion came, it would most likely start in one of these two metropolises, although several smaller centers were considered near flash point, too. Washington, D.C., of course, had the highest percentage of black residents, but both blacks and whites regarded it as riot-proof. One of every four federal employees was a Negro; income levels were relatively high and stable; the ghetto psychology was less an active force; and the new militancy had put down fewer roots. Even as the president talked, though, it became apparent that the nation's capital might be the first American city to "go."

District and federal agencies were monitoring the neighborhoods closely. Reports radioed from Fourteenth Street were ominous. Only blocks from the White House, crowds were gathering at major intersections; windows were being broken, businesses being closed, and fires being started. The District's three-thousand-man police force was stretching thin. Security agencies quietly began reinforcing protection around the perimeter of the Executive Mansion, and the president had a new concern. "Keep the men out of sight as much as you can," he ordered the Secret Service. "If we get pictures of armed guards at the White House gates, it'll only be more provocative."

The spasm eased, and Washington grew quiet. Near midnight the president finally sat down to eat in the family dining room. He had asked me to remain at the White House overnight, and I joined him for the meal. Present, also, was United States District Judge A. Leon Higginbotham, Jr., one of the ablest black jurists on the federal bench. President Johnson valued Judge Higginbotham's counsel and had been conferring with him during the evening. When the light dinner ended, the president rose from the table and asked the judge to come with him; together they walked through the dark second-floor corridor to the east end. "Here," the president said, turning on the lights in the historic Lincoln Bedroom. "I want you to sleep in this room tonight."

On Friday morning, the early reports were far better than anticipated. While disorders had developed in cities of all regions, none approached the proportions of a riot, and the nation's streets were peaceful as the day began. The president, though, thought the calm misleading: Friday night would be the critical time. Once again, it was move, move, move.

Over the telephone before he left his bedroom, he contacted the big-city mayors once more. "Your men," he told them, referring to the police, "didn't get any sleep last night; they're going to be tired, scared, irritable, and trigger-happy tonight." He went on, preaching that "it's easier to stop shooting before it starts," and urging them to assess their needs for federal troops early in the day. "Don't wait till dark to holler for help," he pleaded. But the mayors and the police chiefs were proud of their successes the night before, and unwilling to ask for federal intervention now. "The crisis is past," a midwestern mayor insisted. "I hope you're right," the president replied, "but we shall see what we shall see."

At ten-thirty, President Johnson met in the Cabinet Room with heads of the principal civil rights organizations. Vice President Hubert Humphrey attended, his face drawn and his eyes red with brimming tears. At the president's request, each of the black leaders spoke: all recognized the danger in the ghettos, and all reported their organizations at work, striving to placate the seething unrest; none, however, was confident that a convulsion could be prevented. This matched the president's own assessment. "If I were a kid in Harlem," he told one of the leaders, "I know what I'd be thinking right now: I'd be thinking that the whites have declared open season on my people, and they're going to pick us off one by one unless I get a gun and pick them off first."

It was imperative, he thought, to use the presidency to communicate that the senseless slaying at Memphis had outraged white Americans as well as black. With the black leaders gathered around him, the president addressed the nation on television. "Violence," he declared, "must be denied its victory."

At the last minute, before he faced the television cameras, the president decided his statement did not say enough. More action was required. He summoned Secretary of Defense Clark Clifford and myself to the Cabinet Room; he wanted a line added, promising that he would address a joint session of Congress on Monday night to present a comprehensive program for meeting the crisis of the cities. Secretary Clifford and I both hesitated, silently questioning whether such a program could be developed in so short a time. The president read our thoughts, and his eyes flashed impatiently. "Goddam it," he snapped, "this country has got to do more for these people, and the time to start is now." He dictated his own line, and Clifford penciled it into the prepared text.

When noon came, the presidential limousine led a long procession of White House cars to Washington's National Cathedral. Martin Luther King had occupied the pulpit there on Sunday morning, but now the nation's highest officialdom gathered to hear him eulogized. After the memorial service, a vigil began on the second floor of the Executive Mansion. Special assistants, key figures from the administration, and others gathered around the president to wait out the day. When the noon meal was served, the president himself said the blessing, adding the earnest injunction, "Help us, Lord, to know what to do now." He smiled when he raised his head. "I thought I'd better get specific about it, fellas."

Crises are never seen by a president; they are delivered to him, tersely written and neatly typed on yellow sheets of paper from the message center. Today, however, was to be different.

At the beginning of the meal, the messages being laid beside his plate told an encouraging story: the television statement was well-received; the major cities were calm; mayors confidently advised that there would be no need for federal troops. But then a different sort of word began to filter into the room. White House secretaries, returning from noontime shopping, called to report that downtown department stores were being quietly cleared; floorwalkers circulated among white customers whispering for them to return to their homes. Fear mounted toward panic. A special assistant's wife telephoned to say that whites in the business district were surrendering the sidewalks, walking only in the streets. One member of the group pushed back from the table and stepped to the windows, overlooking Pennsylvania Avenue.

"Gentlemen," he called quietly, "I think you better see this."

On the tall trees rising from the White House lawn, young leaves shimmered in the soft spring sun. Across the way, Lafayette Square bloomed brightly with the color of the new season. As always, it was a view of beauty. But between the trim green of the White House grounds and the graceful symmetry of the square, there ran an ugly flood. The eastbound lanes of Pennsylvania Avenue, carrying traffic toward the shopping district, stood starkly empty, but the westbound lanes were a river of fright, bumper to bumper, curb to center stripe, with Washingtonians surging out toward the sanctuary of their suburban homes.

No one spoke. The sight below told a story the yellow message sheets could not tell. We could only stand mute and motionless, watching a nation divide.

An assistant leaned forward, peering around the columns of the White House façade toward the east. The rest of us followed his gaze. Through the pale leaves, beyond the gray buildings, smoke leaped into the sky, and we could see the first flames. The convulsion had started.

President Johnson did not leave his chair. He needed no view through the windows to understand what had begun. Anxiously, he attempted to establish contact with municipal authorities of the District of Columbia. In the president's mind, no doubts remained: if peace was to be kept in the capital, Washington's outmanned police force would require support from federal troops by nightfall. Yet the commander in chief could not summon the forces without a request from local officials; he wanted to "suggest"—he could not constitutionally do more—that consideration of such a request begin at once. But contact was not made.

Only the previous year, the president had chosen as the capital's first mayor an able black administrator, Walter Washington. It was one of Lyndon Johnson's proudest boasts in private: "Washington is the first big city in the country with a Negro mayor, and I appointed him." But he had told Mayor Washington, "I want you to stay close to the people," and now the mayor was doing just that:

going among the people, trying by personal persuasion to turn the rising tide. The president's call could not be completed.

A crisis occurring far away permits illusions. Orders transmitted to another continent, another country, or even another city seem to be action; once the decision is reached, the message phrased, and the communication dispatched, those at the center of command can feel that the challenge is met. The crisis developing in Washington permitted no such illusion; it was too near. Communications were awkward, fitful, and intermittently impossible. When decisions were reached, the decision makers had only to step to the windows of the White House to witness how cumbersome and uncertain was their implementation.

On Pennsylvania Avenue, automobile traffic came to a standstill. The bridges across the Potomac to Virginia were clogged; motorists idled away their gasoline supplies, then abandoned their stalled vehicles and continued their flight on foot. Someone down the chain of command requested presidential permission to close government offices early and dismiss federal employees for the remainder of the day. The president looked disgustedly out the windows. "Who in the hell," he asked, "do they think is still around to dismiss?" He did not authorize the formal closing.

The president moved from the dining room to the sitting room area at the end of the corridor. A window had been opened, looking out on the serenity of the Rose Garden beside the presidential office in the West Wing. Almost immediately, a light afternoon breeze wafted in, bringing the odor of burning timbers. The president glanced down the long hallway toward the east side of the White House and motioned for us to look: through the arching window at the far end of the corridor, we could see heavy black smoke rising from the business district.

Several times more the president attempted without success to reach Mayor Washington. Overloaded communications equipment at the District building was breaking down. On his own authority, the president ordered troop units readied for duty and dispatched to the city's perimeter. Then he called the Pentagon for General Harold K. Johnson, chief of staff of the United States Army.

"General," the president said, "I know I've been over this with you before, but I want to go over it one more time. Number one, are you sure of your commander? Are you sure he has control of his men? Are you sure he isn't one of those who is willing to use a little more force than necessary, just to set an example? Number two, are you sure of these troops? Sure none of them are trigger-happy? No question of discipline? Remember, General, this is the capital of the United States. The whole world will be watching tonight. I don't want anybody—repeat, anybody—shot if it can be avoided. You understand that, don't you, General?"

The president listened intently, then his forehead wrinkled into a sudden frown and his face fell abjectly. Angrily he snapped the receiver into place, bolted from his chair, and strode alone down the long corridor away from the group. When he returned, he fell into the chair, his face a study in disgust.

"Gentlemen," he said, shaking his head slowly. "I want you to know you can sleep well tonight. The commander in chief of the armed forces of the United States has just concluded five minutes of instruction to the chief of staff of the Army of the United States, talking"—and his words became bitingly sarcastic—"over one of the goddam military's supersecret, hotline connections, direct to the war room of the mighty Pentagon. And when the commander in chief finished, the good general said, 'Gee, I'm sorry, sir, I can't hear you on this line. Let me see if I can borrow a dime from some little private around here, and I'll call you back from a phone booth outside.'"

It was exaggeration, of course, but only slightly. When the chief of staff reestablished the call from another telephone, he received his instructions in the iciest of tones. The new secretary of defense, Clark Clifford, only thirty days in office, hunched down in his chair, drew his coat over his face in mock embarrassment, and told his friend the president: "Sir, it's *your* Army."

Shortly after four o'clock in the afternoon, Mayor Washington called. It was no easier for him than for other mayors to concede that his own forces might not be able to police the city, but the need was past denying. Mayor Washington formally requested federal troops. Assistant Attorney General Frank Wozencraft had been waiting at the president's side for more than an hour with the necessary orders; now he held them forward for the president to sign.

As twilight crept over the April afternoon, all of us stood together in silence at a south window of the White House, watching troop carriers unload beneath the trees bordering the Ellipse beyond the South Grounds. By midnight, Washington was an occupied city. Residents were ordered into their homes under curfew; jeeps and foot soldiers patrolled the streets; and slowly the convulsion began to release its hold.

The president asked me to return on Saturday to draft his message to the joint session of Congress on Monday night. "It'll need a lot of Churchill," he said, repeating his familiar goad, "and I want it to be another Gettysburg, too." Others who heard the instruction smiled about it later, joking that Lyndon Johnson must think of himself as "another Abraham Lincoln." I had to explain that, in his usage to me, "Gettysburg" referred to his own speech there in 1963, not to the remarks of 1863. When I saw the president again, however, I knew there would be no speech to Congress.

Throughout the evening on Friday, and again during the morning on Saturday, the chief executive pressed the departments for the "program" he wanted to present to the Congress and the nation. But as he handed me the sheaf of recommended actions, his face was sad. "We don't have the ideas we used to have when I first came to this town," he sighed. "These things"—he pointed to the departmental and staff memoranda—"are all vanilla; they wouldn't begin to touch our problem." Forlornly, he concluded that he could not make the Monday night appearance.

"Until we all get to be a whole lot smarter," he said, "I guess the country will just have to go with what it has already."

I suggested that it might be desirable for him to speak anyway, without presenting a legislative program; after the trauma of the last forty-eight hours, appropriate words from the president might have a healing and reassuring effect. But his reaction was negative. "Words without actions isn't leadership," he said. Then, after reflecting for a moment, he added: "I guess Roosevelt and Kennedy and maybe some of the others could do what you're talking about, but pretty words aren't my style."

He seemed very tired, and I left him alone at the end of the week which ended his political life.

20

"WELL, SEE YOU AGAIN, SOMETIME"

It was January 20, 1969, Inauguration Day in Washington. At high noon, on the plaza before the East Front of the United States Capitol, Richard Milhous Nixon would become the thirty-seventh President of the United States of America, and for the first time in almost thirty-two years, Lyndon Baines Johnson would become a private citizen.

Shortly before seven o'clock in the morning, the telephone rang beside my bed. At that hour, on this day, I knew before I answered who must be calling.

"Mr. Busby," the White House operator said quickly, "the president."

There were none of the usual switching sounds. He was already waiting on the line, but he did not speak immediately. In the background, I could hear a familiar sound: the rustle of pages while he turned through the morning newspapers. It was a long moment before he spoke, and when he did, he began without a greeting or salutation. "Have you seen the *Post* this morning?"

As always, his tone was edged with the mixture of indignation and resignation he reserved for his daily encounter with *The Washington Post*. I had only just awakened, though, and did not know what he might have found in his customary morning reading.

"No, sir," I told him, "I haven't seen the papers."

"Well, let me read you the terrible things the *Post* is saying."

Over the past twenty years, hundreds of my days, perhaps even thousands of them, had begun this same way, listening to Lyndon

Johnson argue with the morning newspapers. His own position did not matter, nor did the newspaper. Whether he happened to be congressman, senator, majority leader, vice president, or president— and whether he happened to be reading the *Washington Post, New York Times, Dallas Morning News,* or *Austin American*—the ritual remained the same: he had to go through the pages, talking back to the columnists and editorial writers, rewriting the headlines, and playing editor with the news stories.

The grimly serious adjective evoked a smile. I doubted very seriously that anything in this morning's *Washington Post* quite deserved to be termed "terrible." As he read through the offending article, my suspicions were confirmed: he could find only an occasional adjective or verb with which he disagreed. Otherwise, most of the article about his departure was quite generous and kind, and he even paused once or twice to reread exceptionally well-turned phrases, conceding, "I guess that's pretty good for the *Post.*"

Lyndon Johnson was playing editor, but he knew that it was for the last time, and he could not pretend it really mattered so much. He soon abandoned his desultory reading of the first article and turned on through the pages, repeating headlines at random and beginning but not finishing columns which caught his eye. I remained silent, listening none too attentively. He had not called, I knew, only to share the contents of *The Washington Post.*

After five minutes, or possibly longer, his voice trailed off, and I could hear the newspaper being folded neatly back in order. There was silence on the line.

I had become curious while the president was reading as to where in the White House he might be. On this final morning, would he still be lying abed, starting the day with his usual round of telephone calls? Or had he gone to the Oval Office in the West Wing for the last time to clear his desk? When he did not speak, I asked him, "Where are you now?"

The president misconstrued my question. Quickly, with a tone of offended dignity, he replied: "Why, I'm still at the White House, of course." Then, realizing the intent of my inquiry, he chuckled. "At least, I am for now."

As usual, he could find some humor in the irony of his own situation. Now he began whispering confidentially. He was still in the presidential bedroom on the second floor of the White House, but "they"—the moving crews—were "all around" trying to hurry him out. "They are watching every move I make," he confided in high good humor. "If I lay a cuff link down on the dresser, a hand comes reaching around the door and snatches it up." Then he laughed at his own imagery. "They," he said, still speaking of the White House moving crews, "know I'm not going to sign their next paycheck."

The humor continued for a few moments, then subsided. Again there was silence on the line.

I knew by now that this must be a personal call. It was thoughtful of him, and I appreciated it. But he seemed far from certain what he had telephoned to say, and I had not thought at all of what I might want to say to him. Neither of us said anything for a long and awkward minute. Then, when he spoke again, his voice was quiet and subdued. "You got me out of town," he said. "Are you still planning to stay?"

There was no purpose in disputing his remark. It was quick and passing and only a manner of speaking. I chose, instead, to respond to his question. "Yes, sir. I suppose we will be here for a long time."

"I'll be going back to Texas about three o'clock. You still don't want to go?"

"No," I told him. My decision about that was firm.

"What are your plans?"

"I have a lot of starting over to do, Mr. President," I answered. "It will be a while before I know what I am going to do."

There was a long pause on the telephone. "Yes," the president said, "I guess all of us can say that."

The sounds in the receiver told me that he must be moving around, most likely rising from the bed and beginning to pace the room as far as the long extension cord would permit.

"What is your judgment?" he asked. "Do you think I'll like teaching?"

The newspapers had been filled the past several days with reports firmly announcing his intentions to begin lecturing during the spring semester at the University of Texas and other institutions. Although these plans might be definite and firm, I answered his question honestly. "Not really, Mr. President. Not for a long time." Then I spoke more as one does to a congressman or a senator than to a president. "You have a long time to go, Mr. President," I said. "I hope you won't be in a hurry to commit yourself to teaching or anything else."

The answer pleased him. "That's the way I feel too," he admitted brightly. "When I get back down to that ranch, I'm going to get up every morning and do just exactly what I've always wanted to do for forty years." He paused for effect, then laughed heartily as he added emphatically: "Nothing."

I joined in his laughter. For as long as I had known him, Lyndon Johnson had worked longer and harder than any other public man of my acquaintance: fourteen, sixteen, sometimes even twenty hours a day, six or seven days a week. Back in boyhood, he had been told by his father that he had "a lazy streak," and he had lived out his public career fearful that someone might think he did not "work hard enough." This was the first time, however, that I had ever heard him admit how he actually wanted to spend his days.

This just might be what he would do. The realist who had removed himself from the presidency might also remove himself from public view, leaving to others the stage on which he had had his own full term. In five more hours, for the first time in his adult years, he would be free at last—free of politics, free of "the eyes," free of measuring himself and being measured by others' standards. These freedoms of private life would not be readily surrendered by this most private man.

The talk flowed on about the ranch—about the bright, warm sun and the clear, starry nights and the stillness along the Pedernales River. It was talk I had not heard from Lyndon Johnson since that night in November 1963 when he was getting ready to leave Washington for Texas to prepare for President John F. Kennedy's visit two weeks later. But I made no references to the past.

Since the start of the conversation, I had been wanting to say something worth saying. Words, though, were elusive, darting in and out among the many memories and emotions of twenty years. Others, I knew, might have no difficulty using the superlatives which come so readily in political life. They could say something about him being "a great man" or "a great president" or about the "honor" of having worked with him. I knew the words, as well as anyone, but I also knew the man and my relationship with him. If

I employed such formal and stilted words, he would only interrupt with some scolding remark like "Buzz, come on now, you're just making a speech."

Whatever each of us felt about the other, probably neither of us knew, and it was best, perhaps, to leave such thoughts unspoken. Nonetheless, I doubted that I would ever know another president, certainly not as I knew this president, and I finally made the attempt to say something appropriate for this occasion. "I hope," I said with some caution, "that you find great happiness."

It was wrong, very wrong. He did not want such sentiments, at least not from me. Immediately he began to flee. "Yes, uh, yes," he answered, uncertain and uncomfortable. Then his voice rose and he spoke hurriedly. "Well, like I said, if you ever change your mind about coming back to Texas, let me know."

I assured him that I would.

Again he paused. "All right," he said, stretching the words and seeming to think over other things which he might want to say, or perhaps to leave unsaid. But there was nothing more. "That's about all, I guess."

Without thinking of my actions, I rose from the bed where I had been seated and stood beside the telephone table as I had so often stood beside the desks in all his many offices. He continued to hesitate, but if he was searching for more words, he did not find them. Speaking hurriedly again, the president brought his call to an end.

"Well, see you again, sometime."

I went on through Inauguration Day, watching on television at noon as the new president took his oath at the Capitol and turned to address the nation. At midafternoon, I drove to the CBS studios in downtown Washington. The network had invited me to be a panelist for a discussion of the inaugural address. When I reached the studios, however, the television screens were showing a scene from Andrews Air Force Base, where Lyndon Johnson was about to depart for Texas aboard *Air Force One*. I asked that we wait before proceeding with the taping, and I sat alone in a small studio to watch these last minutes in Washington.

In the crowd gathered at the air base, many of my friends and most of my former colleagues at the White House were visible.

So, also, were many faces out of Lyndon Johnson worlds of the past, men and women whom I had virtually forgotten; they were crowding around him, seeing him in person again for the first time in five years or even longer. I had said my own good-bye in another way at another time, but I watched this scene in fascination.

Oblivious to the cameras, Lyndon Johnson moved exuberantly among the gathering, embracing the old friends warmly and talking excitedly. The freedom of only a few hours ran through him, and he was boyish and enthusiastic as he plunged happily among the crowd. When he began to shake the same hands more than once, however, I realized that he was postponing the climb up the ramp to board for the last time *Air Force One*, the craft where his presidency had begun.

Once he moved tentatively onto the stairs, but he retreated to the touch of the admiring and affectionate crowd and lost himself in still more farewells. At last he could delay no longer. He took his grandson in his arms and started firmly toward the aircraft's door. Midway up the ramp, he stopped and turned, facing northward toward the low, dim skyline of the capital city. The camera crews focused in very close, showing only his face.

Once, for a while, Washington had been Lyndon Johnson's, as much as it had ever been any man's, and when he held the moment, he used it boldly, to complete in his last office the works to which he had committed himself in his first office. He had left his mark, he had kept the flame, and his work was done. Now he was returning to the place from where he had come. But it remained that as Washington once was his, so Lyndon Johnson would always be Washington's. He could never belong wherever else he might be.

A strong January wind blew his hair and the cold must have been severe, but he continued standing on the ramp, his eyes searching the horizon of a lifetime that he was leaving behind. The face on the television screens became intensely private. It was the face of another Lyndon Johnson, one whom I would never know. I turned away and signaled to the young producer that I was ready to go with my part of the network's program.

The day that had begun twenty years before was at its end.

A NOTE ABOUT THE AUTHOR

Horace W. Busby, Jr., was an adviser, speechwriter, and confidant to Lyndon B. Johnson throughout his political career. Mr. Busby served on LBJ's staff in the House and Senate and at the White House, where he was secretary of the cabinet from 1963 to 1965. He wrote many of the president's landmark speeches, including his civil rights orations and the announcement of his decision not to run for reelection in 1968. He also played a key role in drafting much of LBJ's Great Society legislation. After LBJ left the White House, Mr. Busby remained in the nation's capital, where he built a successful business as a management consultant, political analyst, and publisher. His best-known newsletters were *The American Businessman* and *The Busby Papers*.

Mr. Busby was born in Fort Worth, Texas, in 1924. He attended the University of Texas at Austin, where he was the editor of the student newspaper, *The Daily Texan*. He left the university without graduating and worked briefly for the United Press International news service in Austin before joining Congressman Johnson's staff in 1948 at the age of twenty-four. He died in Santa Monica, California, in May 2000. He was preceded in death by a granddaughter, Blyth Ann Busby Wilkinson. He is survived by his children, Scott Busby, Betsy Busby, and Leslie Busby, and a granddaughter, Eleonora Maccabruno.